Other Books by Sam Sorbo

Gizmoe: The Legendary Journeys, Auckland

They're YOUR Kids

Teach From Love

Let There Be Light

Share the Light

SamSorbo.com

By Kevin Sorbo

True Strength: My Journey from Hercules to Mere Mortal –
And How Nearly Dying Saved My Life

Share the Light

KevinSorbo.net

TRUE FAITH

EMBRACING ADVERSITY TO LIVE IN GOD'S LIGHT

Kevin and Sam Sorbo

REVEILLE PRESS

True Faith

Scripture quotations are from New King James Version®. Copyright © 1982 by Thomas Nelson.

Cover design by Sam Sorbo

Cover images by Kerry Corcoran

Published by Reveille Press

ISBN: ISBN: 978-0-9828001-1-9
First Printing: February 2020
Printed in the United States of America

First Edition: February 2020

WITH THANKS TO GOD

This book is dedicated to married couples
and parents everywhere.

What Others Are Saying About This Book...

"While so many in this country are praying to the small 'gods' of government, Kevin and Sam show us the power of faith in the one True God. I thank them for standing strong, and sharing that strength with the world."

Governor Mike Huckabee

"Nothing bonds a marriage more than following God together in faith, and Kevin and Sam Sorbo have shown that strength time and again as they've moved through life's trials and onto triumph together in their work as filmmakers and together at home. (True Faith brings you into their story in a personal way, sharing the testimony of God's provision in their lives and helping other couples find abundance in every aspect of married life.) Lose this part."

Jerry L. Falwell, Jr., President, Liberty University

"This may be one of the best home improvement books I've read!"

Tim Allen, Actor, Producer

"In their new book, Kevin and Sam Sorbo take you on a very personal journey of trials and triumphs that will refresh your spirit as they teach you how to grow closer together as a couple through life's difficult seasons."

Kirk Cameron, Actor, Producer

"It's great to have Americans like Kevin and Sam who have so ability and who use their talents to glorify the Lord! I love their work! This is a great read."

John Rich, Singer

"Thank you, Sam and Kevin, for standing strong for our faith, for our families, and for our country."

Lou Holtz, Legendary Football Coach and Inspirational Speaker

"One wouldn't think that people in the entertainment industry would be writing a profound book on the art of marriage. Today's culture is designed to tear marriages apart. Kevin and Sam counter what the world thinks marriage is. In True Faith they give transparent testimony, insight, and helpful advice that could save marriages and help guide them in the right direction."

Sheryl and Alice Cooper, Rock Star, Married 44 years

"Thank you, Sam and Kevin, for standing strong for our faith, for our families, and for our country!"

Eric Metaxas, Author of *Bonhoeffer* and *If You Can Keep It*, host of the Eric Metaxas Show

"Wow! Powerful, poignant, and purposeful. The Sorbos' faith may help you rediscover yours."

Dr. M.G. "Pat" Robertson, Founder/Chairman, Christian Broadcasting Network, Inc.

Table of Contents

Foreword

Faith is a Place

I like to think of faith as a place, a state of being. Faith can be a gentle repose, a calming breath in the middle of a storm. Jesus spoke of faith that heals. When challenges beset us, strong faith allows us to rest in the knowledge of the Supreme Being Who oversees all and who works all things together for the good. Faith, reliance on the one true God, can set you free from worry and fear. But if faith offers us shelter, it isn't a refuge where we run and hide when we are fearful. We should live there daily, in the sanctuary of the Most High.

Kevin Sorbo understands this. He is someone who has looked death straight in the eye, has suffered without understanding, has wrestled with God. In his first book, *True Strength: My Journey from Half God to Mere Mortal and How Nearly Dying Saved my Life*, Kevin recounts how his illness forced him to reconnect with a faith he hadn't previously needed. Playing the strongest man in the world on television required a herculean strength, but ultimately, it wasn't sustainable. The fourteen- to sixteen-hour days proved too much for the mere human, and Kevin collapsed from three strokes.

God uses challenges to draw His children closer to Him. During his recovery, Kevin discovered a state of faith in which he could endure the symptoms of his brain injury, and allow healing and recovery. He is a man I admire, a role model for many.

I met Kevin when he was promoting a dramatic movie called *What If...*—a faith-based picture about a man who was not fulfilling God's plan for his life. In the film, God plucks this wayward Christian out of his financially successful situation and deposits him into a new reality via a curmudgeon angel played by John Ratzenberger. Kevin's character, at first reluctant and even antagonistic, eventually entirely redefines himself in this new life. He learns to embrace God's design for him, instead of what he has built for himself. He finds himself in his faith.

In our largely secular society, we are tempted to build our own towers of Babel, much like the character in *What If...*, and much like what Kevin Sorbo himself had built in his own career before he suffered three strokes. We define ourselves by what we accumulate and our roles in society, instead of our relationships with God. But when trials come, and they always do, we typically discover that the trappings of this world offer little shelter and even less solace. We need faith.

After 9/11, the churches and synagogues were full. People in this country actively sought comfort from above. They needed faith in their time of hardship. But faith is less a commodity or covering. It is more than a blanket to keep the cold at bay, a favorite easy chair in which to relax. Faith is the plug that recharges and renews, and it is most effective when we remain connected to the source. That is why I view faith as a destination, the place we connect with our Creator, receiving unearned grace, being in a loving relationship.

The journey to faith is sometimes a struggle. Those who take that journey surely find their egos too heavy to bring with them. To enter into faith requires humility, and often, some encouragement. Trusting in God through faith is necessary, and it's easier when someone shows you the way. Throughout this book, Kevin and Sam focus on the fortitude of their faith, sharing their struggles and triumphs and offering reassurance and inspiration. Join them on their journey and allow them to lead you in discovering the place where your faith resides.

Dr. M.G. "Pat" Robertson
Founder/Chairma, Christian Broadcasting Network, Inc.

Prologue

Kevin

It was a beautiful sunny day in the desert when Sam drove home from what was supposed to be a routine checkup at the doctor's office. She had left the house that morning full of energy and joy. She loved being pregnant, and it looked good on her. The glow of life growing inside her, but doubly-so. Sam had miraculously conceived twins, after a long-fought battle with infertility. This confounded me, yet filled me with pride. Not just pride. Hope and *faith,* too.

I battled my way back to health after suffering three strokes and their aftermath. My health struggles, including panic attacks, anxiety, depression, dizziness, vertigo, loss of vision, migraines, and insomnia, are well documented in my first book, *True Strength.* These challenges—both physical and emotional—seemed to prevent me from starting a family, which strangely, was the one thing I had thought of as I staggered into the emergency room of Cedars Sinai Hospital that fateful September morning. "God," I thought, "This is so unfair. I wanted to have kids. But instead, I will die today."

I cheated death that day, and every day since, and as I healed, the idea of having children grew more into focus. But life is never easy, and so although Sam and I tried to conceive, well, this pregnancy wasn't on our timing.

Then, finally, we had some good news to share. We were elated to be expecting, and we told everyone early in the pregnancy.

Telling my parents had been such fun for this Minnesota boy. "So, Mom and Dad, we do have some news to tell you." My parents looked suspicious, patiently waiting to hear the exciting news, but unable to bring themselves to guess about it, lest they were wrong.

"It's great news that both Sam and I want to tell you..." I continued to lead them on. "Dad, think about baseball for a minute."

"What has your big news got to do with baseball?" he pondered, then scrutinized me. Mom weighed in, "What is it? I'm not getting it?"

"Woohoo! You betcha! It's twins? The Minnesota Twins!"

"Oh, for heavenly days!" Mom cried. "Is that right? Praise the Lord!"

Sam's grin was as wide as her beautiful face. My parents beamed. We all hugged. Life was wonderful.

Ten weeks later, bubbly and animated, Sam left our house for her twelve-week checkup and returned home devastated and inconsolable. "What's wrong?" I asked the moment she walked in the door. She stood, mutely shaking her head, and I jumped to the worst possible conclusion.

"What? What is it?" I asked, walking to her, fearing the horrible news, daring her to say it out loud.

"They're gone! They're just—" She turned and walked the length of the hallway to our master bedroom. I numbly followed, unwilling to accept the news, but just to the doorway. I stayed there, wanting this not to be happening, wishing away the nausea and desperation that enveloped me.

Sam moved to the open curtains, navigating the gym equipent that occupied the sitting area of our bedroom. The Las Vegas sun shone brightly through the large glass sliding doors. Sam drew the heavy panels forcefully across their poles, shutting out the light.

I stood watching, pinned in place by grief. Was this somehow my fault? Because I wasn't entirely well yet?

This couldn't be happening. After surviving three strokes, I suppose I imagined myself beyond the reach of tragedy. Hadn't I earned a "pass" for additional misfortune? I accepted my illness, the hardships and limitations, but figured I merited a pardon from other challenges. I desperately wanted to convince myself this was my imagination, but there is a part of me that is all too willing to believe the worst.

Still, I didn't move. I watched, hoping there would be some sign this wasn't real.

Sam didn't undress. She just flung back the covers and crawled into our bed, then pulled the comforter over herself, covering all but her tear-streaked face. Then she quietly sobbed.

I went to her. I knelt by the bedside and took her hand. "What happened?"

"They're gone. The twins." Her breath caught in her throat. "Kevin. They aren't there—they're just... gone." Another round of sobs emitted from her lovely mouth. "The doctor told me after we did the ultrasound, in the other room. She was crying. I couldn't believe it. I made them take me back to the scanner so I could see with my own eyes. They did the jelly again and scanned my belly, looking for them. I saw the two little tiny—where there used to be fluttering little hearts—but now, nothing but lumps. Two small, still lumps. No heartbeats. No... They're gone, Kevin, and I'm so sad. I'm sorry."

"It's not your fault. It's isn't," was all I could say. I felt tears run down my cheeks as I kissed Sam's.

On my knees already, I felt myself praying, so I said the words as they came.

"Father, please help us understand. Jesus, give us... faith."

Doctor's Office

Kevin

Sam and I both knew doctors' offices all too well. I had cultivated a healthy resentment of them as a survivor of three strokes and their ensuing side-effects. Not that I disliked my doctors. I hated my *need* for doctors, and, particularly, this one. We chose this doctor to treat us as a couple, but I was sure there was nothing wrong with Sam, my gorgeous and loving and *healthy* wife.

I sat in his barren waiting room simmering with both indignation and trepidation. Sam sat next to me, seemingly oblivious to my fuming, but nonetheless aware of it. Sam had cultivated a healthy habit of refrain from engaging in – in my pessimism and general negativity. She was the yang to my yin. It was simultaneously unnerving and comforting, a contradiction that ingrained itself into our relationship. A similar paradox also resulted from my strokes. I could blame them for so many things, which allowed me to escape blaming myself for anything. It was as much a comfort as a distant whiff of barbeque to a hungry construction worker. And like that laborer, I needed sustenance, not smells. I was a work-in-progress, still in recovery, still reconstructing my life and our marriage. Most important, I was attempting to forge a family, despite what appeared at this point as insurmountable setbacks.

Doctor Korde specialized in fertility, and Sam and I sat waiting to receive our test results. As we contemplated our hopes and desires in the fluorescent-lit, pistachio-green waiting room, Sam held my hand and stroked my arm like I was some lost puppy. It bothered me she could read me so well, but I was comforted. We both knew this was my fault, though that would never cross her lips. We had tried for two and a half years to have a baby, with Sam counting days, taking temperatures, employing all the fertility tips known to mankind. This had made our intimacy clinical and beat the passion out of our relationship entirely. Each month led to more disappointment and rising suspicions.

On our first real date, in a movie theater in Auckland, New Zealand, Sam and I had talked about marriage. Marriage! On a first date! To call our meeting "love at first sight" is almost to do it an injustice. We were instantly attracted to each other, and I pursued her with my whole heart. Sam surprisingly divined the small chapel in the Austrian Alps where I had always pictured my wedding. It turned out she loved that chapel, too. My next assertion was about the children I saw in my future I wanted three: boy, boy, girl, in that order. She laughed, nodding in agreement. "That's funny, because that's what I'm having, too! Boy, boy and then a little girl!"

Our compatibility and similarities were uncanny and undeniable. Despite the long distance between her home in Los Angeles and mine on the set of *Hercules: The Legendary Journeys* in New Zealand, we were engaged only six months after we met. It helped that my producers liked her initial performance as Hercules' love-interest Princess Kirin so much they invited her back for a three-episode arc later that same year. I also saw her during filming of *Kull, The Conqueror* when I flew her to Croatia to spend time with me on set. And, while I know she began our whirlwind courtship waiting to discover how I was not the knight in shining armor I appeared, I was always certain she was the only one for me.

I had waited long enough—so long I had assumed the title of "Confirmed Bachelor." I stopped believing I would ever get married, but meeting Sam changed that with surprising haste that made my head swivel. During our first dinner out, with the show's main production team, we talked and enjoyed each other's company, nearly excluding the folks around us. That weekend, I couldn't stop thinking about a life with her, even while entertaining my older brother Tom and his son Craig, both of whom I had flown in for a visit from the US. I had buried the hopeless romantic side of myself, but here it came in full bloom. That weekend, images of quaint clapboard houses and white picket fences, with swings in the front yard, repeatedly floated into view. She was, undeniably, the *right* one, and so the pursuit began.

Eventually and quickly, I won her heart. She spent the Christmas holiday with my family in Minneapolis, where she met my mother for the first time. (She had already met my father when she visited me on set in Bratislava that fall.) Then, after a magical ski vacation in Aspen with my grade- and high-school buddies and their gals, we returned to my little townhouse in Vegas where I finally gathered my nerve.

I can't explain why I was so nervous about proposing, but I was. We were sitting in the living room watching TV. A "Friends" rerun was playing, and it switched to commercial. I grabbed her hand.

I had wanted to propose several times over our holiday, but never found the proper time. You know how that is, right? It wasn't for lack of opportunity. I just wanted to find a special moment. I didn't have a ring, and while that might sound unromantic, it was only because I knew better than to choose something for her. As a guys' guy, I never understood jewelry, and who was I going to ask? I figured, go to the source, and let her choose a ring she wanted.

But now, time was waning. I would leave soon to return to New Zealand, and, while she would soon join me below the equator for a brief visit, I was eager to have our future together settled. I also knew she was expecting this of me.

I pulled her hand up to my lips and kissed it. I was nervous. She looked at me, smiled, then turned her attention back to the commercial.

"You know, this really works. You and me. Maybe we should make it a bit more... permanent."

Sam took the remote and turned off the TV. Then she trained those deep brown eyes on mine. She spoke in a soft low voice, "That's an interesting idea."

"What should we do about this?" Normally I'm so cool under pressure, but this woman had me in a state. I remembered when I first met her on the set of *Hercules*. Our first scene was the goodbye scene in a Hercules love story. Under a deep night sky, as we stood on the castle bridge over a misty moat, bathed in the warmth of tremendous klieg lights, Sam and I ran through our lines. We were surrounded by grips, makeup artists, and all the people who worked on the set, but we were alone in a magical film-fantasy-land that only actors understand.

Sam wore a magnificent floor-length green and gold royal gown. Her wavy flowing brown hair, enhanced by extravagant hair extensions, added to the romance. She was stunning. Poetry flooded my mind – but not with words – with emotions. What was it about her? I was tongue-tied. I repeatedly stumbled over and uncharacteristically forgot my lines! Sam observed my behavior suspiciously, which made me even more anxious about impressing her. What's a guy to do?

The whole story is in my first book, *True Strength: My journey from Half-God to Mere Mortal and How Nearly Dying Saved My Life.* Of course, now we are married, so you already know how that turned out.

On the couch here in my living room, Sam was again in front of me, with a similarly skeptical look. Though I might have been less tongue-tied, I had more riding on this conversation. I was nervous, as I smiled at her.

"If you are thinking I'm going to ask *you* something, you are going to be sorely disappointed. I'm a traditional girl."

The gig was up. "I'm sorry," I apologized hesitantly. "I've just... I've never done this before."

"Mm, hmm. That makes two of us," she assured me.

I descended from the couch to kneel before her, still holding her hand in mine. "Sam, you are the love of my life. Would you marry me?"

Tears glistened in her eyes as she smiled. She reached both hands around my neck and hugged me. "Silly. I thought you'd never ask."

Two and a half years later, we entered a sterile medical office waiting room in an old building in Vancouver, Canada. There was the typical plant in the corner and some old magazines on the coffee table, in front of white vinyl and steel chairs where we sat. Luckily, it was a slow day for the doctor, so there was no one else in the room. I was nevertheless self-conscious. I couldn't help it. I still struggled with uncontrolled anxiety, a residual side-effect of my three strokes. My brain had lost its ability to fine-tune my adrenalin, causing me unexpected and uncontrollable panic attacks. Although my healing had gradually reduced both their frequency and their severity, I still suffered minor anxiety acutely. As ridiculous as it might sound, I also desperately wanted to live up to my character's reputation somehow. For several reasons, including my own ego and insecurities, I had kept my illness a secret, but that paradoxically added a level of vulnerability I was unprepared and ill-equipped to handle.

But the fact was, Sam and I were desperate for our family, the one we had promised each other. *Boy, boy, girl.* And yet it hadn't happened as planned. They say if you want to make God laugh, plan.

Today was a return visit to Doctor Korde. He was knowledgeable, tall and lanky with kind eyes and an easy smile. Our first visit there, Sam had mentioned that we did not want our visits to his clinic to become public, he got a curious look. "You know, it's quite a common problem, the inability to conceive. There isn't any judgment with this." He spoke softly and with a British intonation.

"Maybe not here," she answered, "but we are private people living a fairly public life, and this is a conversation we choose not to have. This is a difficult enough journey for us, especially given Kevin's health struggles, which also are not public knowledge."

"It's your choice, and we can be very discreet," he had assured us, nodding.

Now we waited to get the preliminary results from his initial tests, and I was worried. What if I had a low sperm count? Then it would be obvious: I was the problem. What if I had no swimmers at all? I already felt like half a man. It had taken great effort to admit I needed Sam when I first fell ill. Then, when my recovery wasn't immediate—I was the strongest man in the world, after all—I had an enormous crisis of faith. Not in God, per se, but in myself, in certainty. My illness shook my very foundations. Our fertility troubles compounded the challenges to my masculinity.

"The doctor will see you now."

Sam and I quietly stood up and walked down the hall.

Dead man walking.

Dr. Korde greeted us with his graceful kindness. We sat casually, as if the information we were about to discuss did not hold our lives, and my fragile ego, in the balance. I smiled, trying to appear natural. "We have your results and the good news is you are both fertile. The bad news is Kevin's sperm is slow, and we believe they have a very small chance of ever fertilizing one of Sam's eggs through natural processes. The great news is that we can try *in vitro* fertilization, where the egg is fertilized with Kevin's sperm here in the lab, then reintroduced into Sam's uterus with the hopes that the embryo will implant itself for a healthy pregnancy.

"The procedure is not without risks, but we do have a very good success rate here – over thirty percent." He smiled and paused.

Thirty percent. I took all this in. In acting, doing thirty percent was like "phoning it in," unacceptable and embarrassing. In school, thirty percent was a failing grade. In baseball, a three hundred batting average is considered great, but I struggled to find another example where thirty percent would be regarded a reasonable success.

I felt like this was a final blow, kicking me while I was down. I sent up a quick prayer to a God I doubted was paying attention. *God, please let me have the children I have dreamed of.*

It's strange to think that my final, stroke-addled thoughts, as I had entered Cedars Hospital that fateful day almost three years before, feeling death wash over me, was of the family I had wanted. "God," I had prayed silently, leaning on Sam for both emotional and physical support, "I thought I had so much more to do. I would have had a family, and three kids. And now you're taking all that away, with one swipe?" I had stumbled into a new paradigm that day. God preserved me, but now I questioned Him again.

"Is this a cruel joke, to keep me alive but not fulfill my desire for children?" My pessimism was getting the better of me again.

Children

Sam

As a young adult, I desired a family, but I could never express why. Biology? Hardwiring? I was the youngest in my family, and I didn't like children. I didn't understand them, and babies had never intrigued me like other young women I knew. I never played with baby dolls or even Barbies. But something inside me drove me to want the whole family life, and that meant children. Finding the right man comprised a necessary component of that equation.

I had not grown up with a dad. My mom packed up four young girls and left my biological father when I was just a year old. She moved us across the country in a VW bug to live with my grandparents. My grandfather was a wonderful influence on me. We used to play Chinese checkers, and he would always let me win. I was four or five years old, and I cheated like the dickens, but he either didn't notice or didn't mind. I would ask him to play again and again, and typically he would, seldom tiring before I did. He was kindhearted and loving, and enjoyed each game, laughing approvingly each time I defeated him. I suspect he knew I cheated. He loved me, all the same.

Mom remarried when I was five, and we moved. I remember little of the man who would 'father' me for the next six years. My strongest memory is of repeatedly begging him to play chess with me. He seldom agreed, although I vaguely recall he must have taught me to play.

One day when I was in fourth grade, I asked him to play while Mom was napping. It was a lazy Saturday afternoon, and I must have caught him in the right mood because he agreed, and we set up the board. He loomed over the game, concentrating as I deliberated, cross-legged on the floor opposite him. Our low oak coffee table chess board was between us. The sun-bathed the room in a soft glow, and I could see the shafts of light through breaks in the window sheers, from the dust particles glinting in the air.

I took my time trying to predict his moves and craft my countermeasures, but my eight-year-old brain strained to compute chess strategy and techniques. About half-way through our game, my stepfather leaned back on the sofa with a laugh and said, "Well, Sammy, either you have a tremendous strategy that I cannot for the life of me figure out, or you've got no strategy at all." He was a large man with a hefty girth. To complement his thinning crew cut, he wore black-rimmed glasses that distorted his eyes into glossy little beads. He removed his glasses and rubbed his face, smiling at me quizzically. The sofa cushions moved noisily under his shifting weight as I returned his stare without confessing a thing.

A deer caught in his headlights, I had absolutely no strategy. So, I smiled at him. He misinterpreted my casual grin to mean I did have some plan. This would be my first lesson in bluffing.

Gauntlet unwittingly thrown, my step-father perched closer to the edge of the sofa and leaned over the board intently, replacing the thick lenses on his nose and investigating my elusive tactics to determine his response. We continued to play.

A few minutes later, after several more turns, my heart was pounding like a freight train in my chest. I softly but proudly announced, "Checkmate." I had analyzed every possible move to ensure that I could unerringly pronounce my triumph. I had *done it*! After examining every possible move on the board, I was certain I had left his king none.

He was surprised, immediately inspecting to undo my lucky move. "It looks like you did," he affirmed, reluctantly. His concession made me immensely proud. Hearing him confirm my triumph felt like a gift.

"I'm going to save the board so I can show Mommy when she wakes up from her nap," I declared excitedly.

He was quietly undone, desperate and seething behind his serious spectacles.

"That's not necessary," he countered, and with a cavalier sweep of his hand he cleared the board, knocking the chess pieces to the carpet below.

It was the last time we ever played chess, and it was a second lesson for me about fatherhood.

I am forever grateful to God for my grandfather and his countless lessons in patience and selfless ego, and I long ago forgave my step-father for his petty, vindictive temper. They both taught me something about fathers. Earthly fathers come in all shapes and sizes. Thankfully, we have One in Heaven who performs faithfully, loves unceasingly, and forgives completely.

We have two opportunities to create a parent-child relationship on earth. The first time, when we are children, we have little control. But for our second chance, we should strive for the knowledge and devotion to succeed, specifically where others have failed us. Maybe I craved the family bonds I lacked as a child, or perhaps I wished to recreate the ones I did have. My desire was responsible for that surprising and prophetic first date discussion of "boy, boy, girl."

But more than two years into my marriage to the man of my dreams (life-threatening illness aside), I remained frustratingly, desperately barren.

I determined if we couldn't conceive, we would adopt.

What was the procedure in Vancouver? The first step would be a home study, our entry portal into parenthood, performed by an agency I identified after a few phone calls.

I enrolled us and dragged Kevin to the informational meetings and interviews that the government required. Our case supervisor, Jessica, was a sweet, middle-aged woman with a matronly gaze. She was doggedly methodical, meeting with us several times, as mandated by law, to complete a dossier on us. It was her job to document our suitability to adopt, and she scrutinized every aspect of our lives. She assured us she would be discreet. But it was a probing process that left us feeling simultaneously vulnerable and deficient.

We went to the police station to be fingerprinted for a background check by a stern uniformed man with a paunch. He was longsuffering and perfunctory, graceless and mechanical. I couldn't help wondering why so many children are considered "unwanted" when individuals and couples who desire children are forced to undergo dehumanizing procedures just for the opportunity to adopt. I thought, somewhat selfishly, *adopted children have it in spades*. Adoptive parents are screened to determine if they qualify, and adopted children are some of the most desired children with the most grateful parents. Of course, this is not always the case. Also, many children go unclaimed, demonstrating the tragedy of our hyper-sexed and wanton culture.

We had nearly finished our home study, and I was researching various countries and their adoption policies. Kazakhstan looked interesting. Russia, in contrast, had recently closed its doors, creating consternation and disappointment among would-be adoptive parents, some of whom had already been matched with children. That was a snake pit into which I wouldn't put my hand.

I still needed to locate a reliable agency. This project of building a family the hard way was taking its toll on me. I was stressed and exhausted, but I continued working as if my life depended on it. In a sense, it did.

Kevin wanted a family. I knew that was in his last thoughts, after he stroked out right in front of my eyes on his labored walk into Cedars that ill-fated day. I saw it as my job to provide that for him. Even if he was too damaged to contribute, and the jury was still out on whose "fault" it was that we failed every pregnancy attempt, I was determined to give him children. I threw every iron I could think of into that fire. It's what I do.

But sometimes a girl just needs to get out and shop to distract herself and gain some perspective. Besides, I wanted some kitchen gadgets for our sparsely furnished rental.

I left Deep Cove, the steep, gray, treed suburb of Vancouver to head to IKEA. Gizmoe was on my lap, as usual. She loved to join me for errands.

The sky was granite, with heavy clouds threatening to discharge a deluge any moment, but I knew once I drove only a short distance from the Cove, the overcast sky would clear. That was the Deep Cove secret and part of what kept the town, built on an inlet between high, steep slopes, from growing bigger. Its protective mountains trapped the clouds, so the entire area was often shrouded and somber. I typically looked for excuses to drive out of the gloom.

The sun smiled on us within fifteen minutes of our drive. Giz repositioned herself on my lap to take better advantage of the warm rays as I drove. My spirits lifted, and I considered motherhood and my efforts in that direction. God knew I wanted kids. I wanted so desperately to be a mommy to more than just my little eight-pound ball of fur. Why were my plans not coming to fruition? The news from the doctor the day before floated through my thoughts. *There was nothing physically wrong with either of us.* Sure, conceiving seemed more difficult for us, but slow sperm was not an insurmountable hurdle, and there were no other issues that might make it impossible for us to have a biological child.

I didn't much care if the child was entirely our DNA. There are many paths to creating a family. For Kevin, however, this was a minefield. Month after month of failure for a man who struggled mightily to redefine himself and re-envision manliness and strength after his bout with death. I knew his heart would embrace any child, but his ego recognized and cataloged the challenges to his virility.

Admittedly, I was also hedging my bets with my adoption efforts. I had heard that adoptive parents who hadn't been able to conceive sometimes inexplicably and 'accidentally' become pregnant after adopting. I had heard that some doctors credited the hormone boost that motherhood provokes, but no one had definitive answers. It seemed like such a roulette wheel.

And I'm not a gambler.

But I am determined.

As I drove, with tears in my eyes from passionate conviction and desire, I made a deal that was more like a demand.

"God," I said, "one year from today, I promise you, one way or another, I will have a child." It was early September, 2000.

Blame

Kevin

"I knew it." It was painfully obvious this infertility was another side effect of the strokes and the corresponding health crisis. My body and brain collapse had left me insecure. I was still suffering repercussions like migraines and fatigue, dizziness, nausea, and overall weakness that I insisted on battling, at minimum, three days each week at the gym. I felt like half the man I used to be, and this latest news of my low-motility sperm reassured me of that assessment. "I'm so sorry."

Sam answered me with her inimitable, positive attitude. I found her approach annoying, but I could read compassion in her eyes. Since it was never pity, I forgave her immediately. "It makes no difference, Darling. It just is. We will get through this, and we will have a family, and that's that. The doctor did say we had better than a thirty percent chance this procedure would work."

"Yeah, I know. But that means more than a sixty percent chance it won't, and then what?"

"Then we adopt. We've almost completed all the paperwork, and I'm just now trying to decide which country. Russia is so unpredictable. We could be a year into it, with a child assignment, and they could just shut down the program again. That makes me nervous."

We were walking in Deep Cove on the uneven, tree-shaded streets. The air was still moist from recent rain, and it smelled woodsy-green, which was soothing. The August sun lazed in the dusky evening sky, but the purplish clouds overhead reflected my mood, despite our invigorating pace. A soft breeze lifted Sam's hair into her face, and she brushed it away as carelessly as she had the news of our lack of fertility. She wanted children, and I was failing as a husband. As if sensing my bitterness, she grabbed my hand.

"Think of it from my point of view," she said. "I *know* we will have children, either through in vitro or through adoption, or both. You know we are going to have three, right? I mean, that was our deal, remember?"

She was referring to our conversation on our first date in the movie theater in New Zealand. So much had happened since then, but it still struck me how strong our attraction was and how closely we fit.

It was still a struggle to hide my resentment for my illness. This was, largely because my symptoms unrelentingly plagued me each day. Granted, I was much improved over the shell of the man that had exited the hospital that last time in Atlanta. Back then, I desperately rejected the knowledge I was walking away from a big-budget movie leading role, and the paycheck and big-budget film career that went along with it. I had resigned myself to suffering. Don't think that I'm being dramatic. At least, if it sounds dramatic, that's because it was. For me, it was like a death – the death of the man I had been. And my rebirth was taking way too long, and it was way too painful. So I allowed myself self-pity, even though Sam rarely did. "Sometimes, things don't work out like you plan, Sam."

"That's true," Sam answered. "But they always do work out!" She smiled. "You want to know the good news?"

I looked at her soft grin with learned skepticism. "Hmm." I considered her. She was serious, but I knew how to read her body language. She reached out and touched my face, ran her fingers through my short hair. I still wasn't used to the short hair, which I had cut as close to military length as I could for the new TV role of Captain Dylan Hunt. I couldn't help comparing myself to Samson, who lost his strength with a haircut. My strength was gone before the trim, but part of me fantasized, somehow, that shearing my locks might reverse the curse and revive my strength. Ha! Fat chance.

Sam was gazing deeply into my eyes. She was going to impart some tidbit of brilliance (in her assessment), and I had better pay attention. We had stopped at the small park on the side of the town's main street by the water. I could almost spit the length of the town, it was so small. The salty breeze filled my lungs. "Okay, tell me. What's the good news?"

Tenderly, she pulled me close. "At least I can blame *you*!"

I pushed her back to look at her face. She was smiling, but tears filled her eyes. "I mean," she continued, "imagine they had said the fertility problem was with my eggs. It would shatter my record of perfection. Then, where would that leave us, right? This way, it's your fault, and I can blame you for everything, still. Thank goodness!"

I couldn't help myself, I laughed. I didn't want to, but she virtually forced me to indulge her in this. I stepped back from her and bowed deeply, feeling the rush in my head from the sudden move – typical of my symptoms but a little unnerving just the same.

"I'm so glad I could come to your rescue, once again, m'lady."

"Yes, Darling. You are a true gentleman!" She offered her hand for my kiss and giggled.

It was a clever strategy. Placing the blame squarely on my shoulders forced me to consider that it changed nothing. It didn't matter whose fault it was; it was something we would face together because it was a problem we shared. And if there was one thing I had learned over time with Sam it was that she bore my burdens. She didn't have the headaches or panic attacks, but she was there for me every step of the way, sacrificing her career, moving halfway around the world just to be by my side through thick or thin. And so, too, with this. Although no one could positively identify what caused my low motility, I was certain it was the overall illness.

Sam's attitude was, So be it. Now, let's figure out the next steps. And for that we turned to God and prayer.

Prayers from both Sam and myself had as yet resulted in nothing discernable. We prayed together and individually. I had learned the grateful prayer long before, during my intense few months of recovery before I began working again. It was challenging to express gratitude and stay angry, and I had found the gratitude prayer very helpful.

A friend who suggested IVF, but Sam was reluctant to try anything that might be outside of God's will. She told me her friend said that IVF wouldn't exist if God had willed against it, which was compelling enough of an argument for Sam to start her research. My, how that woman loves research! She is what I respectfully call a 'shopper,' meaning she won't buy (into) anything she hasn't fully considered and explored. If it's a car, she test-drives all the competing models. This fertility thing was no different. Sam set to work and quickly and quietly found the best clinic in town.

Lacking a definitive answer from God, we invested in both IVF and adoption. Sometimes faith looks like moving ahead despite misgivings, and taking steps in two directions, when no clear single choice exists. It felt a bit crazy, but at the same time it seemed right. If you have a dream, you do whatever it takes to achieve it. We prayed a lot during this time, just asking for guidance, blessing for our efforts, and His will to be done.

In Vitro

Sam

All the nurses and staff at the clinic were compassionate and caring, but Jacquie stood out among them as the bright light with the understanding smile who helped me through the hardest parts of the trial. I call it a trial because my impression was that we were grasping at straws, and the entire procedure had physical consequences I struggled with. First, there were the near-daily blood tests.

I have to fess up; the first day was exciting. Having decided to proceed with the treatment, I waited for that orientation meeting with trepidation and elation. I intently drove the forty-minutes from Deep Cove to the hospital, engrossed in fantasies and possibilities. When life gets aggressive and things don't seem to go my way, and especially once I've hatched a plan to win or at least combat the enemy, I tack toward the positive, set my sights on my target, focus, and deploy. This drive was me, deploying for battle.

Jacquie, with her wavy dark hair that framed her face, her olive complexion and soft gray eye shadow, is the nurse who gently instructed me on how the blood tests worked, how to give myself the shots, which pharmacy to use, scheduling procedures, and all the small details. She left nothing out. We covered the side effects and how careful I had to be. I would be stimulating, using hormone manipulation, the development of multiple eggs in my ovaries. That meant some abdominal swelling that was not without risks, so I needed to treat my body with care. Jacquie gave me my first shot. We used small needles, and though I had overcome my fear of needles years before, it wasn't without trepidation that I approached giving *myself* injections.

Jacquie pulled out a small cooler-bag and explained that the drugs needed to be kept cold. The unimpressive little bag was my gift, which made me smile because the fee for this entire service was high. It came stocked with alcohol wipes in individual packets and starter doses of the medicines. She pulled out the syringe and a vial of fluid for practice. "See the measurements on the side of the syringe? When you call in, we will tell you exactly how much to draw. Take the vial, insert the needle, upend the vial and draw out just the amount of medicine you need. It's that simple."

It wasn't that simple. This was a test of faith. The hormones were about to wreak havoc on my system, with side effects like tenderness and moodiness. Come to think of it, probably nothing out of the ordinary! But I had committed, started on the treadmill, and now my only job was to walk the steps required. That began with the initial drugs, the excitement about what might happen, and incredible anxiety over 'getting my hopes up.' With her glowing smile, Jacquie seemed to put a calm, warm blanket on my shivering ego. I was on my way.

The next month passed in a blur. Injections, blood tests, pharmacy visits, and ultrasounds. The staff made the process as pleasant as possible, but I felt the tension in the air acutely with every visit. Other women were on the same protocol, at various stages. One willowy blond patient was there for her second course. Her first one had ended unsuccessfully. Another came in with a toddler in tow, a triumph for everyone to celebrate. I watched all this with a strange detachment. I had the prophecy and my deal that I was relying on.

Don't let me mislead you. I had no assurances. I simply experienced this with faith it would have a correct ending – whatever that might be. The childless patient filled me with trepidation, which I shoved to the side. The little baby in the arms of another patient inspired hope, which I also pushed away. Reluctant to absorb my cues from my environment, I was relying on faith, which became my guiding principle throughout this seemingly unending, painfully intimate ordeal.

I went back to the clinic for the first ultrasound to see if the drugs were having any conclusive effects. The results were inspirational, but, once again, I took them in stride. But that afternoon, I went to set to have lunch with Kevin, and I was happy to share my news.

We walked to his trailer after collecting our lunches from the caterers. Those guys could put on a spread, but I wasn't hungry. Kevin also seemed eager to hear some good news.

"So, how did it go this morning?" He knew that today would either be a good milestone or it could predict complete failure.

"They counted 14 follicles developing," I said.

"Is that good? I mean, is that better than average, or whatever?"

How do you even know the right questions to ask?

"They told me that was really good, though they don't expect them all to develop fully. But the fact is, we only need one." I smiled. Kevin pulled me into a big bear hug that made my insides melt. I cried. Perhaps it was the pressure I felt. This would be my clutch moment – my time to 'deliver' for my team. It was a relief I had 'passed' my first test. Kevin looked me in the eye. "What? What's wrong?"

I laughed and shrugged. "I don't know – hormones, I guess."

"Never trust anything that bleeds for five days and doesn't die," he quipped. I punched him. "I feel so helpless. You're going through all of this, and there isn't anything I can do."

"Well, that's not entirely true. I mean, one day soon you will need to do one very important thing, you know."

"Yeah, yeah, that I know. But it's not like that's big a deal. Although it is a little creepy when you really think about it."

"So, don't think about it. There. Not creepy at all. Just keep your eye on the prize."

Kevin sighed. I knew I exasperated him with my positive attitude, but that was good for him. It kept the nerves at bay. He smiled at me with those gorgeous blue eyes. "Keeping my eye on the prize, baby," he answered.

They harvested the eggs on a sunny autumn day in a procedure for which I was fully awake. They offered me some relaxing drug, which I dutifully swallowed. But I remember the doctor counting each minuscule egg as it was withdrawn from my body.

Kevin was as good as his word and offered his contribution as my drugs took effect. The staff would mix my harvest with his donation, and we would wait as the desert longs for storm clouds, dry and thirsty.

There was good news from the clinic in the days that followed. Eventually, it was time for the follow-up procedure, placing the multi-celled embryo, otherwise known as a baby, back into my waiting uterus. The report showed that we had several embryos from which to choose, but as they observed the small lives' activities, there were three that looked particularly strong and determined. These were chosen while the others were put on ice. How they determined fortitude in a tiny, barely multi-celled thing is beyond me, but they did.

In late December, we discovered that I was pregnant and due in early September—one year from my so-called deal with God.

There was an intense desert sun streaming through the plate glass window as I worked out on the stair master we had installed on the upper level of our house on the ninth hole of the Rio Secco Golf Course. The room did not have a view of the course, but I was looking out the window to the front, across the street and up into the distant mountains. I stepped carefully, though as fast as I could.

It became too tiring. At eight-and-a-half months pregnant, I had gained nearly fifty-five pounds on my five-foot-ten frame. I'll be honest. Pregnancy was the perfect excuse for me to not concern myself with counting calories or any other weight-control measures, and I welcomed it. As an international fashion model, it might sound odd that I always felt heavy. But maybe that feeling is accepted now because of the focus our society places on weight. Right or wrong, I always somehow seemed about ten pounds too fat. I mean, I was never the ultra-thin coat-hanger type, so I became incessantly concerned with nutrition, exercise, and body image.

But once I started dating Kevin, the workout fanatic, my workouts got more focused and increased in efficiency. Our second 'date' had been at the gym. Eventually I picked up all the great tricks for an exhausting, but effective, workout.

Working out had been Kevin's solace and therapy during his three-year rehabilitation from the strokes he suffered while playing the titular role of Hercules on his hit television show, and I joined him frequently at the gym.

Today the Stairmaster proved too much for me, though, and I stepped off the equipment, catching my labored breath before my allotted thirty minutes were up. I calculated it wouldn't be too long before the baby arrived.

I joined Kevin and our friends at a golf course out at Lake Las Vegas. Kevin's friends, Jon and Julz, were visiting us before the birth, and Kevin had taken them golfing. As big as my belly was, I had no interest in putting, much less trying to swing a club, so I arrived as planned for a lunch date. "I'm so tired now," I said. "That's the real trouble. I couldn't even finish my workout today!"

Our friends were still childless, but Julz sympathized, "Maybe you should go home after lunch and put your feet up."

We got back home around 2:00 PM, and I retired to my bedroom, changed into jammies, and maneuvered my bulk into the bed. But just as I sat down, I felt, unmistakably, my water break. The time had come.

Kevin was upstairs working out on the Stairmaster. I carefully treaded up the pale stone circular staircase and approached him, studiously casual. "How much longer do you think you have on that thing?"

He checked the gauges. "About twenty-two minutes, I'd say."

"Um, no, you don't, actually. My water just broke, and I need you to take me to the hospital." I smiled. He looked at me, calculating but not understanding. "Because we're going to have a baby, now," I explained patiently.

He jumped off the machine, excited. "But… He's still two weeks away, Sam. You're not due…"

"He just moved up the date," I reported gleefully. I hurried my bulging mass back downstairs to grab some things to bring with me. My bag was not packed, yet, because Braeden had chosen to arrive two weeks early, and I procrastinate.

By the time we informed Jon and Julz as they sat in our living room that we were heading to the hospital, my adrenaline surged. It was finally real to both my body and my mind. That understanding manifested as uncontrollable trembling and excitement. It had been a long road to get to this point, and my faith in my ability had wavered but my faith in God's overall plan had not. As my girlfriend had counseled me when I had initially rejected her suggestion to try *in vitro*, if it was God's plan for me not to conceive children, then I wouldn't get pregnant even with *in vitro*. It seemed only to be God's plan for us to build our family in a less conventional, but equally effective, method. At last, we were finally on our way.

Take me to Church

Kevin

I returned to the hospital after a quick nine holes of golf in the early morning. Sam had sent me away once we realized her labor would be slow, knowing I still struggled mightily with sleeplessness. Her friend came to relieve me in the hospital, and I went back to join John and Julz for their last evening in town. When the nursing staff gave Sam labor-induction meds, I could tell her pain was high, even though she tried to hide it from me. It made me uncomfortable and frustrated that I could not do anything for her. When she suggested I go home, I reluctantly took her up on her offer.

John, Julz, and I had a late dinner and talked about our school days. This was probably not as much fun for Julz as it was for John and me. John and I had played football together from grade school through our high school years. We'd grown up in the same small town with the same teachers and classes, and we never grew apart. That's Minnesota-nice values for you. Although, we are different, our Judeo-Christian morals and home-grown fundamental world-view cherishing honesty, steadfastness, and common sense is what binds us. I've held on to many friends from grade school and high school because we all share that common understanding. We all were steeped in this Midwest, Judeo-Christian culture. For me, coming from the success-regardless-of-cost, what's-in-it-for-me attitude pervasive in the entertainment industry, sitting down with friends who share my roots is refreshing and necessary.

It wasn't like I was relaxed however. I was about to become a father. While I had no idea at the time of the specific impact and tremendous shift this would impose on my life, I did comprehend it would be cataclysmic. I was grateful that God had shepherded me to this point, and I was working hard at trusting in His providential wisdom for me.

Maybe it had to do with my nearly dying.

I don't recommend getting married shortly after suffering three strokes. Well, first, I don't recommend strokes.

Really.

No. Fun. At. All.

But right after that, entering a marriage immediately after suffering debilitation is not a great plan. The strain on our marriage, right from the beginning, was certain and harsh.

Then again, it was fire that softened and eventually shaped metal. If I regard it as a test, we passed, but not because we had studied. We applied common sense and logic, with a healthy dose of grace. One thing that grounded us in our commitment was our shared faith. Jesus Christ laid the bedrock foundation for our relationship, which is why Sam insisted on us finding a church. She proceeded gently. In New Zealand, my oppressive illness prevented me from even doing the things I loved the most like golfing, jogging, lifting weights, or even reading, so church was a bridge too far. Sam endeavored to find a church for herself, first. A few times, Sam returned with me in tow. We failed to find one place or pastor that resonated with us enough to draw us back. This was not an honest reflection of the quality of churches in Auckland but likely a symptom of my frailty. It would have to be an earth-shattering service to draw me out, yet there were also small cultural differences to overcome. Mainly, though, I just didn't have the energy.

Much of the reason for my lack of desire to attend church was my inability to process multiple stimuli in my beleaguered brain.

Crowds exhausted me. Music, restaurants, noise of any kind taxed my brain. I would pay for those indulgences for days afterward, with bouts of dizziness, headaches, and nausea. But, over time, I grew stronger. And church, for Sam, was reinforcement, reassuring and reaffirming. I understood her commitment, though I didn't quite share it.

Sam stumbled upon a new church way out in the boonies and decided we should try it together, just for fun, one Sunday. Sunday arrived, cool and misty, but I was feeling more stable than usual, so we dressed and headed out to explore. We got to church early and joined the small group going up the steps into a 1970s-designed, pitched-roof chapel built high on stilts to avoid floods. We took our seats along with a small quiet congregation. After a homey, friendly greeting by the overzealous new pastor, he introduced the main desire of the church: to make friends. With that plaintive introduction, the theme song from *Cheers* played. Sam and I sighed. There was something so corny and desperate with this appeal that we almost laughed. This would not be our church. We needed more substance and less superficial "let's all be friends" stuff. We left the service feeling dissatisfied and discouraged.

The story wasn't new. When I was starting my recuperation in Las Vegas, Sam wanted to find a church for us to attend there, but I could never handle it. Because of my brain damage, fluorescent lights made my synapses crazy. We tried, but many of the young Christian churches were housed in large, new, fluorescent-lit buildings, full of great Christian rock music, inevitably played at raucous levels. I wasn't entirely alone in my misery, though, because the music was too loud even for Sam. We only tried a few together before realizing it just wasn't a great plan. They say the definition of insanity is doing the same thing repeatedly while expecting a different result. But they don't say that, while you are trying again and again, sometimes you change.

While the frequency of my church visits dropped substantially, Sam still attended various services on her own. Eventually, she found a church she enjoyed in Auckland, where I could also join her. We appreciated the animated but thoughtful pastor, the intimate setting, and the contemporary music, which was not so loud as to be uncomfortable. But I still struggled with my illness, so church remained a 'sometimes' proposition for me. Large crowds presented an enormous hurdle for me; surround-sound still confused my brain, as did loud noises, and there was the ever-present "Ape factor."

The ape factor refers to a Swedish phrase Sam taught me, "Alla tjener apan, men apan tjener ingen." Translated: Everyone knows the ape, but the ape knows no one. I was an attraction to people as the famous *Yank* actor filming the hugely successful TV show in their country. They would whisper as I walked by, or smile knowingly. They weren't unkind, but I was already struggling with my symptoms, and feeling the attention and being under the microscope made me uncomfortable.

When we would go back to Las Vegas where I lived when I was in the States, the situation wasn't much better. I still had my symptoms, and people always recognized me – perhaps even more so. We often accompanied my parents to their church services, but I never quite felt at home there either.

If you read my first book, *True Strength,* you know God is essential in my life. My wife knew there was only one way to address the spiritual component of my hardships and that was through an intimate connection with Jesus Christ. Now, you can say you believe in God, and you can even pray, but you cannot pursue a strong connection with God by avoiding church. For this reason, I encourage people to keep seeking a place of worship, to be with other believers who can bolster their faith.

Once we returned to live in Los Angeles, I eagerly revisited the church in Eagle Rock, where Sam and I had attended before I got sick. Mark, the pastor there, married us. In his church, I felt like I was tapping back into my faith. And although at the time I was wrestling with God, going to church became a time of reflection and affirmation in my belief. Church offered a moment to reconnect with God in a way not fostered elsewhere. It was intentional, but also an opportunity for God to work in me, reach me, knead my sorrows, and gently heal me. There is nothing so comforting and confirming which is why I stand by my recommendation to everyone reading this book. If you don't enjoy church, find a new one. Keep looking until you find the right one. Commit to doing so, and ultimately you will be rewarded.

Diapers

Kevin

Now that we had a baby at home, I had even more reason to rush home after work. It was validation, too, of the contract we had negotiated with the production studio for *Andromeda* based on my illness. It had agreed to limit my workdays to five-per-week and twelve hours-per-day, door-to-door. And folks, let's be honest, that's still a full workday!

On *Hercules* I typically worked twelve to fourteen hours each day – on set. If you count drive time and going to the gym for my daily workouts, I would be out for an average of sixteen hours every workday. For the first year of the show, the workweek was six days, excluding only Sundays. I've always had a very strong work ethic, stemming from managing a paper route when I was a boy, which meant getting up at four-thirty each morning, even in the dead of winter, with below-freezing temperatures. My sixteen-hour days were just part of the deal. I loved being on set, and I loved my job and the crew I worked with. I didn't consider my lack of a social life or the absence of 'downtime' to be a hardship. I was devoted to my show.

Then, I had three strokes, and when I finally hazarded to go back to work, I could only give production an hour each day on set. It was all I could handle. Even that exacerbated my symptoms and often left my head spinning, laying me out on the couch. After I worked on set, I went straight back home and rested until bedtime.

Of course, 'bedtime,' used here, is not a euphemism for sleep (or anything else). I didn't sleep well for the first year following my strokes. I suffered from anxiety and panic attacks, which hit for no reason. I saw lightning flashes when I closed my eyes. My dizziness seemed to get worse when I closed my eyes, too, and I had this intense feeling of falling backward, which seemed worse when I lay down. Ah, vertigo, the gift that keeps you falling.

Psychologically and emotionally, I was a wreck, too. Lying down to go to sleep provided me the occasion to consider my disastrous condition, assess all my physical challenges, and worry about my vulnerable future. I dreaded the evenings. I began purposely falling asleep before heading to bed in the den in front of the TV to fool myself about hitting the sack. The distraction provided by the TV allowed me to relax enough to drift off, but it wasn't a deep, rejuvenating sleep, typically. To say my sleep was restless is an understatement.

Beginning a marriage courting these disorders is a sure-fire recipe for disaster, and I hand it to Sam for staying strong and supportive throughout. She had many restless nights, and I would often find her on the couch in the wee hours of the morning, reading because she couldn't sleep. We were struggling but as my health improved, so did the entire situation.

By the time I got into my new show, *Andromeda*, I was working full days, but as I mentioned, we had negotiated a better scheduling deal with my new employer that limited my work to 12 hours each day. Just over two years into my recovery, I was managing my illness better and my symptoms had also dramatically improved. I still forced the production team to honor my 12-hour days for two reasons. First, I needed downtime to recuperate from my continuing intense reactions to over-stimulation. My brain was still struggling. While I could keep it together for the twelve-hour days, I was a basket case on the couch when I finally reached home. I still tried to work out four or five days a week, but that was nearly the extent of my adventures. Going out to dinner at a crowded restaurant or a party was too taxing for my fragile condition. However, our first year up in Vancouver proved to be a positive one, and I felt my recovery picking up steam.

Sam and I became homebodies in the modern home that production rented for us in Deep Cove. The house was all granite, steel and glass. It featured an incline, which is like an elevator set on a slope, because the front door to the house sat about two stories below street-level. While this piece of technology was cool, nothing about the house even approached cozy. What it lacked in hominess it more than made up for with its view. It was a house built on the steep slope of a mountain that formed one side of the cove. The cove itself bordered on being a fjord: sheer sides dropping deeply into the ocean. I enjoyed the natural setting of the house. The view across the dark waters was only mountainside; the opposite wall of the cove was undeveloped forest and rock. The twelve-foot low-tide-to-high-tide change only emphasized the dramatic view.

Although the house was cold and gray, Sam and I endeavored to make it a home. We bought extra furniture, which it desperately needed. And, while it was sparse and chilly, the simplicity of the gray-painted and granite walls, steel, and voluminous glass windows, revealing outdoor greenery's peacefulness, soothed me.

The real downside to living in Deep Cove was the weather. The looming sides of the cove were highly effective in trapping low-hanging clouds, and keeping them. I think they also induced rainfall because Deep Cove was often cloudy and rainy, and a short drive out into Vancouver would reveal sunny, beautiful skies.

We only stayed a year in that little house, determining to move closer to Vancouver, into a more family-oriented neighborhood, or at least a neighborhood with neighbors. The Deep Cove house sat apart from virtually everyone and everything.

Sam found a small traditional-style spec home in an older neighborhood of Vancouver. It was a new construction, and we bought it just as they finished building. She outfitted it with comfy furnishings and warm tones. It had three bedrooms upstairs off a long hallway, and the downstairs had an open kitchen and family room with a separate dining and living room. Because it was long and narrow, the house boasted a loft on the third floor, which Sam turned into her office. The small basement became our quasi-rumpus room then small guest room when the upstairs was occupied. The house was infinitely livable, and although it lacked a view, Sam and I enjoyed our newfound ability to walk to stores and, eventually, neighborhood parks. We traded water and a dock for a small, cozy backyard, and the granite and steel for pillows and drapes. We barbequed almost every night in our snug little backyard and loved it.

Long walks had become my therapy. The gym I found near our new house provided me a mile-and-a-half walk home when I worked out there. My driver, Gail, would drop me off at the gym after work now that I was back to daily workouts, and I would hike home when I finished. I enjoyed these walks while I studied my lines for the next day's scenes or just contemplated my situation. I was so much improved that I envisioned a future free from my symptoms. It had taken a great deal of time for me to do so, unlike my wife, who always had strong faith in my eventual, full recovery. Faith like that might simply be a gift, in which case Sam is blessed.

Finding Faith

Sam

It was a beautiful August day, warming with the intense Los Angeles sun streaming through the windows of my apartment. Kevin had returned from his doctor's office and was about to tell me about his adventure as I placed a turkey sandwich in front of him on the coffee table. He had experienced an odd episode the afternoon before when he called me from his car to tell me the world was going haywire.

"I feel like I'm in an aquarium. There was this lightning storm in my head, and I nearly passed out. I pulled the car over, but I can't see well, and I'm hearing everything in some kind of echo chamber like I'm under water. It's really weird, Sam."

We talked about it for a few minutes, me trying to calm him down, and him working through what we eventually, days later, recognized as his first brain stroke. But at that moment, neither of us understood the significance of this event.

"Where are you?" I asked him urgently.

"I'm on Wilshire. I just left the chiropractor. And it was really strange, Sam, because I was on the table, and he was just massaging my neck, and I heard this very distinct voice, like close-up in my ear, saying, 'Don't let him crack your neck.' He knows I hate that! I never let him crack my neck, but he didn't ask. In eight years, he's never cracked my neck, but today, for some reason, he did. It's freaky because of that voice, Sam."

"I can tell. Let me pick you up. Where on Wilshire are you?"

"No, no, no. I'm doing better now. I still feel odd, but I should be able to make the drive. It's just that everything is kind of blurry – fuzzy. I don't know. It's not too bad, but there's definitely something wrong."

"I'll stay on the phone with you, then. Don't hang up, and if you really start to feel worse, just pull over, and I'll come get you."

His progress to my apartment was slow. Kevin drove cautiously, which, luckily, was easy in the slow mid-afternoon traffic. By the time he arrived, he had a screaming headache and felt nauseous and dizzy. He practically stumbled into my apartment and lowered himself carefully and deliberately onto my couch.

"I don't think I can do the interview tonight, Sam. I feel like crap. Everything's spinning, and my head is exploding. It's throbbing."

The interview was on a new TV show hosted by Magic Johnson, the famous, retired Los Angeles Lakers basketball player. Kevin called his publicist to cancel in enough time, but Andrea answered him in horror. "What? You can't do that! Not this close to show-time! You're the main guest, Kevin, and this is important! Take a couple of aspirin but don't cancel on me."

"It's not like I'm doing this on purpose, Andrea. I'm sick. I'm not even sure what happened, but my head is splitting."

"Are you going to the hospital?" she tested.

"No… no. But my head—"

Andrea, a no-nonsense, professional woman, cut him off. "Kevin, if you cancel now, it's not going to look good for you. You'll look irresponsible. They are counting on you. We all are. You don't know what I went through to get you on the schedule, and if you just crap out on them now, well—"

"Okay, okay." Kevin lacked even the energy to prevail, here. "Lemme see if I lie down for a while, maybe I'll feel well enough."

"Sure, Kevin. You've got a couple of hours. Lie down. Take a short nap. Call me back. I'll see you in a few."

Kevin turned to me, "I'm going to lie down. See if a little sleep makes me feel better."

When he awoke, he wasn't much better, but like a football player gets a shot of cortisone to play a few more downs, it was enough for him to ignore the damage and get back in the game. I accompanied him to the CBS studios, and he did the interview, albeit in a miasma of head pain and dizziness, and we left precipitously.

He slept fitfully and awoke the following morning to a heavy, throbbing head and further dizziness. After trying to watch some television, and struggling to make sense of the sounds, he realized something was seriously wrong, so he called his doctor and walked to his office, which was about three miles away. Walking in LA? Well, the way he was feeling, he wasn't comfortable driving, even just the three miles. He recognized the potential liability he risked by insisting on driving himself home the day before. Kevin also liked being outdoors, feeling strangely bolstered by the fresh smells of a waking day. It even cleared his head a little bit, and he thought maybe he imagined the whole thing or at least exaggerated the severity of it. There was definitely something wrong, but maybe, with a little rest...

Doc found a lump in his shoulder and then Kevin divulged some crucial information: his vision was compromised. Doc sent him to the ophthalmologist, whose office he walked to directly. The eye doctor documented bilateral loss of vision, typically a sign of a stroke. Why he sent Kevin back home is beyond me. I was unaware of that correlation when Kevin sat on my couch, explaining the results of the vision test as simply two inexplicable blind spots in his visual field.

Then, as he spoke, he slurred his words. His face contorted into a confused expression, and he asked me, "Cahn you heah dhat?" It was clear he struggled to enunciate, and failed. His words were muffled and indistinct. My heart pounded strongly against my chest as if to say, "No-NO, no-NO, no-NO!"

My apartment was minutes from Cedars Sinai Hospital. As I escorted him in, I knew the situation was dire. He was leaning heavily on me, and I felt his Kevin resignation. He thought he was dying, and he wasn't wrong. He was well down the road to death. But the objective of a hospital is to provide hope for the patients and their loved ones. They express the hope that the Christian faith has in Christ, which explains why so many of our hospitals were founded by Catholics as charitable outreach.

I grasped onto that hope. I didn't realize then that what I had was faith. Hope is wishing for things to come, but faith is an expectation of them. I had confidence in a good outcome. I held a positive outlook that no matter what, the end result would be for the best. That meant a full recovery for Kevin, regardless of his travails.

When, in the intensive care room, Kevin went into shock, and the nurse yelled, "We have to get him back into surgery or we're going to lose him!" I panicked. I ran to the bank of phones and called his personal physician at his office. That was perhaps my first test of faith, and I failed, but I learned my lesson from that. Doc couldn't do much from his office miles away. He couldn't even reassure me, except to tell me that Kevin was getting the best of care. "Compared to what?" is the only thing I could think of.

Then, I walked back into the intensive care unit, shaken, defeated and despondent, only to discover that the entire incident was resolved; Kevin was calm again, and the hysterical nurse had disappeared. The attending doctors told me they simply had administered some Benadryl. The entire ordeal had been real, and yet, surreal. I witnessed a crisis that was not an actual catastrophe because it was so easily resolved. Sometimes things are not as they appear, and our faith might keep us from accepting them as they are.

I experienced, at that moment, a crisis of faith in the doctors and the medical community. They were not the infallible experts we are all taught. I quietly reexamined my position, reviewing for myself their apparent disbelief that Kevin had suffered strokes when I had told them about his slurred speech. They took more than a full day to discover the underlying problem, the aneurism in his shoulder. Once they found it, they acted precipitously and effectively, thank goodness. They were part expert and part novice. It was the novice element that gave me pause now. I suppose there's a reason it's called a "practice."

I surmised the truth: Kevin would be fine, and I determined not to believe the negative, not to allow it any foothold. So, for instance, later, when the experts told Kevin not to expect any recovery after his third (some said eighth) month in, I scoffed at it. I refused to allow Kevin to focus on it. I casted doubt on the naysayers, instead of giving them power over our reliance on a positive outcome. I relied more on my faith than on faulty human so-called expertise.

Where did I find the fortitude to sustain this conviction? I can only deduce that God was acting in me. The Holy Spirit came and fed me my faith because it never failed me from that moment on. When a friend carefully tiptoed around questioning my choice to marry a disabled man who might never recover, I laughed at her. "Never recover? Of course, he will recover and be better than before!" Even as I appreciated her care for me, I recognized the selfishness of her attitude (on my behalf) and pushed her away. I was committed to him, for better or worse, even before the vows in front of God. The commitment made, I was determined to do my part, proceeding on faith.

Baby Bonding

Kevin

Now, three and a half years into our marriage, we had a third member of our little family – a baby boy, Braeden, who grabbed my heart with both hands and wouldn't let go. He was born late in August, in Las Vegas, where we lived during my off-seasons. We had a quick two weeks with him in Vegas before we traveled back up to Canada for season two on *Andromeda*, which was firmly holding the number slot in syndication. We brought baby Braeden into our new home in Vancouver, and the place looked entirely different. I was a father now. That changed everything.

Sam was determined that my sleep, still fitful and unreliable, would not be disturbed by a crying baby. She set up the guest room upstairs at the other end of the hallway as her temporary bedroom, with the baby in his cradle with her. That way, when he nursed during the nights, she didn't have to go far, and he wouldn't disrupt my nights. Initially, I was uncomfortable with that arrangement. I felt like I was wimping out, not pulling my weight, but I soon saw how clever it was. I couldn't breastfeed the baby and that was his sole interest. I also desperately needed what little sleep I could squeeze in each night. Still plagued by my anxiety and other symptoms, I had not regained the ability to fall into a deep and lasting repose.

During the filming of Hercules, I worked myself hard. Long hours with an exhausting schedule, doing my own stunts and learning, on average, three fights each week, together with the heavy workouts I was used to, gradually pushed me into a shortened and more intense sleep routine. After reviewing my script for the next day, I would typically hit the pillow shortly past midnight. Then it was lights out and dreams on for about five hours before I would wake to start the whole thing over. I habitually slept so hard that I even stopped having dreams. This could have contributed to the whole health crisis.

So, the first month with a new baby, all I could do was look at him and hold him. Strangely, that was enough to hook me. I had always known I'd wanted kids, and when I first had the strokes, I regretted that death would preclude me from having them. Now, I had not only survived my health catastrophe, but God had blessed me with a perfect little boy with the love of my life. Suddenly, there was something more interesting than my career and that's saying something. I would rush home from work, strap on the baby carrier, bring the tiny nugget to my chest, and Sam and I would walk the neighborhood. It was good for me to walk, but the sleeping child added a whole new dimension. I loved him like he was my whole life.

Once we transferred him to his crib, and he started taking evening baths, bedtime became our little ritual. I'd take him upstairs for his bath then put his pajamas on, and we would read *Room on the Broom, Goodnight Gorilla,* and *Goodnight Moon.* Then I would pray over him before putting him to sleep, drowsy and tired from an exhausting day of learning and growing. I'd creep out of the room, leaving the door ajar, and head downstairs to spend some time with Sam before we retired to bed ourselves.

Sometimes, he'd wake and cry. Those were the rare times Sam and I disagreed about child-rearing. I was always ready to run to him, and Sam would often dissuade me, not wanting Braeden to become too needy or demanding. Once, I overrode her and went into his bedroom. He had pooped in his diaper and was standing in his crib, probably traumatized (as I was) by the incredible stench!

It was nearly enough to make me faint! I changed him and went back to bed secure in my invaluable contribution to our child-raising endeavor. Sam was duly contrite. But not before expressing how uncharacteristic it was for him to soil his diaper so late at night. In her defense, it hadn't happened before. But after that, I was on "goodnight" patrol, with last-checks on the little guy. Sam had done full-day duty with him, so, naturally, it was my turn. The combination of her characteristic hard-boiled tough-love approach and my soft, tender touch worked well for us, as I've seen for many couples with kids. It just goes to show why it takes two distinct individuals to cover all the bases – though it's fairly likely even together we missed some angles.

Studies show[1] that children raised in married households perform better as students, and that married families experience less poverty. Statistical research proves that most fathers are better earners at the time of birth than unwed mothers. More surprising is that children in unmarried homes suffer a forty percent greater probability of committing violence than those raised in two-parent homes. "A 10 percent increase in the percentage of children living in single-parent homes leads typically to a 17 percent increase in juvenile crime."[2] Furthermore, "The rate of violent teenage crime corresponds with the number of families abandoned by fathers."

The violence correlation boggles my mind. What is it about the commitment to a marriage that creates the stability that deters violence? Perhaps it is related to responsibility and the integrity of a person's word. Young people from broken families experience weaker connections to their communities and neighborhoods and feel less responsible for them. They are less invested *in* and therefore they *invest less* in their own communities. They more

---

[1] http://www.heritage.org/poverty-and-inequality/report/marriage-americas-greatest-weapon-against-child-poverty

[2] http://www.heritage.org/crime-and-justice/report/the-real-root-causes-violent-crime-the-breakdown-marriage-family-and

easily exploit any opportunity to satisfy their unmet needs or wants at the expense of those around them. This contributes to the disintegration of neighborhoods and communities. Families are the foundational bedrock of society.

Perhaps those who pledge their marriage vows are a different type of person than those who do not—more reliable, more prepared, and more determined to succeed at what promises to be challenging. I don't pretend to know all the answers, but the facts are clear. It's better for children to be raised in two-parent households, economically, emotionally, and for their physical health. Statistics don't lie.

Braeden and Sam often visited me on the set of *Andromeda*, the television show Gene Roddenberry created on the heels of *Star Trek*, back in 1969. Majel Roddenberry, Gene's widow, had approached me to play the lead in the resurrection of the concept, just as we were planning to wrap up shooting *Hercules*. Her timing was impeccable. I was ready to try something new. Being a big fan of the original *Star Trek* series, I was honored to become the first captain created by Mr. Roddenberry after Captain Kirk. Thus, Captain Dylan Hunt was born! As Sam put it, I went from Herk to Kirk.

Production built our set in a rented warehouse in Burnaby, a suburb of Vancouver. I laughed the first time we drove up to the buildings where our production would be housed. The sign out front read, "Ackland Warehouse." After seven years in Auckland, New Zealand, filming *Hercules,* the name coincidence was not lost on me.

For dressing rooms, the production kept trailers and motor homes in the parking lot. My motor home was spacious but nothing fancy. I remember showing up at call-time on the first day of shooting, and one actor complained that my accommodations were bigger than the others. "Ah, socialism," I chuckled silently to myself. I was the star of the show, and its entire lynchpin. My manager had negotiated the best deal for me, including those twelve-hour days I grew to love. Of course, my dressing room would be the biggest – it was my show! But it does sound a bit presumptuous or arrogant to explain this to someone you've just met, so I answered, "Well, I just picked the first one I saw when I got here. What time did you arrive on set? Maybe you just got here too late." (Yeah, I know. I've always had that smart aleck attitude. It came from competing with three brothers growing up!)

When I'm on set, I like to have fun. Unfortunately, the stress of our move to Vancouver, combined with my injured brain, resulted in increased sensitivity, which made me more reclusive. On *Hercules,* I would usually eat with the crew and other actors. I would also goof around on set and off.

But after my health crisis and slow recovery, my brain demanded quiet time, making me appear, to my chagrin, antisocial and distant. On *Hercules,* my acquired reclusiveness was understood. First, I had a fundamental transformation that everyone witnessed. The delays in shooting, my significantly reduced shooting schedule, and weight loss from not lifting at the gym, everyone was acutely aware something bad had happened. The crew and cast were all just walking on eggshells hoping it would work out all right. They were rightfully in fear for their jobs if I couldn't perform.

I'm unaware of how the producers handled the explanation of my absence and my illness. Everyone knew I had been in the hospital, but the extent of my injuries was publicly downplayed. Universal Studios insisted on that. The crew sure were careful around me when I resumed filming in New Zealand. And the joyous ambiance that had characterized the set before was replaced with a somber, wary, and quiet atmosphere.

As I gradually increased my hours on set each day, over a period of about eight months, the mood and tone lifted. But we never quite regained our previous *joi de vivre*, and although I loved the work, it became more like work than ever before.

In Vancouver, no one I know of, save my executive producer, knew my condition. I put on a good face on set because it's important for morale, and the star of the show largely establishes the tone on set. I wanted to have fun and for others to enjoy their work, even though I struggled to achieve my previous level of enthusiasm.

I worried about how the cast and crew might interpret my seclusion. I may have seemed antisocial or withdrawn. Perhaps they would think I was stuck up. When some of the crew or other actors ventured to ask me to sit with them at lunch, and I turned them down, I can only imagine what went through their minds. The fact was, I simply had to go back to my dressing room and lie down to rest my brain.

Once we got into a groove, with my schedule of 12-hour days dictating regular hours for everyone, set became a mostly happy place. We worked as a team and enjoyed ourselves. It soon became clear I had worried needlessly over how people might view my desired solitude. This gradually changed. By season two, I returned to my old form, and the set developed a fun, light-hearted functionality, with cast and crew constantly cracking jokes. This was a wonderful chapter in my life, watching my long dark tunnel lighten with sunshine.

The first year we lived in Vancouver, Sam had tried to find work, but it wasn't meant to be. She eventually discovered the actors' union instructed casting directors not to audition foreign (meaning American) actors for local parts, as a form of protectionism for local talent. This had also been the case in New Zealand. But down there she was too busy to pursue her career with any gusto because my illness was so overwhelming.

Sam had found an agent, who apparently worked with the union and convinced Sam she needed some special union dispensation to work as a local hire. It turned out, we found out later, that the union had sent a letter around to all the casting directors instructing them not to audition any foreign talent for jobs cast in Vancouver! Yet one casting director resolved to hire her on a television show to spite the union. This director resented union bosses telling her what to do. How American of her.

When this casting agent called Sam with a job, we had just discovered Sam was pregnant. Sam and I conferred and decided it was too risky for the pregnancy and inconvenient with my schedule, so she rejected the job offer.

By the time Braeden entered our lives, I had an established routine for work and exercise. Sam was as happy as a kitten with a bowl of warm milk to be a new mom. The baby fit right in from the start. So, while the timing was not perfect waiting for the first few years of our marriage, until my recovery was both underway and more assured, the delayed gratification benefitted us both.

Less than three weeks after Braeden was born, the Twin Towers and the entire United States was attacked by Al Qaeda. I was headed in to work with my driver, Gail, when I heard about the first tower on the news. I immediately called Sam and woke her up. It was about 6:00 AM Pacific Time. I told her to turn on the TV to see what was happening. The moment I got off the phone they reported the second plane on the second tower. Inconceivably, we were under a terrorist attack.

Gail, normally chatty and smiling, was somber as she finished the drive to our warehouse-set. I dropped my bag in my camper and made my way into the offices to find many of the crew standing dumbfounded by the horrendous news. They were glued to the televisions, which were showing hopeless, frightened victims jumping to their deaths from hundredth-story windows. Terrified people ran in the streets, covered in the white chalky dust of the destroyed towers. As a producer on the show, I conferred with our executive producer and agreed to initially postpone shooting for an hour or two, and then consider if we should even cancel for the day

Everyone was grief-stricken and emotional, to say the least. Most of us were in shock. There was a lot of discussion of how far this might go. We learned of more planes, the Pentagon, and the Pennsylvania field, but no one knew how to react, or what to do. We all felt helpless. Some of us had friends in New York but couldn't reach them. Sitting around waiting for more news, watching repeated footage of the buildings burning left us exhausted and frustrated.

After I called her, Sam immediately got up, gathered the baby and his things, and came to the set. She arrived and joined the rest of the stunned cast and crew, watching the television screens in the big room. Everyone hugged and cried, though none of us were directly affected by the tragedy. Each of us, even the Canadians, took it personally. This was an attack on all western countries that believe in freedom. Sam's sister lived in New York, and she tried calling but couldn't get through. All the lines were jammed.

President George W. Bush urged Americans to return to work. Don't allow the terrorists to win by changing your lifestyle or behaviors.

As I look back, with the benefit of twenty-twenty hindsight, I'm uncertain I would agree with this advice. While we did go back to work after a short delay, our lives were unavoidably and fundamentally changed by those attacks. I now question whether "normalizing" them, which became tantamount to ignoring them by returning to work, may prove, eventually, to have been some of our undoing. Denying their impact is one thing, but it seems like we ended up accepting them. Every time we take off our shoes or succumb to a pat-down to get on a plane, they win, and this is a war, not a grievance or dispute. I like to characterize it as a war between progress and regress.

Examine the culture of those who attacked the US and our unmatched, unabashedly successful capitalist system. There is a reason they targeted the World Trade Center. First, observe what even just the name of the buildings stands for. World stands for— what else—the world, i.e., equal opportunity for all nations worldwide. But the extremist Islamic attackers resent the world because it lacks or eschews Muslim dominance. So they seek to assert their supremacy through a war with the non-Muslim world. The second word, Trade, means wealth-producing, which is why America has led the world in wealth creation for two centuries. The trade of goods and services enriches all parties through freely-negotiated exchange. As a simple example: If a baker can't farm, but a farmer, who can't bake, supplies him grain in exchange for baking, they both get bread. They are both enriched. We have facilitated wealth creation with money, which complicates the concept, so people often strain to comprehend it. The Islamists who attacked the US do, however. They attacked wealth creation itself. And where did they attack that wealth? At its so-called "center," the third word in the title of those buildings.

The attack on the World Trade Center was an assault on wealth, the immense prosperity engendered by our western values, which are distinct from those espoused by the Islamists. We value freedom because it allows wealth creation and personal resolve. We value wealth because it allows us to retain our freedoms, and it advances humankind. They attack wealth because it is intertwined with the freedoms they disdain. They seek to eclipse progress with their regressive vision.

To say I took the WTC, Pentagon and intended White House attacks personally is not an overstatement. I'm a science fiction nut, and I've often daydreamed about having superpowers to travel through space and time to thwart deadly attacks and vanquish bad guys. (Why do you think I do the TV shows I do?) Boy, in the days that followed the attacks I had some real rage boiling under my skin. It infuriated me. I kept envisioning scenarios in which the perpetrators were stopped in heinous ways. This wasn't healthy, but it was the best I could manage. I suffered insomnia for months after the terrorist attacks. I found it impossible to sleep, with all the anger and hatred seething through my body.

Once the news of the attacks began to simply repeat and the threat seemed finished or at least suspended, people started realizing the futility of our situation. The news reports were incessant and sinister, and we soon felt we could take no more. We needed time to process the event, but as a producer, I knew the old adage, "The show must go on." Because there was nothing else to do, we got back to work.

The guys had some lighting to do, so I headed back to my camper with Sam and The Boy. I lifted him in his car seat into the motorhome and set him on the floor. Sam followed me up the stairs, pensive and brooding. Her eyes were glazed with tears.

I reached down into the car seat, unstrapped Braeden, and picked him up. He smiled at me. He was just a bendy, floppy baby who couldn't even hold up his head. He was vulnerable and precious. I was hit with the reality that although my job in this world was to protect him, I was powerless against a spiritual evil that dedicated itself to extinguishing freedom, progress, and the welfare of billions of people. How was I to protect this adorable bundle I held in my large hands?

It was a question I threw into the universe, immediately answered by God.

It's odd when you think of it, but the evil of those who would so wantonly destroy – what, exactly? Buildings that represent prosperity and a community that embodies the freedom that engenders prosperity. That's not just a grudge. That is an attempt to snuff out humanity. That is anti-creation in the sense it seeks to destroy the fundamental product of the created: its handiwork. That isn't a small evil. It's the depths of evil. It's the evil that proves the existence of God. Because if evil can be so devoted to destruction, then there must exist the counterbalancing force dedicated to design and creation.

We used this logic in my movie, *God's Not Dead*. I've joked about the atheists out there who are so hell-bent on disproving something in which they don't believe. If they really didn't believe it, there would be no reason to argue against it. Their spurious quarrels about the idea of a creator express His very existence.

This line of reasoning eventually provided me with relief, facing the small boy who didn't even know his own name, but for whom I was entirely responsible. I loved him with a ferocious tenderness, and I wanted the world for him. And our enemies passionately desired to violently deprive him of that world.

First, I resolved to do my utmost to stop them. Second, I realized, again, that I was not in control. However, it looked like I needed a refresher course on what that meant because rather than soothe me, that acknowledgement enraged me.

I looked at Sam leaning her shoulder against the wall of my motorhome, stoic and strong yet still vulnerable. Carrying some tenacious baby-weight, she wore yoga pants, a workout top and jacket. Her head bent toward the window, she crossed her arms and took a deep breath, as profoundly affected as the rest of us. As if reading my mind, she said, "You know, Kevin, we really aren't in control."

"Why do you say that?" I asked, barely concealing my overwhelming, unanswered rage. She had nothing to do with my fury, but it was there and ready to explode onto the scene.

"There's a bigger battle waging. Our job is to fight and have faith in The One Who sees all and judges all." She paused, considering. "Sometimes, you get knocked down."

"You think I don't know that?" My skin was crawling.

"That's not what I meant. I just meant..." she started in a placating tone.

I cut her off. "I'm sorry – I know what you meant. You mean that we live to fight another day. What I don't get is, why fight? I mean, why is there ever a need to fight? Why are people such a-holes?"

She smiled, laughed a little and nodded. "Yeah. Why does evil exist? Umm... it must exist. I don't have any other answer except to say that the only way to have good is for evil to exist. So, naturally, true evil endures because if it didn't we would cease to have anything good."

"I don't give a crap about theory and theology. This is insanity."

"True, and you cannot apply logic to insanity. But have faith because there is a broader picture."

"Okay, fine. But right now, I'm looking at a little boy who just inherited a completely different world than the one I intended." She moved to sit next to me. I was in a mood unlike anything I had experienced before. She was also prickly, feeling just as jarred as I was, I'm sure.

"The world was always there," she said peaceably.

"And now it's here."

"And now, it's here," she repeated, definitively.

A crew member came and knocked on the door. "They're ready for you, Kevin."

"Okay. I'll be right there." I looked at Sam.

She extended her arms to receive the child, saying, "He's hungry, anyway. I'm going to stay here for a bit to feed him."

"Sure. But then come on set, too, okay. Or I'll come back when they need to light."

"That'd be good."

I grabbed the jacket of my costume to head out.

"It's hard, Kevin. I'm so sad for the families of the victims – those people jumping from the buildings…" A lone tear slipped from the corner of her eye and descended her cheek. I kissed it. And, though I didn't feel the emotion, I said the thing I knew she needed to hear. "It's going to be alright. Different, but alright." I walked away.

"Love you," she lobbed as I was closing the door.

I stuck my head back in to say, "Love you, more. Both of you."

The show must go on.

Twin Towers

Sam

Once society had absorbed the attacks, President Bush urged everyone not to allow them to permanently disrupt their lives—almost as if nothing had happened:

Terrorist attacks can shake the foundations of our biggest buildings, but they cannot touch the foundation of America. These acts shatter steel, but they cannot dent the steel of American resolve.

America was targeted for attack because we're the brightest beacon for freedom and opportunity in the world. And no one will keep that light from shining...

The functions of our government continue without interruption. Federal agencies in Washington which had to be evacuated today are reopening for essential personnel tonight and will be open for business tomorrow.

Our financial institutions remain strong, and the American economy will be open for business as well.[3]

This was all well and good, but everyone knew our lives would not go back to normal, nor should they. Our entire way of life had been attacked by a vicious predator, and turning our backs would be the worst thing we could do. I believe the country took Bush's words too much to heart. By returning to life-as-usual so quickly, we allowed the attack to become normalized. They attack, we ignore.

I'm not implying that our military didn't do their utmost. Nor do I intend to relitigate the validity or necessity of the wars in Afghanistan and Iraq. Those are separate and distinct from our response to an attack on the US mainland by a foreign enemy.

Overwhelmingly, the response from ordinary citizens was to show up at church or synagogue. These institutions were packed immediately following the attacks. "By some estimates, on the Sunday following the terror attacks, roughly half of the adult population in the United States attended a religious service. But the attendance dropped off starting in November."[4]

It turns out that the people seeking some supernatural or at least religious explanation for the evil we witnessed either found the response unconvincing or inconclusive. Studies showed that similar numbers of people who prayed and went to church before the attacks did so a few months after. The incredible surge in church attendance was more of a knee-jerk reaction.

I'll take it a step farther. I believe our churches often fail to address the fundamental issues at stake. This stems from the misunderstood "separation of church and state" phrase and the Johnson amendment, which seeks to preclude pastors from

---

[3] http://edition.cnn.com/2001/US/09/11/bush.speech.text/
[4] http://www.foxnews.com/story/2002/09/11/church-attendance-back-to-normal.html

51

speaking on politics from the pulpit. (This amendment has never been prosecuted, by the way.)

I was on a plane the other day, and I had the pleasure of sitting next to a clergyman. Irresistible! I asked him about himself and learned he pastored and that he and his wife worked in an afterschool program with inner-city kids in the Detroit area. I asked him if they used the Bible as a reference for instructing those children, and he said they didn't. "But, you're a pastor," I thought to myself. He believed it would be compromising his mandate to use religion on the youngsters. Wow.

I suggested it was too bad we didn't teach the Bible and Biblical principles in our schools anymore.

He responded, "Then we'd have to also teach the Koran."

"That's actually incorrect," I countered. "This is a Judeo-Christian nation. It has succeeded and will only continue to succeed as long as we adhere to our founding principles, which are based entirely on Biblical teachings."

"Well, they still can't be teaching the Bible in schools because of 'Separation of Church and State.' It's in the Constitution, after all," he said, shrugging his shoulders.

I was dumbfounded, and it's often difficult for me to hold my tongue. "You are terribly misinformed. There is no mention of even the idea of separation of Church and State in our Constitution," I immediately asserted, challenging him.

He regarded me with consternation. "I'm sure there is. That's what I've heard."

"May I suggest you read this document instead of taking someone else's word for it? Because this idea of separation came from a letter that Thomas Jefferson wrote, and it dealt basically with keeping the state out of the church's business. As a pastor, I imagine you understand that we are all under God's law, including the government. The state should not be over the church any more than man should dictate to God. The founders understood that the intrinsic nature of governments of and by men is to grow and usurp power. Jefferson was simply emphasizing the need for the government to have limits placed upon it, especially regarding its power over the church and the conscience of a freely worshipping populous. Surely you must see the reason in that."

"Well, I don't know about that. I just know that we need the government and the government's help. For social welfare, for programs for the kids, you know…"

"Only because the church is not fulfilling its charitable role."

"Charitable contributions are down, and need is rising."

"Because the government is overtaking the church's role in society. It's a downward spiral. We allow the government to construct these 'social safety nets,' and that suggests to taxpayers that their taxes are like charity, dissuading them from making charitable donations. They think, "Let the government take care of them." But that's a losing proposition because the government bureaucracy is typically completely inept." I paused to give him the chance to respond, but he held his tongue. This was all new to him, apparently. What a sad state of affairs in our churches when the pastors are unfamiliar with the very subjects they should understand intimately!

He just looked at me, so I continued. "Did you know that government social programs are typically much less efficient than private charity? I've heard some say that the government absorbs 90% of the money it takes in, and 10% goes to the programs it administers. Did you know that church organizations typically are the reverse? They spend 90% or more of their charitable donations to alleviate suffering and use the remainder, typically less than 10%, for management of resources. The reason is that competition will always insist on better results, and the government removes the competition."

I was making him think, but he still seemed unconvinced. He had been immersed in an environment that supported big government and taught him to use its resources and navigate its maze to his benefit. He was too accustomed to relying upon government largess. Although he was clergy, he failed to recognize that government's ultimate objective is to become the only power and to obliterate the church.

Consider the reverse: What if everyone were staunch, churchgoing, devoted followers of Christ and all the teachings of Judeo-Christianity? If you examine the Ten Commandments, they are clear-cut about what is wrong. Don't kill other humans, and don't lie or steal. All the commandments about God come first in numbers one through five because without faith and belief in the God who created the Universe and its laws, it'd be so easy to just start breaking them all immediately! That is sort of where we are today.

If nobody broke any of those original tenets, would we even need any of the laws we have? If we all were internally convicted to help the widows and the poor, would the government ever have to step in with the safety net of social programs? If people worked for the interests of others and not just for their self-interests, society would be infinitely better. Unfortunately, man is self-serving, selfish, and sinful, so sometimes he does bad things. For this purpose, governments are instituted to protect the innocent and punish the wrongdoers.

So, "Why do we need church?" the non-believer asks.

Our values govern our actions, especially when no one else is looking. Most Americans are good people because they've been taught Judeo-Christian morals in one way or another. Thus, when they break a commandment or a law, they feel a sense of guilt at the very least.

Ask yourself this: Do you trust the government? Think about the following existing laws[5]:

- In Ohio, underground coal mine operators must ensure an "adequate supply" of toilet paper for every toilet.

---

[5] http://www.businessinsider.com/most-ridiculous-law-in-every-state-2014-2

- Indiana prohibits liquor stores from selling chilled water, soda, or milk, but they may sell uncooled water or soda.
- Minnesota prohibits capturing a greased or oiled pig as a game.
- Nebraska forbids marriage for anyone afflicted with venereal disease.
- In North Carolina, no bingo games may last over five hours.
- Rhode Island dictates imprisonment for anyone "voluntarily, maliciously or of purpose" maiming or mutilating another.

Some of these seem ridiculous, and others are so obvious, you wonder why we pay these people of the government to write them. Rather than discuss the merits of these laws, I'll stipulate that all good laws are moral laws, which means they basically reiterate in one form or another the Ten Commandments. For instance, in Washington, exterior doors for public buildings must open outwardly. The reason for this is clear: to avoid congestion during an emergency. This law represents the commandment about protecting human lives.

John Adams said[6], "Our Constitution was made only for a moral and religious people. It is wholly inadequate to the government of any other." He was also convinced that "human passions unbridled by morality and religion…would break the strongest cords of our Constitution as a whale goes through a net."

Why? Because people who don't believe they answer to God are hardly going to answer to government. In other words, they will do whatever they want, as long as they don't get caught and only if they don't feel guilty about it. A mind, untethered from moral convictions of right and wrong, is free to impose whatever evil it desires. Once a society starts down that road, there will be legal infractions too

---

[6] http://www.john-adams-heritage.com/quotes/

numerous to possibly hold them all to account, at which point the culture we know and love will cease, and chaos will reign.

Unfortunately, our airplane landed before I had convinced the misguided pastor, but at least I gave him food for thought. Once you have enough facts in front of you, it's not difficult to figure out the situation.

If you need further proof of the conflict between the church and government, understand this: Christianity teaches that Jesus came to set the captives free, meaning freedom for every man and woman. This is referenced in our founding documents as liberty. The founders began their declaration with the right to life, granted by our Creator, because liberty isn't much good if you're dead. Over the past two centuries, while the church continued to impart this message of freedom as enshrined in our founding documents—and those same papers describe the formation of the government, its purpose and limitations—our government insinuated itself into the business of educating our children.

At first, things went very well. Parents had their time freed up to pursue wealth creation, and kids learned to read, write, and understand the morals and values upon which this country was formed. Much of public school was Bible-based. Teddy Roosevelt said, "A thorough knowledge of the Bible is worth more than a college education."

I'll shortcut it for you: they took the Bible, our greatest collection of historical documents and the world's best-selling book, out of the government's schools. They stopped teaching not only proper moral behavior but civics. Civics is the study of government and how it works. Contemplate that our government schools no longer teach about our government or our foundational documents, the documents that ascribe the power over the government to its citizens. Consider that the government may not want its citizens to assert their power, and the easiest way to assure that is to withhold the information: of the people, by the people and for the people.

Studying our Constitution for a couple of weeks doesn't count. In a 2012 study by Xavier University's Center for the Study of the

American Dream [7], 85% of US citizens tested did not understand the meaning of "rule of law," and 75% couldn't explain the role of the judicial branch of government. If we fail to understand the basic doctrines of our government, which exists primarily to safeguard our freedom, how can we recognize when they are being undermined and our liberty is at risk?

Only 2% of youth who grow up in the church proclaim they intend to continue in the church when they leave home.

In our government schools, we are depriving our children of Biblical faith, yet asking them to rely blindly on the State without understanding the role of government in our lives. This is a recipe for the elimination of religion, specifically Christianity, but it does bode well for government, as our youth is increasingly taught that government can replace God in their lives.

Pastors should be more aware of this than I am, but unfortunately for my seatmate as for so many others, they fail to recognize the subtle assault on their culture and values.

I enjoyed our chat, but I had other things on my mind, namely the twins growing in my belly. After Braeden, Kevin and I had pursued another course of in-vitro, and we were doubly successful this time.

It was a beautiful spring morning in Las Vegas when I went into my OBGYN's office in Henderson, Nevada, for my twelve-week check-up. I was in week thirteen, a week late because we had been traveling, but I was feeling great. With the first trimester down, my morning sickness had abated, and I was energetic and thrilled to be pregnant with twins, excited at the prospect of two for the price of one. I've always been a deal shopper.

The nurse brought me to the back and weighed me. I had lost some weight.

---

[7] https://webprod.floridabar.org/wp-content/uploads/2017/04/1890-benchmarks-raising-the-bar-on-civics-education.pdf

"Have you been vomiting a lot? Having trouble keeping your food down?"

"Not really. I had pretty bad morning sickness up until about two weeks ago, but since then it's been smooth sailing."

"Well, you've lost a bit of weight," she said casually.

"I have? That's odd. I feel great, so *I'm not concerned.*" Those words just tripped so easily off my tongue, but they would haunt me later.

She gave me the cup to use the facility and told me to go into room three when I was finished.

Dr. Mayr, tall with red hair and a kind, generous disposition, knocked softly and entered the room. She loved her job and seemed particularly excited about my babies. She had delivered Braeden, and I trusted her and liked her. She asked how I was feeling and then took out her Doppler to hear the heartbeats of the twins. Then she casually told me she wanted me to go have an ultrasound and called the nurse to take me to the other room for the procedure.

Sonograms are easy, and I'd had plenty, so I went in without any insouciance and lay on the table. The tech put gel on my flat belly and moved her scope around, taking the snapshots as they do, and I lay back, thinking of what was to come with two little babies on the way.

The tech finished, got up, and said, "Just stay here. I'll be right back."

That was a bit odd, but as I had said before, I was not concerned.

Dr. Mayr came into the room with the tech, who showed her some of the research she had just done on my babies. Everything started moving so quickly at that point.

Dr. Mayr turned to me, and tears started running down her face. "They aren't there anymore. They've passed away, Sam. The twins. They... they're gone."

I went cold, frozen. There was something about her crying in front of me that prevented me from crying. I looked at her accusingly, daring her to repeat the gruesome news. "What?"

She shook her head. "I'm so sorry, Sam. I'm so sorry. They... there's no heartbeat, for either of them."

It started to sink in, that putrid, lead, feeling of loss. My nausea returned, increasing with every thud of my heart. I tried to think, but my brain was stagnant. I couldn't believe it. I hadn't had a care just a moment before, and now my entire world was crashing down around me.

"Show me," I demanded.

"Of course," Dr. Mayr agreed, and the tech, who had quietly witnessed my complete destruction, scrambled to facilitate.

The tech grabbed the wand and placed it on my belly, pushing and manipulating the dials, and showed me two small masses as the doctor explained what we were seeing—and what we were not. We were *not* seeing a heartbeat in either of those lifeless clumps. The wand moved to get a better vision of each tissue corpus, pushing and prodding, as if she were trying to get a reaction from them. They weren't home—they were *home* already.

To be thorough, the tech went back to the first one again. Dead tissue, no longer pumping or fluttering. No longer filled with life. No longer anything. The second one was even smaller, having already started to shrivel up, my hopes and dreams within it. Meaningless blood and cellular matter, destroyed, like the twin towers. Edifices that no one could imagine might one day fall, I liken now to the loss of my twin babies. They had disappeared into a vacuum of space similar to that left by the tremendous collapse of the two buildings in New York City.

And I remained, looking down into the gaping chasm.

I had embraced a plan that was more than half-way to fruition. Kevin's health had much improved, and there was little remaining doubt about his complete recovery. Our promise of three children, boy, boy, girl, was nearly fulfilled as well. I had convinced myself that the twins would emerge from my belly, one way or another, first boy, and then girl.

Now, that promise was suddenly and brutally snatched from my gentle grasp. My composure shattered in mid-air on the words of my doctor, like a thousand tons of steel and glass on the streets of New York, and I coughed on my tears.

Where was my faith? Hiding. It understood I needed to process the grief before grappling with the aftermath. I didn't even look for it. In a hurricane of raw emotion, I was too busy trying to comprehend the cataclysm.

Dr. Mayr told me I would likely need a D & C—dilation and curettage. They would clean out the detritus, for my health, but what would they do for the smashed fragments inside my heart?

I ran out of the office, crying, struggling to compute the enormity of the seismic shift that rent my entire life in shreds at that moment. I sat in my Jeep for 15 minutes, until it got too hot and I had to drive, just for some air circulation. I proceeded slowly, zombie-like, casing the road carefully through my tears. I knew, at the same time, that I was indulging myself and that my grief would pass eventually—that this moment would fade simply in the course of time. But I didn't care. I was living this moment, and I was wringing it for every drop, feeling every sting of the loss with all my self-pity and righteous feeling of betrayal. God and I had made a deal, and this wasn't part of it, and I was angry, frustrated, and bereft.

It was a short drive back home, where I retreated straight to bed. My grief consumed me. My hopes lay in an irreparable wreckage on the bleached floor of the doctor's office, and my typically unhesitating faith in the future, questioned.

Loss

Kevin

Braeden turned from a newborn into a baby into a toddler. When I returned daily from work, there he'd be in his high chair with an excited greeting that made me feel like I was the king of the world. I'd finish feeding him and take him out to play and wrestle. Then came the days he might greet me on the steps of our little townhouse. He had an engaging, outgoing personality. He would perch on the front stoop, waving and greeting passersby with a big smile and giggles, while munching on grapes from a little plastic bowl. As much as he liked to be outside and see the world go by, he was waiting for my return, showing me with an excited hop as I descended from my car. Or he'd be waiting so see me walking up the street on my way back from the gym. He'd run to me, "Daddy! Daddy! Daddy!" Sam would be peering through the curtains right next to the front door. She was never far away from the child she called "The Boy."

It was during these early days of his childhood that Braeden adopted his nickname. I'm not sure how he hit upon it. Young little Braeden decided that he preferred to be called Biwa. He was patient but convinced that he should have this new name, and Sam obliged, but his nickname never sat right with me.

61

"My name is *Bee-wah!*" he would demand in his high-pitched little voice. Sam found it cute, especially the way he said it with the persistent glimmer of mischief in his eyes. How could she resist? But it just sounded odd, and I had chosen Braeden for its tone of masculinity. The funny thing was he held on to that nickname until he was about fourteen years old, although I steadfastly refused to adopt it.

As stubborn, sweet and sublime as my first-born was, the loss of our twins devastated the fragile new optimism I had been building since my brush with death those years earlier, my subsequent battles to recover my balance, sight, and sense of self. I was no longer Hercules, that much was sure, but wasn't I at least a man? Braeden had helped me discover the father I always hoped was inside me, and looking forward to twins was an exciting and daunting proposition.

Now they were gone, and ripped from somewhere deep inside me was my budding sense of peace. Waves of fear swept me out into a roiling sea of inadequacy. I had no idea why we lost them, but I was certain I was to blame. Why not? I was the one who had been ill, who was still in recuperation, although my recovery was more certain than ever. But we had struggled the first time to conceive, and this time had been no different. We had used the same method; Sam went through all the same blood tests, syringes, and doctor's visits. It had been as smooth a trial as the first time. She was a trouper and strong through it all. And I waltzed in on the final day and did my small part. I remember waiting to hear about the results: seven fertilized eggs, only three progressed, and they chose to use all three of those for the procedure. Now I saw how lucky we had been to have Braeden.

Well, at least I did have one child, but I was greedy. I wanted more. It was what Sam and I had confirmed to each other that very first date in the theater. Now, that promise seemed to have been betrayed. The two we had been assured were only dust in the wind, and my dreams were in shambles. Is it odd that this experience devastated my ego? Perhaps it's simply because my ego was so frail from the strokes, or perhaps the strokes, having made me much quicker to anger, resulted also in my hyper-sensitivity and self-centeredness.

It almost didn't matter that Sam was taking it harder than I was, because it was killing me.

Fortunately, or not, I didn't have time to contemplate my failures. Suddenly, it was my turn to take care of Sam, but I had no idea how. She was sequestered in the master bedroom. Having divulged to me the bad news, she announced she was headed to bed, she needed to sleep. I'd left her alone, but after about an hour, I simply couldn't stay away. I knew she was suffering, and I was ready to try to take some of the weight from off her shoulders. I went into the bedroom and sat on the bed with her. She was curled up on her side under the covers, facing the other side of the bed. I just knew she wasn't sleeping.

She looked small.

"You know, it's not your fault," I said softly.

She nodded, under the covers. I reached over and gently pulled them back so I could see her face. It was puffy, and her eyes were red.

"What can I do?"

She shook her head, saying, "There's nothing you can do at this point. They're gone. They're gone," she repeated, more softly. "I was feeling so good." She sounded confused by that. "I was such an idiot!"

"No, you weren't. This is not your fault. This is just what happens. This is just the way it goes." My words sounded tinny and hollow and were as effective as feathers cutting diamonds.

"Kevin, I made them show me so I could be for sure. I needed to see. There were no more heartbeats. There were just the two lumps of tissue, with no life in them at all. They had just... left. And now, they're gone."

"I know," I said, although I felt like maybe I was dreaming, that this wasn't happening, that maybe, somehow, I could fix this. Then again, I was all too familiar with the cruelties of reality.

I leaned over and held her close. She clung to me fiercely.

I couldn't help myself. I said, "We still have Braeden."

"Yes, we do. And we will try again, Kevin. We just have to have faith that somehow, this is the way it's supposed to be."

I wished, then, that I did have her faith, even what little that statement represented. Sometimes, when your own faith is too small, you need to hold on to someone else's conviction and give yourself a break. I didn't know what my failure had been. I suppose I wanted to place blame. It might have made it easier if I or my illness were clearly responsible, but there existed no proof. For the first time since laying in that hospital bed and depending on nurses and doctors to revive and repair me, I felt completely helpless but in a new, more profound way, because now it affected not only me but also Sam, my parents, even the would-be older brother. I mourned our mutual loss but also realized that life would go on, and there was work to be done.

Sam and I would figure this out, we would power through, and we would persevere to have the family we both envisioned. Sometimes, things are difficult simply because they need to be, and although I don't have a better explanation, coming through to the other side can prove the usefulness or ultimate necessity of our challenges.

I don't value my children more because of this—I couldn't possibly value them any more than I already do—but I guess I value life a bit more, with a deeper, more visceral understanding of just how precious it is.

Denise

Sam

My doctor insisted that I have a D&C to clean me out, out of concern that any remaining dead tissue might cause other problems. It is basically an abortion, except the baby is already dead. Let's put it this way: I was in no position to argue.

It's a weird thing when you have unborn children die. Because of the widespread acceptance of abortion-on-demand and the argument that a child is not a human life until it emerges from the mother's womb, society seems to be at a loss as to how to respond to grieving parents of children who never matured to birth. Mother Theresa once said that abortion kills twice. "It kills the body of the baby and the conscience of the mother."[8] Her staunch convictions, which I share, are unacceptable in many of our social circles these days. Politicians and pundits lecture us that abortion is very much empowering of women, when, in fact, more than three-quarters of its victims are female, because over half the abortions, world-wide, are gender-discrimination. They are undesirable females, and, of course, mothers are all female. So, when over half the abortions kill

---

8   https://sites.google.com/site/faithfulcatholics/Home/pro-life-quotations-of-mother-teresa

females, and the abortion itself kills the mother's conscience, how, exactly, is abortion a "boon" to feminine empowerment?

I liken it to shackles of enslavement. I've witnessed and spoken to too many women who have been scourged by the memory of their abortions. It tragically ensnares young women with the promise of never having to think about it again, and once they've done the deed, it seizes their every thought. And, of course, the havoc that the abortion movement has wrought on society's young men is beyond compare. That the child immediately becomes the woman's decision alone sends the overarching message to young men of their ultimate insignificance.

Since I first began to determine my own opinions as an adult, I've been pro-life. Now, after becoming a mother, I understood more viscerally why. But it wasn't until losing a child and needing an abortion-like procedure that I truly realized the demonic intensity that is the abortion industry in the United States and its proponents. But you need not just take my word for it. Mother Teresa said it better than I possibly could:

America needs no words from me to see how your decision in Roe v. Wade has deformed a great nation. The so-called right to abortion has pitted mothers against their children and women against men. It has shown violence and discord at the heart of the most intimate human relationships. It has aggravated the derogation of the father's role in an increasingly fatherless society. It has portrayed the greatest of gifts ~ a child ~ as a competitor, an intrusion, and an inconvenience. It has nominally accorded mothers unfettered dominion over the independent lives of their physically dependent sons and daughters. And in granting this unconscionable power, it has exposed many women to unjust and selfish demands from their husbands or other sexual partners. Human rights are not a privilege conferred by government. They are every human being's entitlement by virtue of his humanity. The right to life does not depend, and must not be declared to be contingent, on the pleasure of anyone else, not even a parent or a sovereign.[9]

It took several days for me to equate my D&C with an abortion because I was reeling from devastating loss, and I was trying to make sense of a confusing, heart-wrenching tragedy. Kevin and our nanny were picking up the slack, feeding Braeden and taking him to the park. They silently and graciously afforded me the solitude I needed to process my grief. At one point, I realized I needed to inform everyone we had told about the twins, so I sent a mass email to everyone I could think of who already knew we were expecting to inform them of the miscarriage. I summed up my missive with the news that I would be having the D&C the following day and returned to bed, usually my place of respite and recuperation, now transformed into a place of mourning.

My faith in God remained unshaken, but my faith in this life, in myself, and in my plans, was in serious jeopardy. When I was growing up, I had an unshakeable, irrational fear that my two front teeth would be broken in half. I had over-sized, prominent buck teeth that had been only mildly reined in by braces. There seemed to be no discernable genesis for my fear, it was simply ingrained. I could never imagine how my teeth would break—I pictured myself tripping, but could never properly calculate any trajectory resulting in cracking only my front teeth, in half, on the ground. I wondered if it might happen tripping up the stairs. That would be weird but possible. Not that I obsessed over it, but as a fear, it had been present since my teeth had grown in.

When I shipped off to Sweden as a teen, the group of students went out on the lawn to play some soccer during a break in the orientation. I was a mediocre soccer player, and there were a few students from soccer nations (Brazil, for instance) who were very good. Of course, I got hit in the face with a well-kicked soccer ball.

---

[9] Blessed Mother Teresa of Calcutta , "Notable and Quotable", Wall Street Journal, 2/25/94, p. A14

Don't laugh, please. It literally knocked me unconscious! When I came to, lying flat on my back, the group was gathered around me as I gazed up toward the sky—just like in the movies.

"Hey, you okay?" they asked.

I looked at them as my tongue slipped over my front teeth, probing to be sure they were still there. Yep, I was just fine.

Like my teeth themselves, my trepidation about my large front teeth stayed with me, however. When I was in my twenties, as I was crossing the street in Paris, a small service van hit me. Yes, it was on purpose. I had forgotten the general traffic rule in Paris that motorists like playing chicken with pedestrians. With my New York sensibility, I saw the driver of the van, and he saw me, and I looked away, and he pressed the gas. It was entirely my fault (not!).

The van shoved my hip to the side, and my head smacked down on top of the roof, which knocked my lights out. I woke up, sprawled in the gutter, surrounded (again) by foreign faces leaning over me. I ignored them and slowly ran my tongue over my teeth to discover my nightmare-come-true. Each of my front teeth was broken in half. Luckily, my half-teeth were still in my mouth. Aside from a sore hip and a concussion, that was the only damage I sustained when I *got hit by a car.*

I found this an absolute reassurance. My fears had been acknowledged and answered in the most specific and remarkable way. Not only that, over the years, I had grown to regard my overly large and curved teeth as a liability. I had even floated the idea of modifying them somewhat to make them appear smaller, but I never worked up the courage to mess with them. I had the ambulance drive me to a dentist, whose name I acquired by calling a new acquaintance from the shop where I fell. I'm sure to the innocent bystander, this all appeared very odd. Tall brunette gets hit by car, makes lisping phone call, departs in ambulance to dentist. But to me, because of my persistent premonition, it just came as "par for the course."

The lesson I learned from all this? To rely on my instincts, in the sense that those odd things you "just know" are really soupçons of things to come. To trust the shadows and hints of the future. This is partly why I put so much faith in the "boy, boy, girl" scenario. It was confirmed, and my conviction depended on it as reality.

Losing the twins shook my self-confidence on a profound level. I needed my faith in God to pull me through.

Lying in my comfortable bed, in my self-imposed isolation and self-indulgent self-pity, I prayed for strength and understanding, and then I turned outward. I prayed for my son and my husband, for God's consolation in their loss. Braeden might never understand it, but Kevin was certainly heartbroken and needed some provision. I prayed for forgiveness, and I prayed for my babies up in heaven. I prayed for patience and for my reliance on Him. I prayed for serenity and acceptance of things I could not change. I prayed for confidence. I prayed until I fell asleep.

Somewhere in the wee hours of the dawn, I made peace with my circumstances and settled in for the long haul. This would be part of my life, so I may as well accept it and figure out how to step forward into a new day. "So be it," I reasoned, "Life's too short, so get up and get going."

The following morning welcomed glorious sunshine, as if in celebration of the terrible thing that was happening to me or maybe as condolences and approval of my acceptance of it. Kevin was sweet and doting and brought me to the facility. We sat in the waiting room, a sparsely appointed white room with plenty of old, worn, hospital seating in blues, aquas, and purples. It was chilly, or I was nervous, or both. I picked up an old magazine I didn't care for and pretended to read. I tried to put on a bright face for Kevin, who was clearly reeling, going through the motions. Everything we did felt like it had been remotely programmed. Concentrating on anything was a challenge. We sat in silence.

There was a young woman sitting alone in another part of the large office space, also reading a magazine.

A short, pudgy nurse wearing scrubs with purple flowers opened the door to the waiting room and called, "Denise?"

Kevin and I looked up at the only other person in the room. She was looking at me. The nurse glanced at each of us, waiting expectantly.

My gaze fell back down to my magazine.

The nurse, confused, asked again, "Denise? Denise."

No answer from either party. I recognized the welcome distraction from my pain and watched the young nurse check her sheets again, flip a page over and back again. The other young woman was studiously ignoring the nurse, but she glanced at me as if to say, "Weird."

The nurse apparently realized her mistake. "Oh! Sandra Sorbo?" she asked, pointedly looking at each of us waiting ladies.

"Uhm, that's me, but I don't want what Denise is having, thanks."

"No, no. That was my mistake. You're Sandra? You're who I need, okay? Please come with me." The nurse seemed more definitively resolved, now.

Kevin and I checked in with each other and then followed her through the doorway into the area beyond, where she showed me to a gurney between hanging creamy draped panels.

"Here is your gown," she pointed at the baby blue cloth on the bed as she pulled the curtains around the bed. "Go ahead and take everything off, and we'll come back to get your IV set up in a minute." She hung her clipboard off the bottom of my bed

I did as I was told, with Kevin collecting my clothes into a plastic bag, and I quickly retreated under the sheets, shivering, my adrenaline pumping overtime.

A new nurse, tall and lanky, approached us, trailed by the first gal. Stretch moved quickly and seemed infinitely more competent. She glanced quickly at my chart, and confidently greeted me, "Well, hello, there, Denise!"

"No..."

"No, no!" countered the first nurse quickly, and picked up the clipboard to point to something for the Stretch to see.

"Oh, I'm sorry. It's Sandra, isn't it?"

"Yes," I answered warily.

"Okay, good. Sorry about that. I'm going to put your IV in. How are you doing today?"

I tried to bring some levity. "Well, today is about a negative two on a scale of ten, for me, so—"

"Yeah, I guess so." She worked on finding a vein in my hand while I pondered the strangeness of this whole thing. Kevin was being stoic and supportive, feeling helpless as a toddler, I'm sure, but glancing over at him, I felt his strength warm and support me.

The anesthesiologist stepped into our small space to chat. He picked up the clipboard, which held all my pertinent data and more, apparently.

"Okay, Denise! How are you doing today?"

"You're kidding, right?"

I was interrupted by the nurse trying to correct him on my name. I waited for her to finish and then lost my patience. "Now you'll need to explain, please, what is going on here?" I knew I sounded frustrated, but honestly!

The nurse demurred. "It's just a clerical thing…"

"No, no. Three times now you've called me Denise, and I really would like to know why, please."

The nurse took pity on me and sheepishly showed me my chart, at the top of which was my condition, "Fetal Demise." The problem was that everyone assumed my name would be at the top of the chart, and so they were reading it as "Fetal, Denise." You might guess this wasn't the first time for that horrible mistake, that someone would have already fixed that problem—but you'd be wrong.

Well, as Kevin will attest, humor is truly some of the best medicine. We finally had something to laugh about. A simple misunderstanding, a weird quirk of the paperwork, and some honest embarrassment on the part of several healthcare workers got me through into the procedure, which, although it wasn't at all painful physically, was not as simple and easy as the abortion industry would have young expectant mothers believe. General anesthesia is no picnic, and recovering from it is also a drain.

Kevin took me home, straight back to bed, where I stayed for a couple more days.

The day after the procedure, I was recovering in bed, watching TV, when the phone rang. I knew Kevin had taken Braeden to the park, so I chose to answer it.

"Sandra Sorbo, please."

"This is she," I answered.

"Hi, Sandra, I'm calling from the clinic where you were seen yesterday as a follow-up to make sure you're doing okay and do a quality control check to see how your experience was. Please let me introduce myself. My name is Denise."

I burst out laughing, which, of course, demanded an explanation for poor Denise, whose name alone likely had never engendered such a response before. She was good-natured and caring, apologizing for the odd way I had been called Denise and then inquiring about my health. I gave the entire experience a good review, despite the name issue, because, even though it was in response to an outright tragedy, my treatment was good, and my recovery, at least physically, would soon be complete.

But as I contemplated that certainty, I thought about the ramifications of what I had just been through—that invasive, thorny procedure. I considered that there are so many young women who are deciding to do this same procedure for completely different reasons. They are sold a story of freedom, of empowerment, or hope, like Snow White taking a bite of the apple, like Eve in the Garden of Eden. After she tells the Snake she may not eat of the tree of knowledge of good and evil because God told her that, the Snake questions, "Did God really say that?" and plants that first seed of doubt. Through that crack of doubt, the specious and spiteful song slithers out, "My body, my choice." It feels so good, it must be right, right?

Wrong. But I remember growing up and being taught that same mantra, "My body, my choice," and thinking that abortion was always the fail-safe option, never mind the consequences. In fact, as I recall, consequences were never addressed or even recognized. Now, I knew the truth, from three sides of the equation: mother, parent of deceased children, and patient.

I hung up with Denise and started to pray for the young women who were, even in that moment, being deceived into the shackles of the abortion industry and coerced into snuffing out a life taking form inside of them. What must traverse their brains as they recover? And how to recover from that? What kind of gymnastics does a woman's mind perform to indignantly deny another human being its life, while still demanding the same right for themselves? My heart wept for those women making such decisions, and it still does.

Yet through it all, we have a God Who understands, Who walks with us in faith, and Who is ready to guide us out of the slavery of our poor decisions. And although I wasn't ready to be comforted by some over-arching meta-narrative just yet, I understood a possible deeper meaning to this ordeal. And that gave me faith.

Whoa, Baby!

Kevin

To say we were walking in faith is not to put too fine a point on things. The miscarriage, the struggles with infertility, my brush with death—all had brought me to wonder about meaning and purpose, chance or destiny? The strokes nearly took my life, but here I still was, standing and fighting. Infertility tried to claim ownership, but we had denied them, twice. Then the twins disappeared in a cloud of confusion. We had become comfortable, where God clearly had not wanted us. Now, we needed to rely on His timing, His judgment, His ways.

Sam asked me if I wanted to have a small ceremony for the lost souls of our two angels. I immediately agreed. Just the two of us walked outside and stood in the setting sun in our backyard and grieved. We talked to them both, even though they didn't have names yet. But mainly, we spoke to God. I struggled to be grateful despite my grief and bewilderment. The warm Vegas breeze brushed across the hair on my arms. I held Sam's hand and watched the sun sink behind the red hills in the distance.

Life goes on, as they say, and so we went back up to Vancouver, and I went back to work on the show. Sam did another round of fertility treatments, undaunted it seemed. She has a knack for acceptance that still challenges me. I tell people about her tough love when I was in the worst of my recovery, where the world simply appeared dark and foreboding to my addled brain.

She would say, "It happened. What are you going to do now?"

Well, what she was going to do was to get pregnant again, apparently! She promptly re-enrolled and executed the protocol, and the short version is, we found ourselves expecting baby number two shortly thereafter.

For this pregnancy, Sam ate completely differently than with Braeden. I couldn't help observing that with Braeden, Sam had craved salads and salmon. She was the epitome of the health nut with that child. Now, with a second child on the way and a toddler, Sam was completely remade. She ate chocolate and cookies and you-name-it. And while with Braeden she had gained fifty-five pounds all over, this time Sam had an enormous belly, only. From the back, she appeared as always, long and thin, but when she turned sideways, there was the disturbing protuberance.

Toward the end of her gravidity, people unknown to us would address her and ask if she was carrying twins. "No," she'd answer, at which point they inevitably asked when she was due, expecting an answer along the lines of, "Tomorrow" or "Last week." When she would respond three or four weeks, they looked horrified.

"Why don't you induce? You look so uncomfortable!" One woman in the grocery remarked to us.

But the doctor wasn't having any of it. "Inducing runs you the risk of needing a C-section," she explained, and she wouldn't do that unless there were mitigating factors. Apparently, an enormous belly wasn't "mitigating" enough. Sam even mentioned she knew the baby was extra-large, but the doctor didn't believe her.

When the time came to have the baby, Sam went into labor naturally on his due date. After going about her business for most of the day and breathing through the contractions, Sam decided they were close together enough to warrant a trip to the labor and delivery ward of the hospital.

Most of the story of Shane's birth is in *True Strength*, but I'll reiterate here that Sam ended up needing the C-section.

And as I was in the room, at the head of Sam's bed, I watched the team pull out the largest baby any of us had ever seen.

"Oh my goodness! Look at the size of this baby!" someone said.

They held the baby for us both to see, then took him over to the heat lamps to clean him up a bit.

Sam turned her gaze to him and said, "He looks fine to me."

Tears streamed down my face because I'm just a softy. He was beautiful and perfect and *huge*.

The hospital staff organized a quick pool to guess his weight. I followed the nurse out with Shane Haaken to watch him being cleaned and weighed, camera in hand to mark this moment in history. His body was off the scale—his head hanging over on one side and his feet flopping off the other. I snapped a photo to beat all baby photos, with the scale reading "12.6" and the baby boy so large it looked fake.

We went back to the operating/delivery room, and the nurse made the announcement: "Twelve pounds, six ounces!"

Nobody had guessed over twelve pounds, of course, so nobody won. Except for Mom and Dad.

I was overcome with elation and amazement. I leaned into my lovely, amazing wife and whispered in her ear. "Twelve pounds, six ounces, Sam... it's the *twins*."

God had delivered on His promise, in a way neither of us could have imagined. We would not have dared imagine, truly. To this day, Sam plays a game with parents of twins. "How much did your twins weigh at birth?" She'll ask, all innocence. When the two figures are added together, the answer typically does not exceed Sam's twelve and a half pound second child. She smiles at the unsuspecting mother. "I guess I beat you!" Sam says, laughing.

In the larger sense, Shane was an answer to a fervent prayer, a recompense for what seemed to be an unfair loss. But what constitutes "fair" in a world that is both physical and spiritual? How can we, as mostly corporeal beings living predominantly in the material world, ever hope to reconcile what's fair with what is experienced when we see not the spiritual battles but only feel their effects, if at all?

A massive baby? It seemed like God had a great sense of humor. At least, I chose to see it that way. Job lost everything, but then God restored him to health and prosperity and even gave him a new family. I sat questioning God after the loss of the twins when I should've spent that time praising His glorious power and wisdom. But as He did with Job, God forgave me for questioning and then blessed me despite my desperate misgivings. That is a wondrous God.

When we are in the moment, questioning, uncertain because the world seems to shift in all the wrong ways, to misbehave and refuse to follow rules we want to impose, sometimes we need to step back and trust, with faith, that the one Creator who made everything has a bigger plan than what we can perceive. Our job, then, is to step forward in faith and reliance on Him and rest assured that, even if we hesitate, His faith is enough.

Golf and Football

Kevin

There is one thing that I always return to for my inner peace: golf. Mark Twain famously remarked that golf is a long walk spoiled, but I vehemently disagree.

Since I was a little boy, my dad worked summers at the local public golf course, Lakeview Golf, when his teaching duties ebbed, and I often went out to the golf course to watch or help. It was inevitable that the golf bug would bite me with that near-daily exposure and Dad's encouragement. In between little league practice and games, I got hooked early. All through my junior and senior high school years, I golfed most every day, often barefoot and shirtless. True, that's frowned upon at your more prestigious *private* golf courses, but at Lake View, we struck a more relaxed tone, where shirts and shoes were optional. There was something magical for me about being out on those closely mowed fairways and greens, surrounded by hills and trees, with the sound of the wind rustling through the leaves. The smell of fresh-cut grass takes me back to those days and always brings a smile to my face, melting the years away. I become a child again, playing a child's game.

My high school friends used to tease me about golfing because no one really viewed it as a "jock" sport. I grew up in a very athletic little town where football, basketball, hockey, and baseball were the 'manly' sports, and their players were kings. Now that my high school buddies started picking up the sport as we've aged, most of them wish they had started earlier. Golf is a life-long journey, and one you can play well into retirement age if you stay healthy, which is more than can be said about football and basketball.

I like to begin my golf rounds early in the morning, with the dew still playing on the leaves and the sun peeking over hillsides and low through the bushes. The day yawns itself awake with the crisp sound of the club on the ball. Whack! It's me, alone with my thoughts, focused on a little white ball rolling on a soft green carpet of grass. I love the scent of the course and the creatures that come out to witness: deer, rabbits, coyotes, frogs. I am at my simplest, communing with nature. I love my mornings, the dawning of a new day with the promises it holds.

Golf gave me serene moments during my recovery that I struggled to maintain off the course. My eyesight was compromised by the strokes. I lost almost fifteen percent in both eyes. Basically, I have a blind spot in the upper right quadrant of my sight, an empty hole in my vision that wreaked havoc in my injured and addled brain. When I first returned to the golf course months after my strokes, I scored more on the first nine holes than I ever did on an average round of eighteen holes. (Remember, in golf, it's all about fewer strokes to win the game. It's the only game I can think of where the fewer points, the greater the chance of winning! Some might ask, why play at all? Because a zero would be the ultimate score...)

My game was gone—along with my balance, vision, and stamina—and I vowed right then and there to fight to get it back.

The thing was, when I addressed the ball with my club, ready to swing, if I turned my head just so, the ball would literally disappear. It was like a parlor trick but with no funny business.

You know the science demonstration they show kids, where if you look at the circle, you see there's a piece missing, but if you look at the dot in the center of the circle, the brain fills it in and makes you think the entire circle is there? My brain was like that, but in reverse, because it literally could not see whatever fell where the blind spot was. It was a Lite-Brite with ten percent of the lights not illuminated. But while compromised vision is, of course, superficially challenging, behind the scenes, my brain was confused by the loss and aggravated, causing me dizziness, nausea, and anxiety. Sam was convinced that my brain would learn to adjust, to fill in the missing parts and stop getting confused by what it failed to see, like on the children's circle experiment. Although I lacked her optimism, I gleaned some solace from her faith.

After the births of our first two boys, Braeden and Shane, it was clear that she was at least much more right than wrong. My recovery was well into its final stages, and I was feeling almost back to normal. Which meant I still loved golf.

Golf courses were my sprawling, verdant bastions of tranquility, and so, it was an amazing experience to have one of the most exciting events in my professional life happen there.

But I've got to back up just a bit, first. *Andromeda* was wrapping up, and I called my manager to see if he had any ideas for my career moving forward. I told him I envisioned myself in a sitcom.

Situation comedies are the best job in the business for an actor. It's pretty simple, really, and it's mainly to do with logistics, particularly the schedule. On a typical sitcom that shoots on Fridays, the cast walks in on Monday morning around ten am to do the read-through. This is a relaxed day that focuses mainly on allowing the writers to hear the lines out loud, listen to how the actors envision them being delivered, and start tweaking them for the most impact. After an hour or two, the cast is dismissed, and the writers get to work on the script. Tuesdays begin again around ten for a run-though, and that may be a four-hour day. This might include wardrobe checks and blocking, going through each scene typically more than once. Wednesdays and Thursdays are longer, maybe six or eight hours, max, and involve more rehearsals, blocking, costume fittings, maybe shooting some pre-shoots as inserts for the show, and more discussion. Each night, the actors will likely see new scripts delivered to them. Writers write, and write, and then write some more. Sometimes, they write so much that a joke that began on Monday and was discredited evolves all the way back around to exactly how it was written originally! When Friday arrives—the day of filming—it's all out. They bring in the 'studio audience' and they film, encouraging the clapping, laughing, and cheers of the fans there. They may shoot until very late at night, just to get the scene the way the director envisions them. The point is, with only one day of late-night work, for an actor, it's a cushy, stable job. Plus, sitcoms often take every fourth week off, as well.

Eric loved the idea of getting me into a sitcom. He asked me if I had any ideas for one. I mentioned I thought it was about time for one that focused a bit on some kind of sport, and that, as an athlete, I could play a retired or retiring athlete of some kind. He loved it. He said, "How about football?"

"Absolutely."

We bounced this idea around and fleshed it out on paper before bringing it to ABC. The execs at the network thought it had potential and told us to find ourselves a showrunner, someone with a track record of having run a TV show, which means head writer and the director of writing on the show—the visionary for the show, basically. Eric reached out to Barry Kemp, the very accomplished TV writer responsible for *Coach* and *Newhart* (among many credits). We met with Barry and sold him on the concept of the show.

After a week or so, the three of us went back up to the executive offices at the ABC tower. It was cool in the glass-enclosed corner office overlooking the Disney studios, with Warner Bros. and Universal competing nearby. The three of us waited as a few more stragglers walked into the already crowded room and took seats at the long conference table, leaving three seats open for us at the opposite end. One young man in a button-down shirt with no tie and no socks, sat on the arm of one of two large black leather desk chairs, at the far end of the room. All told, there were more than a dozen executives in the nicely appointed room. As the latecomers settled in, all eyes landed on us, expectant and impatient. There was something jaded about their faces, like they'd seen it all and were bound to be unenthusiastic and unimpressed.

I was nervous, but I didn't let it show. Eric was smooth—he was one of them. And Barry, well, he held all the cards. It was his moment to shine, and he was up to the task. He didn't even have notes.

Nothing speaks louder than experience. Barry regaled the committee with the story of Bobby Cannon, the man with a cannon for an arm, the star quarterback of the champion Chicago football team, who we first meet at his bar and restaurant, appropriately named Cannon's. Through Barry's storytelling, we also meet the gal a publisher assigned to ghostwrite Bobby's memoir, who he immediately hits on, until he is distracted. It's the NFL draft, and Bobby watches intently, wondering who his team might choose. Another blocker, to protect him in the pocket, or a wide receiver, to improve the team's passing game? He is gob-smacked to learn his team just chose a young, upstart quarterback, obviously planning to groom the kid to replace—you guessed it—Bobby himself!

The room was quiet during Barry's masterful pitch for the show. They chuckled at some things, smiled at others, but they were, in a word, subdued. There was no real way to tell if they liked what they heard or if they were just being polite. I had experienced the auditions where they shower you with compliments just to get you out the door. Was this another case of "don't call us, we'll call you?" I couldn't tell. What I did know was that the show would be a hit if we could just get the green light.

We finished the presentation, answered a few follow-up questions, and left the room. Nobody spoke on the elevator down. When we got to the parking garage, we felt free to talk.

Barry said, "The first time I pitched a show, it was me and two executives. I swear each year they bring in more people. It's like everyone is afraid to make a decision."

Eric laughed. "I thought it went really well. No way to know until we hear, but they obviously are interested, or why would they bring everyone and his assistant into the room?"

"My thoughts, exactly," I said. "I kind of felt like so many people in the room is a good sign."

"It could be. But so many cooks can also spoil the soup. Let's hope more liked it than didn't. The one gal in the blue didn't seem to have a sense of humor at all." I could read Eric.

One moment he seemed positive and assured, and the next he had given up. It was odd, but I had faith in the idea of the show and was certain it would find a home somewhere.

About two weeks after that meeting with the ABC executives, I headed up to the Lake Tahoe Celebrity Golf Tournament. Famous athletes (mostly) are invited to play with a few high-profile actors. I had been available to play in it for three of the previous five years, and I had really enjoyed myself. I was paired with Marcus Allen, the football Hall of Fame running back who I had known for years by that point, and Carson Palmer, the quarterback for the Arizona Cardinals.

Wow. I'll be honest—I idolized these guys! This was really a dream come true for me. The format was straight golf, with no funny business on the scoring side of things. We played in threesomes with full TV coverage and large crowds of spectators walking with us and watching our every shot. To say there was pressure to play good golf would be an understatement, but that's the kind of stress I enjoy. It's the part of the challenge of sports and competition that I learned to adore. I remember before football games, I would feel like throwing up. I craved that exhilaration that came from the game rivalry. I felt it in Tahoe, too, and I played some very good golf—though never good enough to win—and I thrived in the atmosphere of competing.

I was walking with my caddy on the way to the tenth tee box on the second day of the three-day tournament when my phone vibrated. I normally wouldn't have even answered—typically, it's poor etiquette on most golf courses—but since there was another group teeing off, I knew I had ten minutes to kill. Tournament play is notoriously slow, and this was no different. I never would've done this in a PGA game as the atmosphere is much more rigorous. I've golfed with everyone from Arnold Palmer to Greg Norman, and I never even have my phone with me at a professional event. This situation was obviously more relaxed, so my caddy didn't even blink an eye as I pulled the phone out of my pocket.

"Hello?"

"Hey, Kevin. It's Eric. Is this a good time?"

"I'm on the golf course in Tahoe, but I have a few minutes before our next tee shots. What's up?"

"I've got some good news."

I smiled. "Really? What's that?"

"ABC called. They're good to go. They bought the show! I'll be negotiating a nice deal on this for you over the next few weeks, but they're ready to go on this, so how's the beginning of next month sound to get started?"

"That's what, ten days away? I can make that work."

"Great. You finish up golf and call me later. I'll have more details then. Have a great round!"

"I will now!" I hung up the phone and let out a whoop, but quietly, because I was still on the golf course. I shared my great news with Marcus and Carson. I told them about the show, and as football players themselves, they loved the idea. I quickly called Sam and told her the good news, and she shared in my excitement.

I was on my way to achieving my next dream. After the illness, I had struggled to make sense of life, faith, and hope, but God had seen me through. It seemed He had better plans for me now that I was healing and stronger. I put my faith in the new adventure, breathed a sigh, smiled, and proceeded to hit a perfect drive straight down the middle of the fairway. Yep, this back nine was the start of a whole new life for me and my family.

While we were developing my sitcom, Sam was pregnant with our third baby, the little girl we had always planned on. Surprisingly, there isn't much of a story to this pregnancy, except perhaps that it happened the old-fashioned way. Relocating to the US after wrapping *Andromeda* in Vancouver, Sam and I decided to remain based at our house in Vegas near the grandparents, and I would commute to Los Angeles, where things were proceeding full steam ahead with the show. It's a short flight from Vegas to LA, and I didn't mind coming back home to the tranquility of living on a golf course and playing with my babies in the pool and at the park. I met with the writer, producers, my manager, costumes, hair and makeup department, set design, and set building. I would commute in for two overnights, cram the days with meetings, then fly home and relax.

Life was good and exciting, and I was thrilled to be looking at what I was sure would be a hit show on a network—the Holy Grail of Hollywood.

At the same time, small doubts crept around inside my head. I wasn't entirely thrilled with every line of the show, every outfit, every piece of scenery. But who was I to impose my opinions on others, especially those who had been in the business longer than I had, or if not longer, then at least closer to Hollywood then me? After all, my shows, *Hercules* and *Andromeda* were hits, but syndicated successes as opposed to network blockbusters, and consequently, they were marginalized and snubbed by the Hollywood elites. For instance, *Hercules* never got an Emmy nod during its seven years of production, but our costume designer, Ngila Dickson, went on to win an Academy Award for her work on *Lord of the Rings.* The same thing happened with our creature creators, Richard Taylor and the WETA Group. They also went on to win several Oscars after cutting their teeth, honing their skills, and perfecting their techniques generating beasts on my show. While *Hercules* was the number one show in the world, Hollywood saw its star, me, as just a beefy guy running around in a loincloth and assumed I couldn't act. And while I bristled at this misapprehension—for one thing, I wore very heavy leather pants, not a loincloth!—a part of me, especially after the strokes, bought into the lie that I was inferior goods. I was trying to learn from the Hollywood professionals when I should have been asserting myself, trusting the value that I brought to the show.

Despite some inauspicious beginnings (we had several casting sessions looking for the right female costar for my character's love interest), we put together a solid cast and a great production. We were ready to film the pilot.

Sam invited a few of her girlfriends for the taping, which was on the CBS Radford lot. Sam flew in for the show, five and a half months pregnant. She sat in the audience with her friends, excited and happy. It may seem odd that it was on a competing network's property, but sometimes the studios rent out their space, and others need any space they can get and disregard affiliations. It's a business, after all.

The stand-up comedian did an awesome job warming up the audience. At one point, he introduced the cast, and we all walked out to greet the crowd, to their enthusiastic and resounding applause. I thanked everyone for being there and told them we were going to have some fun, and then went back to calm the butterflies in my stomach. There was a lot riding on this night. The script was great, and I felt confident in the incredible collection of talented individuals both in front of and behind the cameras. Barry Kemp was old-school with directing and was at the top of his game. Still, I felt like it all rested on my shoulders, even with the best of the industry supporting me. I could still fail, but that's the environment in which I thrive. The challenge was issued, and I was determined to answer the call.

Our show *Bobby Cannon* was a sitcom about a nice-guy Chicago quarterback nearing the end of his career. He owns a popular bar and has a lot of friends, but playing football and being a star celebrity in Chicago consumes him. Bobby's world implodes when he discovers that his traitorous agent inked the deal for the young quarterback that his own team just drafted as his replacement. The pretty biographer who arrives in time to witness the cataclysm unwittingly punctuates Bobby's jeopardy when she assumes he has a retirement plan—he doesn't—and then she rebuffs his advances.

The funniest lines in the show are when the young quarterback tells me he's a virgin, and I answer, "Uh, a what?" as if I don't understand the word. He is a young football player, after all, and can probably get all the dates he desires (like my character certainly did and does). Then I turn to the gorgeous twins who wanted me to invite him to their party, basically to gloat that they're barking up the wrong tree, but I'm still available. Unexpectedly, they volunteer that it's totally cool, and even "hot," that the young abstinent quarterback doesn't mess around. This turns my entire world on its head. "I'm outta here!" I grumble, and when my agent asks why, I say, "Because if that's the new definition of 'hot,' that's a train I can't jump back on!"

By the end of the show, though, Bobby rediscovers his fire and sets out to reclaim his glory on the field and elsewhere in the book he plans to collaborate on with the writer.

I loved the 'phoenix rising from the ashes' aspect of the script, for obvious reasons. I loved the humor, both situational and physical. The taping went without a hitch, and we were all very excited.

Immediately after the recording of my show, Sam's girlfriends, blown away by the humor and intelligence of the show, leaned over to her to ask if we were prepared for the immense success this new series would be and what that would mean for our personal lives and privacy. She smiled. She's fairly unflappable, but she knew we had a hit show on our hands, and she was proud of me.

A few months later, ABC flew the entire family to New York City for the Up Fronts. This is the public announcement by each of the networks about what shows will complete their fall line ups. The night before the Up Fronts, my manager confided in me that my show was "on the bubble." What the heck? It was a great show that tested first in its class across the boards for ABC, how could it be on the bubble?

Eric used a conspiratorial tone and low voice to tell me, "That's all I can say—it's all I know. I just heard it through the grapevine."

Well, grapevines are what they are, and Hollywood bureaucracy is what it is, and the soon-to-be-deposed studio chief decided not to pick up my show for production. Never mind that every single one of the seven shows that they put in our stead hadn't tested as well as mine and that each one was canceled within months of its own launch, that's Hollywood, and politics, and sometimes, just plain (bad) business. We waited for an announcement that would never come, and we returned home empty-handed and deflated.

Getting back to work without a show meant pounding the pavement again. It amazed me that with fourteen years of full-time television under my belt, I was nearly back at square one in terms of auditioning for roles. I write 'nearly' because, in fact, I had kind of a black mark against me. As I mentioned before, Hollywood had no respect for my number-one-world-wide-hit-show *Hercules* because it was a syndicated show. Suddenly, I began hearing that I was "too recognizable" to cast. This set up something of a conflict with my representation, and both my manager and lawyer basically fired me. Which is funny, because I was their employer, a nuance they failed to appreciate.

The scene with my manager, a driven go-getter I signed with during my fourth year on *Hercules*, is a scene out of a Hollywood movie, pardon the expression.

After *Bobby Cannon,* he asked me to come in to discuss and regroup regarding the future of my career. I was knocked down by the colossal blow in New York, but I was a fighter. I hadn't stopped calculating where I wanted to go from there. I thought simply working on developing another sitcom seemed promising, so I was all too happy to head over to the glass and steel high rise office building where Eric perched. His assistant showed me in to his modern, crisp office with the expansive views of Beverly Hills and beyond. The sun was sinking in the late afternoon sky.

"Kevin, I called you in because we need to chat about your future," he said, after greeting me with a warm handshake and a smile.

"Sure, I'd love to consider your ideas. I have a few of my own." I was eager to get back up on the horse, if you know what I mean.

"Kev, since the show got canned, and because of the exclusivity of it, we can't shop it around, so it's basically dead now. I just don't have anything for you. You can't do movies, and your TV career is washed up. There's nothing more for me here, so I'm cutting you loose." He almost seemed giddy telling me this.

"What?!" I was dumbfounded, hurt, punched in the solar plexus. I thought we were friends, and in that, I had clearly been mistaken. He had confided in me about his serious heart condition, which had required heart surgery, but apparently, he had failed to tell me that they had *removed* it.

"Look, I've got Jim Carrey, Ellen DeGeneres, and I'm a busy guy. I just don't have the time to devote to someone I think doesn't have a career anymore. You've peaked, and you'll never have a movie career."

Welcome to the ethics of Hollywood. I hired this manager when my career was already going gang-busters to represent me on the deal for *Andromeda.* He collected a great paycheck for five-years-worth of episodes and then supervised the sitcom deal with ABC. There were a couple of other bookings in between, like *Who Wants to Be a Millionaire,* but not a lot of effort for the return he got. Yet, this is how he repays me—with a pretend friendship he discards like a used tissue.

"After one rejection? Just because one guy at ABC who's clearly running ABC into the ground didn't pick up a great show that would have been an eight-year hit?" I was angry and lashing out, frustrated at my inability to control the moving pieces. "This makes no sense…."

"Well, it makes sense to me," he cut me off, impatient. "Look, I gave it my best shot, and it didn't work. I'm done. I'm out. Good luck to you, Kevin, but don't think you've got a movie career ahead of you, because you don't."

Honestly, was that parting shot really necessary? I couldn't help but think there was some satisfaction for him in his pronouncement. As I walked back to my car, reeling, I thought to myself, "Well, that didn't go as planned."

I called Sam from the car. "You aren't going to believe what just happened."

It wouldn't be until I got back home and slept on it that I fully digested her response. "Kevin, he obviously doesn't know you. He's a jerk who was looking for an easy payday, which he found with *Andromeda.* Now that that show is done and this new easy paycheck has dried up, he's got other things on his mind. Would you rather he keeps you around, making you believe he cares, but not actually doing anything for you? No. He's done you a great favor. Be done with him, and let it go."

Astute words from her, but difficult to digest. I knew she was right, but could my heart convince my brain, which insisted on rerunning the whole scene like a bad movie on an infinite loop? Although Sam contended that his hurtful words said more about him than about me, they were like barbs in my backside, leaving festering wounds even as I tried to pluck them out.

This, of course, is a great commentary on the underbelly of the Hollywood machine and its politics, or if you prefer, religion. You see, you're only valued for as long as you're useful, and when they decide to drop you, friendship becomes a dirty word, or worse, meaningless. The opposite of love is indifference. This was a big lesson for my "Minnesota-nice" sensibilities. I felt betrayed, but of course, it was nothing like that. My sensation of treachery implied a kind of personal relationship, but evidently, I was the only one who considered our association personal. It was business. Only business. It is a business of quiet desperation and handshakes to distract from the hand behind the back that holds the knife.

Sam's analogy was spot-on. I had signed Eric with the prospect of *Andromeda* already on the horizon, and he had driven it into the most lucrative deal going. In fact, the day we signed it, he said to me, "Mark this day, because this is the last deal we will ever see like this in the syndicated world. Television is changing, Kevin, and nobody's going to get a deal even close to this one again. Congratulations." At least that part was true.

He was, of course, congratulating himself, but I certainly don't begrudge him that. He negotiated a lot of money for himself, me, my agents, and my lawyers with this TV show. And he was right; no deal like it has ever come again. I had a forty-four-show (two-year) guarantee, pay or play (meaning I would be paid even if they failed to produce the show) with a great starting salary and all the perks I had sought, including my twelve-hour door-to-door, which I required for my health. For a few hours of negotiating skills, he had hit the jackpot. That's Hollywood. "Congratulations," indeed.

But easy come, easy go. Eric no longer saw a fast buck in me and my career, so he set me free. He only wanted the easy money, and he figured I just wasn't worth the effort. I can't say that didn't smart a bit. I should also admit that it taxed my faith in myself.

But I put my faith in a higher source, deciding to believe there was a plan different from mine, certainly, but better. In hindsight, I realize now that he likely would have led me down other paths than the ones I eventually chose, and those would have been to my detriment. He did me a favor, even as he sought—actively sought, for whatever reason—to hurt me. He even did me a service by trying to hurt me to my face. Although it took time for me to fully appreciate it, he was a cancer in my life, and once he extricated himself from my world, and more importantly, once I accepted his divestment, I felt a freedom I never expected.

Not My Plan

Sam

I can easily say that for the past twenty years, I have been on a spiritual journey.

It was shortly before I flew down to New Zealand to guest star on an episode of Hercules that I had a conversation with God about my husband. I wasn't desperate to get married, but I understood that time was running out, and that my patience and pickiness were becoming liabilities to my reaching the end-goal of having a family. Perfectionism can be a problem.

"God," I prayed one day, "I get it. I know there's got to be a compromise. The perfect guy probably doesn't exist, and, on the outside chance he does, how I'll meet him is beyond me." I had been living in Los Angeles for too many years to harbor any lingering hope that Mr. Right lived there, too. "So, please show me what the compromise will be. Will it be superficial or deeper than that? Will he be loving, but dumb? Or will he be wonderfully intelligent, but self-absorbed? I get that there is a compromise, and I'm ready to do so, but I humbly ask for guidance…"

It was, I thought, a futile prayer. I had always imagined that I would know when I met the right guy. In fact, I was absolutely certain of that small truth, just as I was certain that I would have three children in the order of boy-boy-girl. The prayer, heartfelt as it was, was an acknowledgment of weakness and insecurity. I had relied on myself for so long, made my own money, paid my own bills, and executed my own decisions.

I was growing in my faith. At the time, I thought, *I might as well. If I agree that God is sovereign, then He must know better than I.* And so, seemingly against my own judgment, I placed the burden on God.

Only a week or two later, I flew down to New Zealand, not realizing, of course, that God's plan had already been in motion before my prayer.

I met Kevin Sorbo while shooting *Hercules,* and the rest, as they say, is history. I wrote the amazing story of our falling in love in Kevin's book, *True Strength*, but suffice it to say that he was, indisputably, the answer to my prayer. Apparently, as Kevin's illness would force me to concede, the compromise I would accept was not in my soul mate, but in me.

It was an easy one. Kevin was lying on the hospital gurney in the intensive care unit at Cedars Sinai hospital in Beverly Hills, unable to move lest he bleed out from the powerful and plentiful blood thinners coursing through his angiogram tube. I had just booked a national network commercial—for ice cream, no less. (Ice cream was my *favorite*!) I stood before him as he lay in agony on his uncomfortable bed and asked him if he would rather I not take the fantastic job that would fly me to New York City for three days.

Kevin didn't labor over his answer. "Yes, I'd rather you stay here with me."

Sure, he was scared, and he was vulnerable, but he was still the strongest man in the world. This admission on his part that he needed me was like a hot bath on a cold day. I melted inside, realizing my purpose in that moment.

"Okay, done. I'll call my agent and let her know."

Kevin had the incredible manners to utter, "Thanks."

"I love you. I know you're going to pull through this, but I'm going to stay, to make sure you're taken care of."

Neither of us realized the extent of the damage the strokes had done to Kevin's brain at that point. While Kevin experienced the strokes, he was in complete denial as to the severity of their deleterious effects. Sure, he was dizzy, but that was maybe because he hadn't gotten out of bed in a few days. He had the "just shake it off" mentality of a jock, and the hardheaded "power through" perspective of a man driven to succeed. He would be the last one to admit weakness. His request that I stay indicated greater physical devastation than I was willing to acknowledge, but it didn't matter just then. What God wanted me to perceive was that my so-called compromise was immediately defined: I would leave my career.

Sitting in that intensive care room at Cedars, the distinction clearly announced like the clanging of a bell, I sent another shorter prayer up to God. "Done, and thanks."

Since that day in the hospital, life hasn't been all flowers and butterflies, by any stretch. Kevin and I waged a three-year battle for his brain and well-being, and although I didn't suffer as he did, I picked up the pieces when he fell apart, offered explanations when the medical community got things wrong, and served as head cheerleader in a game with no spectators. We didn't share his struggles, fearing trepidation on the part of his future employers were we to come clean with his health issues.

For his part, Kevin fought valiantly and overcame brilliantly, just as I purposely predicted and passionately prayed. He *is* the strongest man in the world.

The story of my so-called compromise highlighted for me the way in which God exhibited not only His sovereignty in my life, but also His abundant love for me, for Kevin, and for our family. Because, despite my own doubts, God proved Himself to me, and perhaps because of the hardship we encountered as well, I began marriage to Kevin a more devoted follower. I prayed, read my Bible, and kept a devotions journal in which I wrote every morning after Kevin would go to set. My daily devotions set my heart and gave me strength I did not previously possess.

Years later when we published Kevin's story in *True Strength: My Journey from Half-God to Mere Mortal and How Nearly Dying Saved My Life*, I gained a new perspective on that divinely inspired strength.

Kevin and I realized we needed to move back to Los Angeles if he was to pursue his career and I mine. I found a house in a lovely quiet canyon in Bel Air, a gorgeous little jewel box perched on the side of a mountain. After we bought it, we would jokingly volunteer that we owned an acre of land, but that our acre was vertical. The garage was up a short hill, about a car length from the street. From the charming gate next to the garage, stairs scrambled up to the side entrance and wound from there around to the front of the house. A small terrace received the determined climber, and he could gaze directly down at the canyon street two stories below. There was also a side terrace out the kitchen door where our toddlers and new baby girl would play in a sandbox or the Italianate fountain that edged our property.

The house itself was cleverly laid out, and though small, suited us perfectly. Downstairs, there was a cozy paneled-and-upholstered-walled den, whose window gazed upon the green wall of mountain behind the house. We installed a large TV and furnished the room comfortably, and it became a refuge for me in the evenings when I needed to unwind or at night when I couldn't sleep. I was still struggling to regain healthy sleep patterns after the years of Kevin's recovery, nursing babies, and my battles with anxiety, which often woke me or simply kept me awake.

Upstairs, there were only two bedrooms: a spacious master and a large secondary suite with a tiny, fully finished, bumped out dormer. It was super-cute with its low, double-sloped ceiling. It was akin to a treehouse or clubhouse, but right off the boys' shared bedroom, instead. The boys would play in here, I had immediately decided upon seeing the house, and as I purchased their bunk beds, I also ordered cubbies to run along the two-foot-high walls of the little dormer room. There was just enough room for their train table in there as well. The boys both enjoyed the warm, snug feel and laughed at my inability to stand upright in that space. I would duck my head to enter, then take a seat to converse or play with them.

Being back in Los Angeles was a strange experience for me. It was still the same town—although with more traffic—but I was a drastically changed person and now a mom to three young people. Once we were established, I began to realize that I disliked being away from home for any length of time. It felt like there was a tether between me and my adorable, vulnerable little babies, and the farther away I ventured, the stronger my compulsion grew to return home to them.

It was in acceptance of that invisible attachment that, while Kevin traveled extensively, I would (could) never leave the children to accompany him, always either finding a way to bring them along or choosing to stay home instead. We didn't have the luxury of family to stay in the house with them. Our closest relatives were Kevin's aging parents, who lived in Vegas, and I stood resolutely opposed to leaving the kids in the care of any unrelated caregiver overnight.

Shortly after we moved into the house in Bel Air, I hired a housekeeper to help around the house and watch the kids. This was supposed to free up my time to pursue my acting career, which I had placed on hold since Kevin fell ill and again when I couldn't work in Canada. Now in the heart of Hollywood, I reached out to my commercial agent, a wonderful, supportive friend I had known for years, and she was thrilled to have me back in town. I started auditioning.

As I mentioned, it was hard for me to go out of the house emotionally, but I powered through. An audition typically required preparation. After about a forty-five-minute drive, then waiting for as much as an hour, and the drive home, the total would amount to about a two-and-a-half or three-hour commitment. After my third audition, I walked in the kitchen door and announced, "Mommy's home!"

My wee toddler Octavia came running into the room, pointing her little finger at me, saying, "No, no, no, no, no!" She was reprimanding me.

"No?" I asked her, snatching up her delicious impish form into my greedy arms and squeezing her. "No, no, no?"

"Mmm," she replied, then shifted abruptly in my arms to eyeball the housekeeper, who was nearby, wiping the counters and smiling at us. Octavia put her hand up in the air, opening it and closing it, instead of waving, and she said, clear as a bell, "Bye-bye! Bye-bye!"

It was immediately obvious to me what that meant. While she liked her nanny, Octavia did not like Mommy to be absent

For me, being away brought its own easily discernible discomfort. In an instant, I resolved to abandon my pursuit of acting jobs. I had a husband who provided for our family, and I had the luxury to stay home with the little ones, and I saw that as a strong choice. I was also grateful to be able to see it so clearly. I often speak with professional women who struggle to balance their family life with their jobs or other pursuits. I recommend getting clarity through prioritizing. My priority was first to my family. I had desperately longed to have children, but I also really love acting, and I had bought the lie that today's woman can "have it all." That's like saying you can eat the whole smorgasbord. You can't. And if you try, you'll end up sick, or worse. I've discovered that you should pinpoint, on a buffet, the individual items that you really want, and stick to them. It's healthier, and in the end, you're eating what makes you happy. The same is true about prioritizing your life.

You know the saying, there's no tombstone that reads, "I wish I spent more time at the office." When I put my career second to my marriage, I gained a new, improved focus. Now, holding my wee daughter in my arms, Octavia brought me to a similar epiphany. I decided then to concentrate on my children, instead of allowing my career to pull me away from them. Perhaps the boys would have been fine with a nanny instead of Mommy around, but Octavia wasn't having it, and she was strong enough to make her desire known with her squeaky little voice and her pudgy little hand wave. I thank God that I had the ears to hear her message, ringing like a chapel bell. So after planning my big career comeback for several years, I discovered that my plans were secondary to someone else's, and I was totally okay with that.

Maya Angelou says, "If you don't like something, change it. If you can't change it, change your attitude." I had an attitude adjustment that day, courtesy of my eighteen-month-old daughter. It is a gift I can never repay her because it started me down an incredibly satisfying and gratifying road. While it was a leap of faith for me to abandon my acting career, for what I believed would be the final time, God redeemed it in the long run, and the story I am living is clearly one only He could have crafted.

Soft Cushion

Kevin

We were back in Los Angeles, *The City of Broken Dreams*, and I was back to hitting the pavement, looking for work. I'll be honest—this was hard on my ego. Sure, I got the jobs, but *me*, audition? After two hundred-plus hours of television under my belt? How is that fair—or reasonable?

It was great to be back in the heart of things in LA, but it also represented a drastic change in lifestyle. For one thing, canyon roads were barely navigable from *inside* a car. There would be no evening walks with our strollers, three kids, and a little dog the way the cars came screaming up the twisting canyon road. Our house had very little yard, because although it sat on an acre, most of that acre was vertical! But we did have a large Italian fountain that the kids loved to splash around in, and a nice patio, onto which Sam added a sandbox and easels for painting.

Sam put her garden swing out on the front terrace that overlooked the canyon road from about thirty feet up. Gizmoe, our eight-pound Brussels Griffon, enjoyed traversing the low stone wall that bordered the terrace, surveying her domain, while Sam sat on the swing, reading to the kids, watching them paint, or cuddling them.

One thing that had been lacking in Henderson was a church we felt was our home. Being back in LA, we could attend Sam's church with Pastor Mark Pickerill, who married us. I really looked forward to hearing him speak, and I always left church with a new perspective on life. His sermons were often critical and yet uplifting at the same time. He infused in them his unique sense of humor, and his self-effacing quality seduced the large congregation.

As we settled into being back in Los Angeles, my life began spinning more and more out of control. Gone was the structure of being on a television show with the daily filming schedule, the script review each night, and the production meetings. I was adrift, and, now in LA, I didn't even have my golf course to distract me.

Sam installed a gym for me in the basement of our garage. It was a weird little area, just spacious enough, and she connived to build out a window on the side, which allowed for just enough ventilation to make the whole thing work. She mirrored an entire wall and painted the others white with turquoise, giving the room a very cool, energetic vibe. It was to my man-cave, and I retreated there often. I didn't just need the physical workouts, but also the mental detachment from the disappointment I was still experiencing after the loss of my sitcom. It wasn't like I was moping around all day, but I unquestionably had a depression going under my upbeat type-A demeanor.

Hollywood saw me as a jock who lucked out on a show, based entirely on my physique. My second show, *Andromeda*, never even made it onto Hollywood's radar.

Here was a show that took over the same spot that *Hercules* had occupied for so many years. *Andromeda* debuted as the number one show in first-run syndication and stayed there for all five years of its run. *Stargate* never beat us in the ratings, yet it had a ten-year run, unlike my show. I suppose that might be because my show's parent company declared bankruptcy. Go figure.

I felt like I had been in Siberia for the most recent five years, and symbolically, with my illness, I had, leaving me with a lot to prove upon my return.

This is the bane of the actor's existence: our self-worth is tied much too tightly to our work. At least, that's how it is for me. Don't get me wrong—I was very busy all the time. I loaded up my schedule with meetings and appointments, golf tournaments, and even some auditions. I traveled a lot, mainly because I always had. But underneath the organized chaos, I was foundering, being unmoored from a stable show after 17 years of full-time employment. It was a mid-life crisis of the highest degree, although I would never cop to that.

Sam was busy with the kids, of course, and happier than ever. She had determined to go back to work acting but lost the heart for it after the incident with Octavia. She had found something more important, a profound lesson that would evade me for some time to come. I was relentlessly a doer, my work was my *purpose*, but now it had become elusive and unfulfilling.

Gizmoe, our stalwart Brussels Griffon, was getting old. At thirteen, her sight was fading, and her hearing as well, and she had gradually become more and more solitary and sedentary. Gone were her days of policing her domain from the low wall overlooking the road on the canyon floor. It was sad to watch her decline.

Sam and I talked about Gizmoe's future, and she had Gizmoe tested at the veterinary clinic. They put up some briefcases in a make-shift maze, and Giz just bumped into each one as she went along. She was truly blind. Further tests established Gizmoe's retinal failure, so, even if we removed her cataracts, the vet assured us Giz would remain sightless. On top of that, Gizmoe seemed miserable. She was old and crotchety, scared, and short-tempered.

I was working on various projects, TV shows and some movies, and then one day the phone rang. It was my agent, who said the guys from *Scary Movie* were interested in me for their new movie, *Meet the Spartans,* which would be a spoof of *300*. I laughed. My first thought was that they were going to want me to shave my head, and I would never do that. I was older now, too, and I'd never regained my previous athleticism or great build from before my strokes. I no longer had the body to play a Spartan army officer. I was still in good shape, but my personal bar was very high, and I was nowhere near it.

Sam was not so dismissive. She believed in me, as well as the tongue-in-cheek cunning of casting TV's former Hercules as a funny addition to a spoof on an epic Greek tragedy. She encouraged me to explore the possibilities, and it turned out she was right. Regarding the physical athletic shape, or lack thereof, it didn't even matter. They were painting abs onto everyone, as part of the spoof. They also had no desire for me to shave my head. I accepted the offer.

It was a hot summer day in Los Angeles. The shoot was a few weeks off, and I was in the office working out the details of our living arrangements and making sure they would accommodate our little dog.

There was a slow breeze blowing when Sam brought the kids to play at the park down the street. It was a park she had often taken Gizmoe to, even before she and I had ever met. The kids were excited to go, and I watched everyone load up into the car below my office window.

When they arrived and parked, Sam unbuckled everyone, and lifted Gizmoe out of the front seat, attaching her leash. She called out to Giz, who made her way carefully by following Sam's voice. Slowly, listening for Sam to cue her, Gizmoe grew bolder in her steps and found a nice grassy spot in the shade of a large tree. Braeden and Shane wasted no time meeting other kids to play with on the climbing apparatus. Octavia was more mellow, walking slowly toward the swings with her mom. Sam took a seat in the shade, chatting with some of the nannies who were there with their charges while keeping an eye on Gizmoe, who was lounging near the sandpit. Sam would tell me later that it was the first time in a while that Gizmoe seemed at peace, enjoying the warm sun reflected around her, the cool breeze on her fur, and the children's joyful sounds in her ears.

When it was time to head home for lunch, Sam made her way back to the car with the three small children and the blind eight-pound dog. First, she opened the car door and put Gizmoe on the floor of the front passenger seat. She left the car door open, to allow the lazy wind to start cooling the heated interior, while she went around to the baby's car seat on the driver's side. While Sam was preparing to put Tavi into the car, a man approached the car, apologizing for his dog's defecation so nearby. He bent down to clean it up. The boys stood close, watching this.

"Yeah, I'm so sorry about this. Don't want your kids to step in it, so—," he continued.

Sam wanted to say, "Be careful, because my little dog is in the front seat," but she couldn't seem to get a word in edgewise, as the man continued to apologize and explain himself.

"I'll just get this picked up—"

His dog Duke, a large bullmastiff weighing probably about 150 pounds, must have smelled the diminutive creature not far away. Duke yanked the man's leash out of his hand and leapt into the car's front seat area. He wrapped his immense, salivating jaws around unsuspecting little Gizmoe's head and pulled her out of the car.

The owner was oblivious to what was actually happening. "No, Duke, that's not our car!" he reprimanded, thinking that the dog was simply getting in what he thought to be his owner's car.

Sam knew immediately what was happening. "My dog!" She ran around her car, still holding Octavia, and screamed. "My dog! Stop! Stop it!"

Duke had yanked Gizmoe from the car and started to shake her in his mouth until her neck broke.

"What? Duke! No! Duke, put that down!"

Sam turned away from the violent, gory scene. She couldn't be a witness to what she knew in her heart was the end. She staggered to the fence, her eyes averted, and, holding her daughter, screamed at the top of her lungs, repeatedly, for what seemed an eternity. Scream after scream, arguing with fate, rejecting the inevitable outcome. Scream upon scream, the anger and frustration and the memory of a five-year-old girl watching a German shepherd perform the same instinctual attack on her guinea pig in her front yard. Scream, scream, scream.

The nannies came over from the playground to investigate the commotion. A Filipino nanny walked up to Sam and said, "At least let me hold the child."

And Sam, in her all-consuming anguish, handed off our little girl to a kind stranger. Others took the boys under their temporary care.

Sam recounts hearing an unyielding, soothing voice, under her screams. "This is it. You knew the end was coming. She is already gone, Sam, so mourn the loss of her but rejoice that she is free from her suffering and sorrow. This is the easiest way. She's gone. She's simply gone now. It's done." The finality and the assuredness of the message calmed Sam so she could turn around.

The nannies were trying to tell Sam that it was over, to look, please, now the two dogs were separated.

The owner had wrestled with his dog. His hand was bloody, and he told Sam he thought it might be broken. Gizmoe lay on the dirt like a discarded rag. "Take her to the vet! If you hurry, you have about seven minutes before shock sets in." People will say the most outlandish things when the adrenalin is pumping. Shock was the least of Gizzy's concerns.

The stunned crowd that had gathered watched Sam pick up the bloodied and broken little body as it shuddered its last. Gizmoe hadn't recognized anything after being yanked from the car. Sam had heard her squeal once she felt her head in the vice-like jaws of the massive, slobbering bullmastiff, but Giz likely never knew what hit her. She certainly never saw it. And then, as suddenly as it had begun, it was over.

Gizmoe was gone.

We shot *Meet the Spartans* for two months in New Orleans, and the family, sans Gizmoe, accompanied me. I was working again and having a lot of fun on the set, and in my downtime, I would take the family to the zoo, the aquarium, the park—or should I say, they would take me? We went on a swamp boat and came very close to some enormous alligators. We saw the Mardi Gras storage and preparations. Getting out of Los Angeles did wonders for me and was also quite therapeutic for Sam, who was in a deep depression over her intense, shattering loss.

Did I mention she published a book of photos of that little creature? *Gizmoe: The Legendary Journeys, Auckland* is a lovely coffee table book of photos of little Gizmoe, while she gives the reader a tour of Auckland. And wouldn't you know it, that dog *posed* for the photos. If you page through the book, it's obvious.

Sam desperately needed the recovery period and the travel that my shoot in New Orleans afforded her away from all the things that would remind her of Gizmoe. She would bring the kids to me on set, or to the fantastic Audubon Aquarium of the Americas, or just out for walks, returning home each day by one o'clock for the family nap.

Sam had always been diligent with babies napping. Shane was a mere toddler when he decided, as many young, active children do, he was done with napping. There was too much of interest in this world for sleep!

Sam accepted none of that, because she had a wee baby as well as an older boy, and she understood the value of sleep, especially in preventing what is commonly called "the terrible twos." She tricked Shane into taking naps, and he became our best sleeper, often putting himself to bed early when he feels the need or taking a nap during the daytime, even at twelve years old.

In New Orleans, while I was on set, Sam devoted the diminished little family's afternoons to naps, not just for the kids, but for herself, too. She would put the two youngest down in their beds and set Braeden up with something to color or play with, and then retreat into our bedroom with a book to distract her, falling asleep more often than not. Her afternoons were quiet, restful, and restorative.

I consider those two months we spent heaven-sent. I needed to feel useful on a film set, and getting out of LA made it somehow more weighty and transformative for me. Being an audacious, madcap comedy, the film itself was a blast to shoot, and the talented, creative cast and crew made it a great deal of fun.

We even had the "Pit of Death" in the film that was like the one in *300*. Of course, at the bottom of that pit was a pile of soft foam cubes. The day Sam brought the kids to that set, the two boys had the thrill of a lifetime tumbling, leaping, and dropping into the pit. What joy, to be like my little children, with their unquestioned faith that the foamy sea would gently break their falls. While we giggled and goofed around for a few minutes that morning, I noticed some light and levity come back into Sam's eyes.

Sometimes faith provides the soft landing from a rough tumble. Sometimes it's just the outstretched hand, pulling you up off the ground after a hard landing.

Sam needed a period of recuperation, away from home, to heal and regain her inner peace. I had never seen her lose her calm like she had that day at the park, and the repercussions from that catastrophic event profoundly affected her. There wasn't much I could do for her, but not because I was working long days on a film set. Some wounds only time would mend.

As she cared for the children in a foreign city, exploring new places and not confronted by old memories back home, Sam grieved quietly. I prayed for her healing, and I watched as the time she spent in the hot New Orleans humidity restored her sanguine, serene spirit.

IGWeT

Sam

To understand the prominent role that Gizmoe played in our lives, there are a few important details to know. Gizmoe was the first dog I ever had all by myself, inspiring me to become fully adult by serving her and not only myself. Once Kevin entered our lives, she played another a pivotal role.

For the first several months of Kevin's recovery (and our marriage), walking was the only exercise Kevin could manage. So Gizmoe was our companion each day for our long morning walk. Returning from that activity, Kevin spent most of the rest of the day on the couch, which suited Gizzy just fine. While she was initially quite skeptical about this new, large, intimidating human in my life, she seemed to change when we established this routine. *So, this guy just wants to go for a long stroll and then loll on the sofa all day? I can deal with that!* she seemed to think. She also had an uncanny way of brightening Kevin's mood with her antics, soothing his anxiety, and relieving some of his suffering.

Gizmoe traveled everywhere with me: to auditions, appointments, even to the doctor's office. She had it figured out. She gleefully snuck into her little travel bag and remained church-mouse quiet. People seated next to us on airplanes had no idea she was under the seat in front of me. Once, I escorted a friend to a doctor's appointment, carrying Giz. When the doctor came in for the consultation, Gizmoe could barely be heard. But then she sneezed! The doctor looked down at the black bag on the floor, then at my friend and me. "Is there a dog in there?" he asked dubiously. I had to fess up. Luckily, the good doctor was a dog-lover!

Giz was simultaneously sage and ridiculous, kooky but dignified. After we had moved to New Zealand, where Kevin shot *Hercules,* I eventually found I had time on my hands. I decided to create a book of photos of my adorable puppy showcasing the sites around town. It's called *Gizmoe: The Legendary Journeys, Auckland.* It is no lie to say that Giz knew she was being photographed, enjoyed it, and even insisted on posing for each photo. The proof is right on the pages. Gizmoe wasn't just a dog. She was a collaborator, companion, and caregiver. She was a God-sent best-friend.

When we lost her, it was cataclysmic. Her little wall-eyed expression and crooked nose is indelibly printed in my memory. And though I knew she would eventually leave me, when that day arrived something inside me irreparably broke. It would be almost a year before I could entertain the thought of getting another dog, specifically another Brussels griffon.

I began my search for a new dog in prayer. God, I feel like it's time I got another dog. The kids should have a dog growing up, and I need another furry friend. Please give me wisdom and guidance.

Sometimes, prayer is like trying something on and wearing it around the house to determine its suitability. I felt my bereavement slowly lift off me, transformed into positivity, optimism, and a little excitement. A new family member!

For several weeks, I searched my local shelters. Small dogs are snapped up so quickly it became clear I never stood a chance of getting one there. I searched the web for a few more months before finding the right dog: a small, black, female griff from a reputable breeder and not a puppy mill. This tiny precious creature was square. Like, from the side, she was long in the leg, but her back, butt, head, and front legs formed... the only way to describe her was *square* (and perfectly adorable.)

About six weeks later, at around nine at night, I returned home with the new puppy. Kevin had allowed the kids to stay up to meet the furry black energy cube. They were so excited to welcome her! The puppy was thrilled, moving from human to human, sniffing, getting pats, licking, investigating some more. It was a love fest, with giggles and surprises for both dog and child, and a wonderful new beginning.

For me, however, it was less than spectacular. I immediately sensed pangs of guilt. Granted, it had been a year since Gizmoe had passed away, but I still missed her terribly. How was I to bond with her replacement? I remembered meeting the breeders, a pair of sympathetic elderly women. As I described to them my thirteen-year-plus relationship with my wonderful and devoted Gizmoe, they smiled at me with sympathy. Then the older woman said, "You know, Sam, this dog cannot replace Gizmoe."

It was like a warning. A foreboding. A curse? "Of course! Nothing can replace Gizzy!" I insisted, brushing off the chill the woman's intuition and sagacity gave me. My protests aside, I did hope that the new puppy would at least fill the hole that Giz's death rent in my heart.

I was naively optimistic—and in for a big lesson.

The day after we adopted our puppy, I fell to the task of naming her. Everyone had suggestions, but I wanted a special name, something that was original and quirky. Shadow and Midnight were cute, but they were too mundane and devoid of character.

Kevin's and my office was over the garage, separate from the main house in our quaint homestead in Bel Air. I sat at my desk, ruminating and searching the web for ideas for naming our tiny monster. She had the characteristic pushed-in monkey face, with wide-spread eyes over a down-turned mouth. I looked under *Star Wars* to find names of creatures. "Ewok" was one. Biwa, six, and Shane, four, played by Kevin's desk with their little sister, Tavi, who was barely two. Daddy was downstairs in the basement gym.

Little Biwa found the red "In God We Trust" stamp Kevin had at his desk, and he thought it was a great idea to stamp Tavi's forehead.

She was sweetly oblivious. My little girl wandered over to me as I pondered "Wookie" as a name for the puppy, with that crimson phrase emblazoned on her face above her eyebrows. "In God We Trust." The first letters stood out to me. *IGWT*. I sounded it out.

"Igwet." I smiled. Again, I said, "Igwet!" I liked it. "Iggy."

Tavi scrunched up her nose and said, "Iggy. Wha's'at?" in her cute squeaky voice.

"*That* is the puppy's name." We smiled, like we had shared a secret.

The first few days with a new puppy are always a little stressful. We wanted our new addition to be comfortable, while also needing to beware of establishing bad habits. Needs, desires, and intentions only go so far. I embraced this responsibility reluctantly, having forgotten how intense the early days were. Potty-training required vigilance, as did preventing the kids from feeding the dog from the table.

Every morning, I took some time to work to train her. I took her to obedience classes. It was hard work, frustrating, and I was ill-prepared. Giving lip-service to the idea that this dog would not replace Gizmoe did nothing to prepare me for what a burden and commitment our new dog would be. The stark contrast between Iggy's exigencies and the severe pangs of memories with Gizmoe aggravated and depressed me,

One cheerful warm day in May, the kind filled with hope, birds singing, sun shining, and optimism like the breeze scintillating the leaves in the trees, I reached the end of myself. Despite the beauty in the world, I felt horrible about the new puppy. She was difficult to potty-train, she chewed things she shouldn't, and she was messy and needy in a way completed foreign to me. I just wasn't accustomed to working this hard for a dog and she gave me almost no joy, mainly because I still longed for Gizzy. Gizmoe had developed into an extension of myself. She knew just where to be, how to be (quiet), and what to do. This new dog knew... *nothing!* She was like having another toddler—and I already had three of those at home! I was struggling, not least because I had designed this house of bricks that I felt collapsing on top of me. It was my own fault, and I knew it.

I left the puppy locked up at home, safe, when I drove to pick up Biwa from his little Montessori pre-school. In the car, I had twenty minutes to reflect on my mistakes and try to figure out what to do. I felt bereft. I grasped for some sense of purpose or confidence in my choices. I prayed. Tears streaked down my face as I cast my burden at the foot of the cross. I felt silly. *It's just a puppy!* But in the moment, whatever your struggles, they are *your* struggles, and faith brings the knowledge that He cares and He tends and He heals and He redeems for His purposes.

I offered it all to Him. "God," I said, settling my roaring emotions and clearing my addled thoughts as I sat at a red light, "I know this dog will never be Gizmoe, who I miss every day. This is hard right now, but only for a season. In the long-run, I have faith that Igwet will be the dog that this family needs—the perfect dog for us— because You gave her to us. Thank You for this gift. Amen."

I'll acknowledge here that speaking it and believing it are two distinct things, but the moment I uttered the words that even I scarcely trusted, my confidence grew. There is power in the spoken word that defies terrestrial explanation. Not from my own accord, of course, but from the knowledge of God the Creator. A prayer is spirit, but so are our thoughts, attitudes, and feelings. So, prayer works, especially when we invoke God to liberate us. He is our Deliverer, our Comforter, and the Author of Salvation, and when you cast your cares at the bottom of the cross, the peace that surpasses all understanding does come over you.

My prayer stated, it was, eventually fulfilled. I'm happy to report I never looked back. I persevered despite my misgivings, trained my proposed tormentor and learned to love her for the wonderful, adoring, devoted creation that she was, different entirely from Gizmoe, but distinctly chosen for such a time as that, and such a family as ours. I accepted my responsibility to our diminutive, defiant, delightful Igwet and enjoyed her company in the years to come. She was never Gizmoe, but she definitely lived up to her name—"In God We Trust."

Home Alone

Sam

It wasn't until Braeden had turned eleven and Octavia was seven that I agreed to a trip away from the kids overnight. Kevin and I were traveling up the coast to host his third golf tournament benefitting A World Fit for Kids! We flew out on a Friday night after I briefed my sister Joryn on all the details regarding the children, their playdates, and Braeden's football game. She was already familiar with the house because although she lived on the East Coast, she visited often.

Braeden had a football game early Saturday morning, and I arranged for him to hitch a ride to the game with a friend because I wanted to avoid saddling my sister with needing to wake the younger ones and mobilize the entire house that early in the day.

The coach called my sister at around nine-thirty to inform her that Braeden had been hurt in the game, wouldn't be playing anymore, and wanted to be picked up. It was about this time that I began my tasks hostess of the golf tournament vineyard tour, a special, day-long event for the non-golfers or spouses of our attendees.

Joryn drove to the game with Shane and Octavia in tow, eventually finding her way through the parking maze that surrounded the school. She called me from the sidelines off the field.

"Sam, Braeden hurt his hand in the game today, and he wanted me to pick him up. He says he wants to talk to you. People are telling him he needs to have his hand x-rayed, so just be aware of that."

"Wait, how bad it is? How does it look?" I couldn't help thinking, *the first time I leave the kids, this happens!*

"I'm looking at it, and it looks fine, but he says it really hurts. It could be a sprain or something more serious. It's hard to tell. Lemme put him on the phone for you, and I'll snap a photo and send it." She handed the phone over to my firstborn.

"Mom? My hand really hurts. I got hit really hard, and I'm not sure, but I think I need to get it x-rayed."

"Why do you think that, sweetheart? Does it look or feel like it's broken? Does it look weird at all?" I maintained a composed tone, even though I was freaking out inside. I considered if his hand was broken. I wasn't exactly sure what the protocol was, but I would be flying back to town the following day. I didn't want to burden my sister with all the medical stuff, either. Couldn't this have happened when I was in town, which, up until this moment, had been *always?!*

"No, it looks fine. But a lot of people are saying I should go to the emergency room."

The photo came through on my phone. It was a snap of a completely normal-looking hand. That offered me no help at all. I wanted to scream from the top of my lungs at my ineptitude. I had no experience with this kind of thing. When I broke my arm falling off a horse, I simply got back on the horse and, to convince myself that everything was fine, I swooped large circles with my entire arm about five times as I rode gingerly back to the barn. Though I had no valid scientific argument for how, exactly, I believed this proved my arm was completely healthy. Tears streamed down my face from the pain. I worked, modeling the next two days before boarding a transatlantic flight. It wasn't until five days after my fall that I went into the emergency room and asked them to x-ray it. The doctor seemed utterly surprised. Affixing the films up on the light-board, he asked casually, "When did you say you had the accident? Because your arm is broken."

Clearly, my single experience with broken bones was an excellent indicator of my deficiencies. I needed help! I also needed some reassurance. My nerves were shattering, but I needed to keep everything together because, well, that's what I do. I said a quick prayer asking God for some wisdom and guidance and felt immediately reassured by a calming thought that there was no reason to overreact. I held on to that idea as I spoke to my son. It was a studied essay in cool faith.

"Okay, let me just say this. I'm not saying you don't need it x-rayed. I can't tell that from here. But if you do need an x-ray, then you won't be playing football for the rest of the season. Do you understand what I mean?"

"Not really, no," he answered, and waited.

"I'm saying that if you *need* an x-ray, it's because bones are broken. And if your bones are broken, then you won't be playing any more football because the healing will take a long time. Now, I'm happy to have Auntie Joryn take you to get an x-ray, but you need to think about if you really feel like you've got broken bones, or if you just hurt your hand a bit. It's up to you to decide because I can't see it and the photo doesn't tell me much either. So, what do you think?"

"Well, Auntie Joryn offered to take us garage-sale-ing, and I kind of want to do that, so," he trailed off, distracted by the treasure hunting that garage-sale-ing promised.

I asked him to hand the phone back to my sister. "Hey, so, he says he wants to go with you to some garage sales. Just keep an eye on it for me, and let's touch base after lunch sometime. How does that sound?"

"Sounds like a plan," she responded. "I've got a few sales picked out already, so, maybe the change of scenery will help take his mind off the pain, or whatever."

We hung up, and I returned to my hosting duties, apprehensive, but temporarily reassured. The morning went by slowly with my guests, and although I focused as much as I could on their enjoyment of our tour, and I did try some of the wines at the various places we stopped, I was distracted and concerned. After we stopped for lunch, I phoned my sister again and heard the kids were fine and had enjoyed their morning out. They were off in another room, but I asked Joryn to go check the hand.

She returned to the phone and told me Braeden was busy playing a game with his younger siblings but that his hand was swollen and discolored.

"Okay, so, I think you need to go have it x-rayed, please," I said. We discussed where the nearest urgent care facility was, and she set off, while I remained with my group, worrying and planning for contingencies.

A couple of hours later, my sister phoned to tell me there were two broken bones in Braeden's hand, spiral breaks that would require surgery. I murmured a quick prayer to the Great Healer, asking also for guidance and peace for myself. We were headed back to the hotel, but there were still a great number of festivities left in the weekend. I wasn't concerned for myself as much as for Kevin, whose birthday it was that very day, and who would be hosting the gala event that night.

When I got back to my hotel room, I started making some calls. I got the update from my sister on all the particulars, and then I called a doctor friend I trusted, learning from him first who he recommended as a specialist, and second, thankfully, that there was nothing the specialist could really do until the swelling subsided, probably five days away or longer. That put my heart at ease. There was nothing to be done just yet.

Still, I felt awful for not being at home. It had taken a full decade for me to finally allow someone else to be responsible for my children, and the nightmare became real. To put it into perspective, of course, this wasn't close to the worst that might have happened, but for me, it still resounded inside my gut like a sucker punch from a gorilla.

When Kevin returned from the golf course, he was in a good mood. I was sorry to interrupt his good time, but I needed his support. I had to handle it carefully, though, because when it comes to medical issues, Kevin can be very vulnerable and reactionary. (Something about his almost dying, I figure.)

To begin, I simply said, "Hey, I need you for a few minutes," and he turned his piercing blue eyes on me with his full attention.

He could read me like a book. "What is it?" he demanded with a serious tone.

"Nothing serious," I countered. "It looks like Braeden broke his hand in his football game."

"He what?!"

I could see the scenery collapsing in on him, on us both, so I quickly asserted, "It's just a broken hand, and he can't see the doctor until Monday, plus, I've learned that if it requires surgery, they can't even touch it for a few days, until the swelling goes down. So, there's nothing we can do from here right now."

"Should we fly home tonight?"

"I think we need to fulfill our commitment to the fundraiser first. There's nothing to be done at home, and Braeden understands that, so it's not like we're needed there. They gave him some pain killers, but he says it's not even that painful. He's fine."

"He's fine?" He was asking with sincerity, not his usual sarcasm.

"He'll be fine, and he's doing okay right now. My sister has it under control. We get in tomorrow, and all this can wait till after then. Besides, it's your birthday, so let's celebrate that tonight, and tomorrow we'll take care of business."

"Yeah, celebrate." There was the sarcasm.

"Well," I was exhausted from the tension I'd felt since I first heard there was a problem with Braeden's hand. He should never have been playing center. That position gets hit the most. I wasn't much of a fan of my son playing football, but neither would I stand in the way of his desire to follow in Kevin's footsteps. The problem was with a temperamental coach who had some serious issues, specifically with the son of Hercules. It never helps to tell that kind of insecure person that it's just a television show.

He would say things like, "Hey, who else wants to play, because Sorbo here looks like an idiot out there?" Mind you, the players were nine years old. He was rude to Braeden and picked on him, but Braeden was no quitter. Perhaps serendipity had arranged that

116

Braeden wouldn't be finishing the season with this weak man as his coach.

Kevin put his weighty, secure arms around me. They offered an intense moment of relief, and I relaxed in his embrace. He sensed what I needed, and he provided. He said simply, "I'll change our flight to the earliest flight back tomorrow."

The evening was a success for the foundation and for the guests, who enjoyed the entertainment and the food immensely. Unfortunately, I cannot report the same for the birthday boy, who started feeling ill at the time they began serving dinner. At first, I just thought he was worried and feeling a relapse kind of anxiety, but soon he started looking pale. Such a trouper, he powered through until the end, but by the time we got back to the room, he was sick in the bathroom.

Suffice it to say, we got no sleep that night. Kevin had come down with a parasite, which he'd probably had for a while, but it chose that moment to present itself. We boarded the flight back home, me, bleary-eyed and exhausted, and Kevin strung out from his multiple rendezvouses with the porcelain throne.

We arrived back at the house to find my firstborn with a purplish hand puffed up like a grapefruit. My sister, Joryn, met us at the door, grateful to be relieved of her duty. We hugged, and then I said to her, "I am never lending you any of my things again! You break everything I let you borrow!"

The obvious joke broke the tension and eased the apprehension she had been feeling. Sometimes, it's better to laugh, even when it's serious, and especially when it's irreversible.

Braeden had his hand operated on at the end of that week, and in the ensuing time of healing, he enjoyed the attention. He knows how to make lemons from lemonade.

Education and Politics

Kevin

The way Sam and I complement each other in the realm of childrearing is remarkable. I was always ready to change diapers and help with feeding and bathing, but let's not kid ourselves, I lived in her household. She is the disciplinarian, while I confess to being kind of a pushover. (Although, when Daddy does get serious, the kids listen!) At the same time, our kids respect us both for our strengths, and we each encourage that respect from them.

Of course, we homeschool them, which contributes to the incredible harmony we have in our home. Sam's written a book about it—it's something she is passionate about. Truth be told, I wasn't the biggest fan at the beginning. We moved to a new house for the schools, after all! It took a lot to convince me, but then again, I'm not exactly blown away by any phenomenal results from our public school system. Let's be honest, is anyone? Last I checked, the US ranks around 27th in the world in academic performance.

When Sam hit me up with the idea of trying something different, I was ready to explore our options. Initially, I thought that we just needed to find a "good" school, which was why we had moved. After seeing how things went with Braeden in our local "really excellent" public school, I wasn't so sure anymore. I just wasn't sure bringing education into the home would be the best solution, though. When I heard the price of a private school tuition for a single year, I became easier to convince—just kidding. Sam used the salami tactic on me. She suggested we try it for just a semester, something I know she now advocates for other people interested in exploring their options. She said, "I don't know if I have all the answers, but I'm stepping out in faith, Kevin. I think we are being called to this. I don't think we can fail any worse than the school already is!"

At the time, we were unaware of the Biblical directive to parents, and only parents (and grandparents), to educate their children. I submitted it in prayer, and while I didn't feel like I ever received an affirmation directly from the Big Guy, I knew that Sam had the conviction to experiment. She is thorough and dedicated, and I trusted her judgement.

I'll just say, after the first semester, there was no turning back. The change in Braeden's attitude, his relationship with his siblings, and the closeness I regained with my kids was unmistakable. After being out of town for a short trip, coming home and having the opportunity to spend the mornings with them or take them on errands with me thanks to their flexible homeschool schedule was too precious to give up again. Once I understood that, I was an easy convert. In addition, the ease with which we can all travel together as a family with no interference from the school and its assignments and paperwork is a major plus.

The icing on that cake was that Sam seemed to really enjoy it, although she was plagued with self-doubt. I tried to be supportive, but what did I know? She was easily more qualified than I based on interest, but we both lack college diplomas. She began blogging about her experiences with the kids. Eventually, she decided to publish her experiences in a book called *They're YOUR Kids: An Inspirational Journey from Self-Doubter to Home School Advocate.*

As she worked on the book, she realized that perhaps she needed to make the case to other parents for why they should consider home education. She started researching deeper into what was happening in our schools and discovered more than a few unsavory facts. As we experienced the joys of homeschooling with our kids and the togetherness that it brought to our family, Sam was also discovering the secrets hidden in our system that would spell, she believed, the eventual self-destruction of American education. She had begun homeschooling reluctantly but with excitement; however, the further away she got from the institution, the more committed she became to the process, and the more convinced she was of its effectiveness. What started in a whisper of faith soon became the firm cry of conviction.

I was keeping busy, even if I wasn't working all the time as I had on my two television series. I've never been one to sit idle for longer than a football game. Even then, I'm not just watching the game but am generally working on one project or another. So, when I wasn't auditioning or doing a guest-role on some sit-com or drama TV show, I played in a lot of celebrity golf tournaments.

It was at one of these tournaments, in a classic old Palm Springs hotel, that the host surreptitiously handed me a small slip of paper with uneven sides. There was just enough space on it for an address, date, and time.

"I think you might enjoy this evening's event I've planned. It's a film showing and a special presentation about national security," he told me.

His sincerity was genuine, and I liked him personally. I took the invitation he pressed into my hand, feeling a bit like this was some kind of illicit drug deal. I looked at the date and said, "I don't think I'm in town for that, but my wife loves that stuff, so, if it's okay, I'll give her the invitation."

"Sure, that'd be great," was the happy, quiet reply.

Steve Emerson, purportedly one of our foremost experts on national security, would be speaking at one of the large agency venues in Los Angeles. Sam was excited to attend. Instead of going alone, she invited her friend, a mom of some kids our kids enjoyed, to join her.

The sun was just setting when Sam picked up Sheryl for the 7:00 PM event. Sheryl was a part-time screenwriter working on a screenplay about a group from the United States that travels to the Middle East and contracts a translator for their business dealings. The translator would be a woman, and the show was intended for the premier women's network, Lifetime. Sheryl was busy researching this area of the world so she could write the screenplay as realistically as possible. In accepting Sam's invitation to join her, Sheryl had commented that the timing couldn't have been any better, specifically because of the relevance of Steve's subject matter.

"I'm excited about tonight," Sam said as she eased the car into eastbound traffic on Pico Boulevard.

"Me, too," replied Sheryl.

"I have no idea what to expect, to be honest. I didn't get a chance to do any research on the speaker tonight, to know exactly who he is. Plus, frankly, you know how it is with little ones, I barely had time to put on make-up, let alone look this guy up. I'm just thrilled to have an excuse to go out in the evening with a friend! When does that happen?"

"Never."

"That's right, although I'm not complaining. There's seldom anything that interests me enough to make an effort at the end of a long day!"

"Tonight will be different! By the way, and I'm just saying this, I have no idea where this guy is politically or if this even a political thing. I got no indication of anything from our host. So, we're just going in to see, to learn, you know..."

"Yeah, of course. Let's just go and have a nice time."

Sam says she doesn't know why she made a reference to politics. Although she was conservative at the time, she wasn't heavily involved in either politics or current events. Children will do that to a person.

Sam and Sheryl pulled up to the large fancy Century City building that housed the posh Hollywood agency. This firm represented the biggest names in the business, which was partly what made the invitation so attractive. It wasn't often that Sam was invited into the inner sanctum of the show business machine.

The uniformed valet zipped around the front of the car as the ladies alighted and entered the glass and granite edifice. Signs indicated the direction of the reception. "Emerson Reception," they read.

The foyer of the theater was white, black, and chrome, like a movie from the 1950s. Black and white stills from those very films hung on the walls. People milled about, looking at the décor and waiting for the bartender to mix their drinks. Waiters walked around proffering fancy hors-d'oeuvres. This wasn't a Doritos and beer crowd, at least not tonight.

Sam and Sheryl made their way to the bar, and Sam asked for two white wines.

A tall, dark man standing to the right of them at the bar turned around. "Sam?"

"Michael Nouri!" Sam replied, surprised. "How great to see you!" Michael had aged a bit since Sam had last seen him but in the distinguished sort of way; salt-and-pepper hair, three-day growth, the same charming smile. "You look fantastic! Uh, Sheryl, this is Michael Nouri, you know, from countless movies. He and I shot a movie together in the Philippines many years ago."

"That's right. How are you? I've been keeping well."

"Good, good... Sheryl is writing a screenplay about a female Arab translator, so..."

"Oh, fascinating. Good for you."

"Oh, my gosh... Do you remember the snake? The fifteen-foot yellow python—it was a python, right?"

"Yes! Yes, it was a Python, and I had nearly forgotten that! It was nineteen feet, and you were brave to hold it."

"It was heavy, but I look back now and think, 'Man, what an idiot I was!' I mean, who knows what would've happened if it had decided it didn't like me—or you, for that matter. You held it first!"

"Are you afraid it might have strangled you?" With that, he placed his hands around Sam's neck in a playful move to imitate the snake encircling her.

Sam yelped. "Agh, stop it! That's just creepy!" she laughed.

Sheryl laughed, too. "Wow. I can't imagine. Snakes give me cold-sweats."

"Well," Nouri turned his attention to Sheryl, "Imagine this bright yellow python around your neck." He gently slithered his hands around her neck, but she nearly jumped out of her skin.

"No, no, no! Ew! I don't even want to think about snakes! Let's change the subject, please!"

"Of course, my dear," Michael didn't miss a beat, "What would you like to discuss?"

"Uhm, what are you working on now?"

"Well, it's nice of you to ask. I've got two projects I feel very strongly about right now . . ."

The banter flowed for the next few minutes, with Nouri talking mainly about himself. In Sheryl, he had found a receptive audience. Sam left the two to greet some other friends in attendance.

Moments later, courteous aides ushered the group of about thirty into the adjacent theater. There was ample room in the soft, blue-gray cinema, so everyone spread out in the stadium seating, and Sam and Sheryl, together with Michael Nouri, sat comfortably near the center of the viewers.

"Tonight is a very special night, and I thank you all for joining me in welcoming our guest for the evening." Their host spoke with an intensity and calm forged from years in front of the camera. "I invited Steve here to make this presentation to you because, well, I love this country. I think we all do. And Steve has been witnessing what can only be called the infiltration of an opposing ideology. But more importantly, he's also on the front lines of this because our own government refuses to acknowledge the danger. He tells this story much better than I do, so, please welcome Steve Emerson."

The audience applauded politely as a smallish man with red hair took the stage. Sam hadn't known what to expect, and he certainly fit the bill.

Steve began to tell his story to the quiet audience. He had been a journalist on assignment to Oklahoma City, Oklahoma, back in 1994. Staying at a hotel downtown, he noticed a large group of people attending an event at the convention center. The group was large enough to capture Steve's attention and arouse his curiosity. He tried to attend but was told that no non-Muslims were allowed. This blatant prejudice irked him, so he decided to attend incognito, pretending to be Muslim. What he heard inside the venue was bone-chilling: booths with pro-terrorism literature, Hamas propaganda materials, even speakers calling for "Death to America."

He called the FBI to alert them to the anti-American activities going on right under their noses. Their response was classic. They couldn't verify his report, and they had no information about such subversive activities, so there would not open an investigation.

You're kidding me, right? was roughly Steve's response. Not to be dissuaded, Steve captured some photos and audio and supplied it to the FBI, but he was rebuffed again. It was at this point that he began his research in earnest, the fruits of which he used to produce a documentary film titled *Terrorists Among Us: Jihad in America*. That documentary comprised the main part of his presentation.

It was an excellent film, having already won several journalistic awards, and Sam really enjoyed it while learning a great deal about the atmosphere and conditions leading up to 9/11.

After the film, Steve responded to audience questions for about forty-five minutes. As a whole, the group seemed very responsive and receptive to him, with genuine curiosity sprinkled with mild shock and frustrated dismay. Sam sat with Sheryl and Michael until the event ended, then headed out to collect the car from valet. Nouri escorted the ladies out. Sheryl seemed to have enjoyed her time with Michael even more than with Sam, but they shared some pleasant chit-chat on the way home.

"That was kind of eye-opening, don't you think?" Sam began, once they were seated and driving in the light Los Angeles evening traffic.

"Yeah, it was interesting. Michael Nouri is funny and charming." Sheryl pivoted quickly to a different subject.

"Oh my gosh, when we were filming in Manila, we had a truck for the actors. I mean, this was low-budget, so all the actors had to share this truck. It was like a U-Haul, no windows, and the back door was the garage kind of door that opened upward. But it had air conditioning, so if you wanted to get out of the heat, then this truck was your best friend. Anyway, we all had to share, so the actors all piled in when they didn't need to be on set."

"How many actors?" Sheryl asked.

"Oh, well, it depended on the day, but I'd say five or six on the busy days. Anyway, those days, Michael smoked. A *cigar*!" Sam emphasized the word as if it were the definition of revolting.

"What? Inside the truck?"

"Yes! I literally had to ask him not to smoke inside, and he said, 'Why, does it bother you?' as if it might not. Then, he kept lighting up, when I wasn't in the truck, 'forgetting' that I didn't appreciate it. Nobody else had the temerity to ask him to step outside."

"Wow."

"Of course, he didn't want to smoke outside, because it was so dang hot. That's got to be the best way to give up smoking—go somewhere really hot with no air conditioning!"

Sheryl laughed as Sam pulled into the driveway of the cute Spanish-style house where she lived. "Well, good thing I don't smoke because I'm stuck here in LA!"

"Thanks for joining me tonight, by the way."

"You're welcome. Thanks for driving!"

Sam waited until Sheryl opened her front door before heading back home to pay the sitter. It was a great evening—the start of something that began to boil inside my wife. Her love of country, combined with a mother's protective instinct, ignited her patriotic activism that still roils today.

Incidentally, though she called Sheryl repeatedly after that evening, the young mother of two who hung out often with Sam before that evening, never spoke to Sam again.

The truth affects people in two possible ways. In Sam's case, she runs toward it. Although it's hard to imagine a world in which people hate her beloved country, she saw the proof in the attacks on the World Trade Center and Washington and grew to embrace this new reality, even as she mourned the loss of innocence.

In Sheryl's case, running from the truth can help maintain a worldview that's more appealing, but which has little truth in it. This works if you keep your head buried in the sand, and until the truth comes to find you personally. Once it knocks on your door, time has run out. You are herded into cattle cars, or forced to march through the fields, or they simply cut off your head.

"You know what bothers me most? She never returned my call, never picked up the phone, stopped going to the park, where we would inevitably run into each other. She just cut me off without any consideration at all. I was persona-non-grata, and I didn't do anything!"

"That's Leftism, Sam," I tried to assuage her hurt, but I was inadequate to the task. "Look, this is just something that you've got to learn. Some people don't want to be shown the truth. Nothing is worth the sacrifice of their, uhm, personal, private worldview. You threatened her worldview with that lecture, the movie. That's dangerous to her preconceived notions, which she refuses to allow to be challenged. Therefore, you are dangerous."

"I know. It's just... we were friends."

"No, that's where you're wrong, Sam. You were never friends. Friends don't treat each other like that."

Sam looked at me with those intense brown eyes I loved so much. She smiled, but her eyes were glossy.

"Hey, she did you a favor. You don't need friends like that." I pulled her into a big hug.

"Nobody does," she offered back.

"Nope."

Little did I recognize, this wouldn't be the first time an LA local abruptly rejected and discriminated against one of us because of a political disagreement.

The event focusing on terrorism prevention was an auspicious beginning for a new social network in our hometown. Just as it became the end of one relationship, it ignited several others.

The host began by organizing friendly lunches, where invitees could discuss conservative principles and their frustration at the myopia and intolerance of the Left.

Sam attended those lunches, where she heard stories of how ostracized others had been for expressing diverse opinions. These were the years Bush was in the White House, and the vociferous and vicious Far Left was uninterested in harmony. They were out for blood.

Sam would return from these lunches elated. They offered her strength and support. She often regaled me with some story or another about another attendee's experience "in the trenches." Mao Tse Tung said that politics is war without the bloodshed, and he is a worthy representative of the Far Left.

The most notable lesson from the lunches, for both Sam and me, was the idea that we were not alone in our beliefs. There were many Hollywood residents in the fold who had been casually liberal before 9/11. As we would all recognize, 9/11 substantially changed the world. Sam's new friends were people who did not understand the threat before the collapse of the World Trade Center, mainly because we were all lulled into a kind of somnambulant apathy. Of course, 9/11 changed that, at least for these folks.

When a Leftist professor at Colorado suggested that the people working inside the towers were worse than the terrorists, "little Eichmanns" was the term[10], as a way of justifying one of the evilest acts we have witnessed in modern history, some people recognized that something had fundamentally shifted. They called themselves 9/11 conservatives. They explained that because the attack on the Pentagon, the White House and the financial center of New York were so horrific—watching people jump to their deaths from a hundred stories in the air instead of choosing to burn to death—the

---

[10] https://en.wikipedia.org/wiki/Ward_Churchill

realization that we were at war was too plain. But it wasn't actually something inside of them, as much as it was the reaction of their compatriots that convinced them of the swing. Sure, there were kooks out there who wickedly accepted and even justified the events of 9/11. There was a preacher and others saying the attacks were not only justified but honorable, calling it "chickens coming home to roost."[11]

As in many cases, one can ignore the idiots who showcase their folly loudly, but one cannot ignore those who support them. This became the point of schism from the Hollywood Left for many who attended those initial luncheons, and certainly for the growth of the ranks, once the new group became firmly established.

Some of the founders told the story of how they discovered they were conservative. They had met for a friendly lunch, and when the conversation turned to current events and world politics, they both started to whisper. Whisper! They agreed that something had to give. If the opposing team can make life so miserable that you are *afraid* to express yourself in a civil and respectful way, something is terribly wrong. Why the whispers? Because of fear.

I had struggled for nearly three years, overcoming the damage to my brain wrought by my strokes. My illness introduced me personally to the intense feeling of oneness: the loneliness of struggling unaided, the isolation of pain and suffering, and the recognition that there is no one else who truly understands your personal experience. There is only God, who made you and your experience, and so knows it intimately.

Unfortunately, with all the distractions of life, it isn't often we hit our knees to commune with the One who truly empathizes. It is far too easy for an enemy to isolate us and make us feel small and insignificant, and worse, unjustified and invalid.

That is what happened to those first members in what became the now well-known clandestine conservative fellowship group in Hollywood, called FOA, or Friends of Abe. They named it that

---

[11] https://www.youtube.com/watch?v=2o8t8OuceSg

because they felt like the persecuted, meeting secretly and speaking in hushed voices, lest anyone overhear some conservative or pro-military language. They identified with the old Hollywood types who would call themselves "friends of Dorothy" as code for being gay.

Sam reveled in the early days of long lunches. The people in attendance were few, but they exhibited a strong conviction that buoyed her. I don't think either of us realized the necessity for an outlet where you weren't persecuted for your beliefs, until she found one. Say what you will about tolerance, but often those who scream loudest for it exhibit it the least.

Eventually, the group began conducting general lunches, for which, if you were already a participant, you could sponsor an invitation to someone else who you personally knew was like-minded. This practice was not meant to prevent the free exchange of ideas. Rather, it was for peace. We were not interested in having a shouting match with Leftist loons. It was also for protection. The Far Left is very eager to destroy anyone who disagrees with its position, and so, if anyone had published a list of members, say, their careers would have been destroyed.

Initially, the group was so small that nobody knew about it. Over time, it grew, like the shampoo commercial: if you tell two friends and they tell two friends…

The lunches grew to eventually include forty people. The main host would welcome everyone, and then the focus would travel around the large, squared tables for everyone in attendance to introduce themselves. Guests were all seated on the outside of the square facing in, so everyone could see and hear everyone else. Typically, the inviter would say a quick something about themselves, and the invitee would tell their story of isolation and persecution for their beliefs.

For example, someone told the story of being in the greenroom at an event with other television celebrities. The banter was fun until someone asked them why they lived in Las Vegas, to which he responded, "I moved there to save taxes. No state tax in Vegas!" At that point, an actress in the greenroom taunted, with a loud, sneering voice, "What? Are you a Republican?!" Every head turned. This is the isolation for the kill that the militant Left practices. Nobody else contributed to that conversation. Everyone waited to watch for the blood sport.

"Nope, I'm just a lot wealthier than I would be if I had stayed in California."

"But those are taxes you deprived California of."

"If you know California is hurting for money, why don't you pay more?"

"I pay my fair share!" She countered angrily.

"Well, so do I, so we're even."

It's important to point out you are even with Leftists because they see everything as unfair, and they also perceive it to be their job to balance all the scales so that perfect parity can be reached.

These lunches would often start at noon and continue until after three. After one lunch from which Sam had to leave early, she called the founder to discuss some sort of time limit for speeches. It wasn't so much that she wanted to limit people's full expression, but she had wanted to be able to hear from everyone, and they hadn't made it around the room before her departure.

The founder responded to Sam in this way, "Sam, these people have been stifled for so long. They obviously need the time to express their frustration and their experiences."

"Of course, you're right," she said. "I'm just irritated because I couldn't stay until the end. It's amazing how cathartic this experience becomes for everyone."

"It's so important for people to realize they're not alone in this, don't you think?"

"I don't just think it, I know it. I love hearing these stories and seeing the pent-up emotion breaking out. And even though, at first, I only figured this was a nice thing to do, now I realize that it's therapeutic in a way I couldn't have imagined. You're doing a great service here, you know?" Sam's admiration came through on the phone line.

"All I know is that people need to be able to express themselves, especially patriots who believe in this great country, and they shouldn't have to fear for their livelihood or their careers for holding a different opinion."

"Exactly! That's why we can't be exploring the idea of becoming a public organization. We have to remain clandestine to allow these people safety, or they won't come. You've seen the trepidation in the room, and I've heard stories from some who can't get their friends to even consider attending. I think it's very clever to resist the impulse to shout it from the rooftops, so to speak."

"Yes, I know. This is strictly about fellowship; I get it."

My wife was very concerned for my career, in the event that I became more vocal about my positions on current events and politics. She knew the vitriol of the "tolerant" Left, as well as she understood the need for fellowship and a feeling of belonging. I don't know if it was my brush with death or simply my frustration with idiots, but I was becoming more willing to share my opinions. That put her on edge, and she warned me to be more restrained. I had already been restrained by an illness that I refused to allow to define me, but it was a hardship I could not share with anyone. Perhaps now I was approaching a new kind of therapy, one that encouraged me to share more of myself than was prudent at that time of upheaval.

After all, although the entire world didn't collapse with 9/11 (although I'm certain that was the goal), the world in America was a fundamentally changed world. The odd thing is that it was the conservatives who insisted on adapting to the new, while the liberals resolutely demanded to accommodate the old assumptions, despite all the contrary evidence. For this reason, they sought to excuse the violent behavior of the terrorists, rather than to accede to the new paradigm of good versus evil.

Conservatives understood that we were attacked because evil cannot help but attack good. Their attack on us defined us as good. But to the staunch liberal, it is the opposite. To them, the attacks proved that we were the bad guys.

As happens in most battles of will and morality, things were coming to a head. Bush made the mistake of encouraging everyone to simply go about their business. This was misguided in concept because things were no longer normal. We needed a new normal, and we should have paused to absorb that fact.

In a strange parallelism, I went back to work shortly after my strokes in order to prove to myself that I was still normal, when, in fact, I was anything but. On the one hand, return to normalcy encouraged me to deny my illness any foothold and not give it any power over me. I was insistent that it would not fetter me. At the same time, it did limit me in ways I was forced to confront.

The American people, too, faced limitations in ways we incorporated with little grumbling, like taking our shoes off before boarding the plane and getting to the airport earlier to allow for security searches.

While returning to "normal" allowed our strength to return, like it helped me vanquish my illness, it also promoted the liberal point of view that we deserved what we got, that we were intrinsically evil, and the attackers were justified. Now we have the intensely difficult job of excising the diseased parts of our society that hold those views. And while I did heal from my injuries, over time, my frustration grew as well, and the bulwark I had built for self-preservation and against sharing my contrary views was about to crumble. Frustration had seeped into the cracks and grown, like seeds in asphalt that eventually cause its upheaval.

The FOA group continued to grow over the months, and soon the management felt they had enough people to make an evening event. It was a classy affair with more than a few Hollywood notables at a fabulous sprawling mansion in Hancock Park, a wealthy old Hollywood suburb. The catering was exceptional: bacon-wrapped shrimp and other delectable canapés served with cocktails on the tennis court before we adjourned to a sit-down dinner with several speakers.

Word leaked out about the event, and it was written up in a tabloid or two. Some conservative Hollywood actors gathered at a secret party. What? All three of them?

That first event was about a hundred and twenty-five people. The next event, the following year, we doubled that. When it became apparent that our events were being held at a large ranch outside

LA, the media abruptly stopped talking about us. That's when we knew it was serious.

If the left fears something, they silence it. If they can't silence it, they ignore it. Once we started being ignored, we recognized the power we had. This may be what finally emboldened me, together with my frustration at the terrible untruths that were permeating our culture. Well, that and my faith.

Christ said, "Blessed are you when they revile and persecute you and say all kinds of evil against you falsely for My sake" (Matthew 5:11).

When Pilot accused Jesus of claiming kingship, Christ answered him that "king" was Pilot's word and not his own. Christ also said, "For this cause, I was born, and for this cause, I have come into the world, that I should bear witness to the truth. Everyone who is of the truth hears My voice" (John 18:37). And Christ told his disciples, "If you abide in My word, you are My disciples indeed. 32 And you shall know the truth, and the truth shall make you free" (John 8:31-32).

I suppose, in one way, I recognized this was a fight for freedom and truth. My ultimate allegiance is to the author of both of those. My conviction and faith are what drive my pursuit, and fear is what the left uses to silence the faint of heart. The distinction is clear. I am moving toward something—truth—and the left is trying to scare people away from something—truth.

George Orwell wrote, "During times of universal deceit, telling the truth becomes a revolutionary act." My principles certainly have led me through some uncharted waters. I never imagined that the truth could be so controversial.

I also never envisioned the vitriol and animus that might be leveled at me for some of my opinions, or some of my (purposely) misunderstood statements. It has been a journey of faith to stand on the truth with conviction, and it hasn't been easy or lucrative. But the Holy Spirit bound my heart in verity, and for that, I answer only to God.

This is how it all began... on the set of *Hercules: The Legendary Journeys.* We began a voyage of our own.
Photo by Pierre Vinet; Sorbo personal collection

Gizmoe featured as our flower puppy at our wedding, January, 1998.
Photo by Joe Buissink; Sorbo personal collection

Kids came later, but oh, how adorable they were! Right to left: Braeden (5), Shane (3) and Octavia (1).
Photo Sam Sorbo; Sorbo personal collection

Kevin grew up on in the land of ten thousand lakes, so the kids know a little bit about boating. Even Igwet learned to love the water!

Minnesota-born native, back on his favorite lake, with his family.
Photos Sorbo personal collection

With Sean Hannity, just before filming his scene in the Fox News building in New York. *Photo Sorbo personal collection*

Kevin directing on the set of *Let There Be Light,* with Sam, first AD Chad Rosen, and writer Dan Gordon.
Below: Kevin in character.
Photos courtesy LTBL Productions

Above, another set wedding for the Sorbos, shown with Dionne Warwick and producer James Quattrochi, center.

Left, Daniel Roebuck as Norm.

Below, Donielle Artese plays Traci the publicist, managing the crowd.

Photos this page courtesy LTBL Productions

A family that works together...
Left, Kevin directs his son Braeden on the set of *Let There Be Light.*
Next page: Marriage is a dance...
Photos these pages courtesy LTBL Productions

Kevin has a wonderful sense of humor. As director, he had the art department make this homage to his old TV

show and then he featured it prominently in the film.

Photo below Bill Stewart. Other photos these two pages Sorbo private collection.

The Sorbos serve at more and more speaking engagements, addressing everything from politics to religion.

Below, Sam appears at an event with Sarah Palin, Candy Carson, and Melissa Robertson.

Bottom, Sam and Kevin address an audience on the topic of Hollywood filmmakers' ability to influence cultural norms.

What If...

Sam

I was raised as a good girl, with firm boundaries and strong morals. My mother sent me to Sunday school at our local synagogue, which I distinctly remember for its large sign out front: Save Soviet Jewry. Whenever I saw that sign, I had to clarify in my mind that it wasn't referring to jewelry.

My mother was Jewish by bloodline, but not because she believed in any deity. She didn't. I was probably around ten years old when I figured that out, and I don't remember how I realized it.

When I was five, she married a non-practicing protestant man who is not terribly memorable to me. We celebrated Christmas and Easter in the house, with a decorated tree and lavish chocolate and jelly bean-filled Easter baskets.

This is to say, we were not religious by any stretch, so it should come as no surprise that by my thirteenth birthday, I had had a serious discussion with my mother concerning my Saturday school religious studies. My mother never attended a service, as far as I know.

"Mom, I think I'm ready to quit my Saturday school classes at the synagogue," I said plainly. We had a very open and communicative relationship, something I valued then and treasure now.

"Really, why?" Mom was driving me to my guitar lesson in our beat-up maroon Honda Accord.

"I'm just not learning anything. Every morning the girls talk so much, and the teacher doesn't seem to care enough to get them to quiet down. It's like a clique in that room. The only boy, Ben, quit last month, I just found out. And I don't need to waste my time that way anymore."

We continued in silence for a few minutes as she thought about it.

"Anyway, it's not like you even believe in God."

She had just pulled up to the stoplight, so she turned to me. "What makes you say that?" She sounded distressed and even looked a little horrified. "How do you know that?"

"Mom, it's no great secret. I don't remember, exactly, when I figured it out, but it is kind of obvious."

My mother could be quite dramatic when she wanted to be. "Oh," she answered with an audible sigh. She was disappointed, although I wasn't sure whether in herself or in me. "I tried not to let on. I wanted you to make your own decision about religion." The light changed, and she pressed the accelerator.

"Well, congratulations," I said, with only a modest amount of teenage snarkiness. "I have. And by the way, it doesn't have too much to do with your beliefs. I'm just not that into going early every Sunday to sit with a bunch of rude girls and *not learn* for three hours."

"All right. I respect your decision. I'll let them know." She didn't even sound sad about it, just matter of fact.

That was the end of my tenuous religious instruction, and we never engaged on the subject again.

For a long time, I believed my mother's opinion on religion was that it was a great crutch 'for people who needed that kind of thing.' She also believed that if you were the sort of person who might need to rely on a belief in God, the best way there would be to have your faith begin as a child, rather than as an adult. What she failed to realize is that faith begins at home and that if the parents don't practice actively, the children adopt that attitude faster than anything they might have outside the home. If the parents don't model prayer at home, don't make a practice of saying grace at mealtime, and never crack open the Bible, how would anyone with half a brain expect their children to adopt any kind of faith practice?

My mother had chosen Judaism for her daughters in part because of what she believed to be the ethic of the Jewish people: valuing education, work, and family. I realized only much later that, for her, religion was much more about instilling integrity than any faith. For an atheist, God represents an insupportable adversary.

Years later, after I had traveled the world as an international model, I went on my own personal search for answers to spirituality.

Eventually, after a bit of research, I discovered that the universe could not exist without some kind of creative force behind its existence. I chose to call that thing God. This brought me back to religious institutions.

I began at a synagogue because that is where my religious instruction had begun, though admittedly half-heartedly. I loved the synagogue more for its fabulously intellectual rabbi, but I didn't feel like I belonged there, my Jewish birthright notwithstanding.

One day, I was sitting with a new friend from acting class. "Theirry," I said, completely out of the blue, for this thought had just occurred to me, "Do you go to church?"

Thierry had been raised a Christian but had strayed from the Church during her time in LA, largely because she felt the Church obliged her to evangelize or proselytize, and she wanted no part of that. It made her terribly uncomfortable, and so, she had strayed from attending church regularly for a few years. Recently, she had been invited to attend a church in Eagle Rock, a community not too far from ours. She really enjoyed the service at that church and had quickly made a habit of attending.

Thierry regarded me with what appeared to be suspicion. "Why do you ask?"

I answered guilelessly, "I want to try attending church. The synagogue I attend is nice, but I just feel like I'm missing something."

144

She smiled and gave a short chuckle. Thierry hadn't wanted to proselytize, but having someone ask to join her at church seemed to answer her conundrum. In that moment, she was thinking, "Well, if *that's* what you meant, I can do *that* much!" She said a quick prayer to a God who hears and invited me to drive with her the following Sunday.

That is the short version of how I became a Christian.

I loved that church and did some more research to figure out the Christian case for God and the Trinity, adopting it over time.

It's all well-and-good when exploration leads *not* to belief but instead to an affirmation of the non-existence of God, but if the search for truth ends in finding religion and faith, then the otherwise easy-going atheist, watching a person searching for truth, gets riled. Conviction in faith is a full challenge to an atheist's worldview, and mine was no different for my mother, the atheist. Eventually, my belief in and commitment to God strained my relationship with my otherwise reasonable and broad-minded mother to the breaking point.

When I met Kevin on the set of *Hercules,* I was a practicing Christian, and he was a wayward Lutheran. My burgeoning faith was important to me, but Kevin had been steeped in it with church twice a week and practicing parents who were active in their church activities. So when Kevin left home as a college student, he was happy to break away from the strictures of the Church. Today he says, "I had faith, but I never needed faith."

I challenged that position without realizing it. I think now that Kevin wasn't averse to attending church, per se, but he didn't see the point of it. He had his faith, and that was enough. He enjoyed a limited prayer life that served him in his busy life. But I was much more fervent, being a new believer. I loved going to church. I needed the weekly message, and the service fed me, and I wanted him to share in that. As I took up golf, watching sports, and traveling to see Kevin, he least he could do was to join me at my church, especially because he really enjoyed it, too. We started attending church together when we could, and Kevin admits that experiencing a church that was more vibrant than what he grew up in rekindled his zeal for God.

Years later in Los Angeles, Kevin and I met the nicest couple at an elegant evening event over cocktails. Amanda and Dallas Jenkins were staunch Christians, and Dallas was a film director. When I learned their last name, I joked with them, "Are you my long-lost cousins?" They were related to the Jerry Jenkins of the vastly successful *Left Behind* series of books. Sadly for me, no relation.

Parents to three children, like us, we immediately decided to get our kids together. It's what parents of young children do.

We showed up for a barbeque at the Jenkins's house, and the kids had a blast. They hit it off with each other immediately.

The adults fared equally well. Kevin and I enjoyed the easy nature and unwavering moral viewpoint of this couple. They shared our values, were strong Christians, and even approached child-rearing with similar steadiness and principles. I also admired their obviously strong marriage. Plus, they had named their oldest Sam, so he literally had my maiden name.

During our time there, Dallas spoke about a film project he was working on. He had a few people in mind for the part, but he wondered if he could send it to Kevin for his thoughts on it. Of course, Kevin said he'd be happy to take a look at it.

Kevin loved the script. He called Dallas and said, "Why are you considering anyone else for this role? I want to do it."

Dallas laughed. "Well, we aren't really there yet with preproduction, but Kevin, it's like a $500,000 budget. We can't afford you."

"Try me," Kevin responded, seriously.

A few months later, Kevin received the offer to shoot *What If...* He loved the script and wanted to take the entire family to Michigan for the month of shooting.

"Is Amanda going and bringing the kids?" I immediately queried.

"Dallas just told me to tell you she was."

I smiled. We were going to Michigan to shoot our first faith-based film.

Is God Dead?

Kevin

It was a warm day, especially for northern Michigan. I loved the humid Midwest air on my face and the strong scent of pine. Outside the small, white clapboard church, the crew paused their chatter to allow for filming. Only the cicadas, it seemed, ignored the production assistant's determined voice. "Quiet on the set!"

I was playing a man who had it all from a business and material point of view—driving a fantastic hundred-thousand-dollar-plus Mercedes, dating a gorgeous, though cold and conniving model girlfriend, and boasting a wake of destroyed businesses by my handiwork. I was a mover and a shaker. But just as I was about to claim the big prize of life, which, in my case, was the promotion to partner at my mergers and acquisitions firm and a wedding proposal in Paris, God plucks me out of that life and deposits me into the life that He had foreseen for me: as a pastor with two growing children. God calls on His cantankerous angel, played by the wonderful actor John Ratzenberger, to help Him out and give me some very sketchy guidance, including a couple of knock-out punches.

Needless to say, my character was resentful and incompetent and had to learn how to be loving and giving instead of selfish and devious. Lucky for me, He returned me to my high school love, who, though once forgotten, ushered back my long-lost feelings of devotion and responsibility. But not before a number of funny and quirky events, of course.

"And we're rolling!"

The loving young married couple exited the quaint church and walked to their waiting minivan, for which the young husband had traded in his tricked-out red truck. My character had counseled them effectively, albeit unconventionally, that marriage required sacrifice, in a scene where I unwittingly made a jerk of myself. In fact, I had basically advised them not to bother with marriage, because it was hard, and living the single life was fun, especially for a guy with that boss truck parked outside. Like in the movies, the couple took my dissuasive critique as reverse-psychology and promptly recommitted themselves even more fervently and with greater deliberation to their impending nuptials.

That couple has an impact on my character, as well, who realizes that if you believe in something, it isn't enough to simply believe it. *Faith without works is dead* is really an admonishment to behave as if your faith meant something more to you than just a symbol of resilience.

Kind of like the old question about the tree falling in the forest, if belief fails to ignite any reaction within the thinker or to have an effect on another individual, can it really be belief, or is it simply a passing fancy, a notion, or a disembodied concept? To be a belief, it must carry gravitas. A change in belief should result in some new consequences. Otherwise, why would anyone attempt to convince anyone else of their beliefs, and what difference would it make in which religion people put their faith?

Jordan Peterson has an interesting take on belief and faith. In short, he says he is too frightened of an all-powerful God to degrade Him with his own profession of belief because if he truly believed in Hell and Heaven, his life would necessarily look much different, and his behavior would reflect the seriousness of that.

Is inactive belief really *belief* or simply *ideas* that someone entertains?

There's an old idiom that refers to this: having the *courage of your convictions*. It means to act in a way that corresponds with your professed values, even when others may think you are wrong or misguided.

But in this culture, we are sheep, not deep thinkers, it seems. Perhaps we have always been sheep. It does seem to be our nature to watch what others do and then emulate them. Monkey see, monkey do. In our schools, we have long been teaching the nation's youth they are descended from apes and even fish, but somehow expecting they behave better than that.

Our expansive social media is focused on "following" people, and for people who crave the limelight to earn as many "followers" as possible. We have made stars out of people who are famous for being famous but who have accomplished only that. What good is fame if you provoke a deleterious effect on society and culture? Perhaps the question is better asked, why do we follow (read idolize) people who have accomplished only their own celebrity? We laud selfishness and hedonism.

I wouldn't be involved in that scene if it weren't an exceptional way for me to express my opinions in an attempt to win people over to the side of truth. For instance, I've never paid to get "likes" on Facebook, although I've known about the practice for years. Those aren't the people I'm addressing because they aren't real.

This brings me to the other aspect of having the *courage of your convictions*. I personally do not believe it is enough to simply have convictions or beliefs. Nor is it enough to simply follow them, adhere to them, and withdraw from society, hiding away so that society does not lambast you for your principles. If your beliefs go against the grain, then you must as well.

Christ did not admonish us to shrink from encounters with the enemy but to pick up our crosses and follow him, a reference to the Via Dolorosa and the long agonizing march through the jeering crowds. The enemies of truth never rest. If the light of truth is to continue to shine, men and women must hold it aloft and keep its glow bright.

Shooting *What If...* brought a new purpose into focus for me personally, as a father, a husband, and a Christian. It became an example of life imitating art. I had always loved performance since seeing that first Shakespeare play at the Guthrie Theater in Minneapolis at the age of 11, but my love was based on my personal enjoyment of affecting people in the audience. I loved that aspect of acting and still do.

This movie, however, marked a turning point, and something shifted inside me. I began to understand that my roles could bring hope and healing to people watching, rather than simply temporary entertainment. Entertainment has value, but a lasting resonance brought about by great storytelling of great stories (the greatest of all, in the case of *What If...*), what a blessing!

What If... earned me a Movie Guide award for "Most Inspired Performance," and one might think that the offers would start pouring in after that. One would be mistaken.

I had entered the Hollywood-free zone of the entertainment world. It was twilight. In fact, Hollywood largely ignores Christian movies if they can. And they can, because until *What If...* your typical Christian movie was produced in a garage with five dollars. *What If...* broke all kinds of stereotypes. It was, in my opinion, the first, fully Christian, Hollywood-caliber movie, and if you haven't seen it, I highly recommend it and still do when people compliment me on my other film work. (They always come back thanking me, by the way.)

But Hollywood-caliber means it's a really good movie in terms of the production value, the directing, the photography, writing, the acting—all of it. Hollywood-caliber does not mean Hollywood likes it or wants it to exist. Hollywood wanted to ignore it, and, as the production company was young and didn't market the film effectively, ignoring it turned out to be pretty easy.

So I worked on various projects, primarily independent movies and TV shows, and also kept my feelers out for other Christian projects because there was something special about doing a movie that sought to elevate the human condition and spirit in a meaningful way. I was maturing in my Christian faith.

Nearly four years after *What If...* made a disappointing showing at the box office but proceeded to perform admirably on DVD sales and for enthusiastic audiences, Pure Flix, its production company, called me up to play the titular role in their new project, *God's Not Dead.* We would shoot in Baton Rouge, or, as my kids would learn to call it, Red Bat, Louisiana.

At this point, Sam and I were full into homeschooling the kids, so the family easily traveled with me. Production rented us a fully furnished three-bedroom apartment near the college. We unpacked and got to work.

It was an easy shoot. The crew was great, and the actors were all eager and ready to work, particularly Shane Harper, who showed up having already memorized his long soliloquies! What I wouldn't give for a memory like his.

We shot the death scene (spoiler alert!) in the middle of the street in a rather busy part of town. They blocked off traffic and got all the production ready for a somewhat complicated shot with a crane, large lights overhead, and a rainmaker.

It's raining when my character gets hit by a car and goes down, injured too much to move and nearing death. The pastor character, who Radisson has never met, comes to my aid, but he can only offer me confession. It's a sad scene and playing that takes a great deal of concentration, with all the distractions of the rain and the streets.

But the kicker was we shot this scene on election night. The moment the news broadcasts announced that Barack Obama had won the presidency, this part of town went haywire. There was chaos in the streets. We heard loud cheers and screams, car horns honking, people running and shouting, "Four more years of free s4!%!" These were all hard-core Obama voters, thrilled at the prospect of the government paying for their housing, health care, and cell phones. We paused in filming because there was nothing else to do but let the human energy storm pass.

I knew this movie was special, but I must admit, with the disappointment of *What If...*, which I still think is a better movie, I wasn't holding out much hope that this movie would perform well.

I'm happy to admit I was wrong and sad to confess that my back-end deal reflects my initial skepticism. By the time they launched *God's Not Dead,* Pure Flix and the promotional team they had put together for the film had figured out how to market to their audience. The predominant reason the small, independent Christian movie needed a novel marketing plan was because mainstream media is practically in the business of denying the Christian God. Mainstream media seems unable to laud or promote or even pay attention to any artform that does not express their left-leaning, hedonistic worldview.

For this reason, Pure Flix chose to release a trailer of our film several months before the film launched in theaters. They cut a fantastic, provocative trailer, and the theology in the movie was sound, and we now know how much audiences all over the world crave this kind of wholesome entertainment. The rest is history, in a very real sense.

God's Not Dead performed so well, it broke all kinds of records. We had shot it for about two million dollars, but it earned over sixty-two million in the US box office alone. We opened in a respectable 700 theaters, and it was popular enough to raise that number to 1100 screens the following weekend. Typically, producers hope simply to maintain their number of theaters, but word of mouth about the movie spread like wildfire, and people saw it multiple times, brought their friends for a second and third screening of the movie. They wanted to share the message in the film with non-believers and agnostics. The next weekend saw the number of theaters build again.

At roughly the same time, *Noah*, Hollywood's answer to "faith-based" movie successes, performed quite well for its opening weekend but dropped significantly when American Christian audiences, who were expecting to see an Old Testament story about the man who built the ark, viewed instead "*Waterworld* meets *Transformers*," as my wife Sam termed it.

At a screening of *Noah* that Sam and I attended at Paramount studios the night before the film's premiere, one of the movie's several producers spoke before the show. He issued a mild but undisguised disclaimer about the movie. It seemed like he was apologizing for the lack of adherence to scripture in the telling of Noah's story. Perhaps even he recognized that hiring an atheist to tell a story from The Book could only lead to severe consequences at the box office. Effective advertising and the star power of Russell Crowe could not save *Noah* from a post-opening weekend plummet. That producer himself likely predicted this inevitability, which became clearer after the movie ended, when he took the stage for some questions. One of the stand-out inquiries was this one:

> *In light of the great success of God's Not Dead and other faith-based films, do you think that Hollywood will seek to enter that realm of filmmaking more? That we can expect more faith-based entertainment?*

His answer surprised us only a little, and only in its candor:

> *I think that the independent filmmakers do what they do well and that Hollywood makes blockbuster movies well, and I see that continuing.*

In one sense, he is inarguably accurate. See, the anti-religious Left has the courage of their convictions. They unabashedly influence our culture to denigrate the Bible and believers. We need more people with the courage to stand for what Jesus represented: Truth.

The liars and pretenders and know-it-alls who actually know nothing do what they do really well. We need those who stand for our faith and our beliefs to do likewise. If that drafts you into the fight, welcome to the team!

Faith in Motion

Sam

God's Not Dead performed so well because it touched a nerve. The story is about young college student Josh Wheaton, played by Shane Harper, who unwittingly enrolls in an introductory college philosophy course and must defend the existence of God. The friendly registrar's representative even warns Josh away from that course and from that particular professor when he notices Josh's cross necklace.

"How bad can it be?" Josh muses.

It turns out that Josh's new instructor, Professor Radisson, has a penchant for persecuting believers, though he seldom encounters any resistance. He tells his class they're going to skip examining the ridiculous mumbo-jumbo of organized religion and get right into the better part of philosophy. But he needs consensus from the class. All the students must write on a sheet of paper, "God is Dead," and sign their names to it.

Poor Josh. In good conscience, he cannot write this sentence. As a Christian, he knows the Matthew 10:33 verse in which Jesus admonishes His followers, "But whosoever shall deny me before men, him will I also deny before my Father which is in heaven." So, Josh must disrupt the entire class, inviting ridicule and ire, and write God is *not* Dead, instead.

Professor Radisson, as he walks through the seats to collect everyone's concise, sworn testimony, comes across Josh, who confesses he cannot submit such a paper. Radisson clearly is seldom challenged. Just as obvious is his fervent desire for the opportunity to destroy a believer in front of his class, and so he challenges the hapless, harmless young man to a duel of words, a debate on the existence of God, with the undergraduate's grade hanging in the balance. Without much deliberation, Josh does the right thing and takes the bait.

Throughout the course of the debate, over several class sessions, Josh stands his ground amidst a torrent of Radisson's verbal abuse and derision. It is this posture that we movie-goers find so admirable, almost regardless of our faith. The reason for this is that our culture, inherited from our Judeo-Christian roots, is infused with the knowledge of good and evil. Even if we have largely lost the moral code-giver's address, we still understand that good and evil exist, and most of us prefer good to evil, and forcing someone to go against his belief, especially if you're mean about it, is evil. So, we root for Josh to somehow win against seemingly insurmountable odds.

What was so fascinating about this movie was Kevin's performance as the evil Professor. It takes an incredibly strong and gifted actor to portray the evil character as a three-dimensional, red-blooded guy, but he managed to do it. For the first part of the movie, the audience hates him, but then they start to realize that he has his own story—a sad, emotional one—and that there is an underlying and ultimately justifiable excuse for his nasty attitude towards Josh.

Finally, by the end of the movie, the audience is rooting for Radisson's salvation and practicing forgiveness of his transgressions, seeing parts of themselves in him.

Kevin's character's transition through the film, along with the subject matter of life, death, and eternity, is what allows the film to completely engage the audience enough to make viewers want to return to the theater and bring friends. It's what made the film unimaginably successful, propelling it to the fourth most popular film of all time.

Kevin and I have up-close and personal experience with the weighty effects of this movie. Whereas for a long time, in airports and restaurants, Kevin was noticed and approached as *Hercules* and sometimes for *Andromeda*, after the release of *God's Not Dead* and *Soul Surfer,* a preponderance of fans approached Kevin based on these newer, Christian-worldview projects.

We were flying back from Salt Lake City with the family. We had arrived at our gate to wait for boarding, having grabbed something to eat on the way. This part of the airport was spacious but busy. We were lucky to find five seats together. Braeden, Shane, and Octavia hunkered down with their sandwiches and their books, and Kevin and I were on our phones, checking email, the kids between us.

A nervous young woman approached Kevin shyly. She had dark hair and was dressed in blue jeans and a flowered shirt, her jacket thrown over her arm, and she pulled a roller-bag loaded down with an overstuffed satchel. Her little girl, seven or eight years old, hung back behind her mom.

"Hello, excuse me, but are you the actor from *God's Not Dead*?" she asked nervously, with a vague accent.

Kevin looked up and smiled, "Yes, I am." He was quite used to being approached and is always gracious and charming. He never enjoyed people's unease when they initially spoke to him.

A softness came over the woman's face, and her nerves calmed. "I saw that movie. I wanted you to know I used to be Muslim, but after seeing that movie, I converted. My daughter and I were baptized last week." She smiled with glistening eyes.

"Congratulations," Kevin responded, sincerely. "I'm so happy my little movie made such an impact."

"Yes, it did. I wanted you to know that. May God bless you," she ended and turned away.

I had watched her approach him, but I tend to give fans a wide berth, to allow them to interact with someone they clearly admire— no need for me to be breathing down their necks. I did so in this instance and missed much of their private conversation. So when

Kevin turned to me and told me about their exchange, I started asking questions.

"What did her husband say?"

"I don't know."

"How did her family react when she told them?"

"Sam, she just told me, and then she left. I didn't think to ask any questions like that."

"Oh, right. Shoot, I'm so curious now!"

This is when something happened that I would have never predicted. Once *Hercules* had become a big hit, Kevin realized that his fans loved him in a way that could make things uncomfortable. Aside from weird stalkers, his fans felt like they *knew* him. He was, after all, a visitor in their homes every week, sometimes more than once. Who else do you know, in your life, who you can say that about? Suffice it to say that there is a kind of presumed intimacy between a fan and Kevin, even though Kevin will never have actually met this person before.

So when Kevin got out of his seat to try to track down the mystery woman, I was honestly surprised. But he was curious, also. I got up with him, and we walked around looking, but no dice.

They made a pre-board announcement for our flight. Kevin likes to board immediately, as soon as possible, so we started gathering the kids and their things.

Just then, Kevin whispered, "There she is!" indicating two rows of seats away.

We quickly walked over to her, and I introduced myself. "I'm Kevin's wife, Sam. He told me about you and your daughter becoming Christians."

"Yes, it's true. And my name is Monir." She smiled.

"Monir, I wonder if I can just ask you, what did your family say about your conversion?"

"They are not happy. I have not seen them since I told them," she answered wistfully.

"I see." I nodded and then asked, "What about your husband?"

Her eyes pleaded with mine, but I didn't comprehend yet why. She looked at Kevin, then back at me. "You don't understand." She began pulling up her sleeves to show us her arms. They had scars up and down them. "He tried to kill me when he found out. Do you see?"

The boarding agent announced our flight.

"Yes. I understand. You left him?"

"He gave me no choice. He divorced me. My little girl is flying to Arizona now to see him."

Kevin interjected, "Sam, they are boarding. We've got to go."

"Go ahead. Get the kids, and I'll be right there," I said to him.

I turned back to Monir. "I will pray for you." I couldn't help myself. I hugged her. Her little girl looked at me with wide eyes, so I winked at her. She smiled at me.

I boarded the plane, catching up with my family, but I couldn't stop thinking about this woman, and the incredible knowledge that she was sending her seven-year-old daughter to visit the man who had tried to kill her. I have never been able to reconcile that, and it troubles me still today. I know that a Muslim who converts from Islam is labeled an apostate and that their holy book prescribes the punishment of death for any apostate. It wasn't a shock to me that Monir's husband had reacted in such a manner. He believed he was in the right to do so, and who are we, with our Judeo-Christian morals, to say he is wrong?

Well, that really is the question, isn't it? Can an entire religion be wrong for preaching amoral behavior? Do any of us believe strongly enough to defend our faith before the onslaught of competing and opposing faiths? Are there any Josh Wheatons left to guard and protect our position?

Professor Radisson was one challenger, but he used only words. At the end of Kevin's movie, the production ran a credit roll documenting twenty-eight cases of persecution on American college campuses—cases in which a professor challenged not just the beliefs of a student but students' very right to believe freely.

In the world today, we have many who challenge not just the right to believe freely, but the right to live, believing differently than the powerful. There are those who insist on doxing people who believe differently than they do. That means they disclose the names and addresses and other pertinent, private information about people who dare to stand up, thus subjecting them to the threats and violence at which the Left excels. What would really happen if those people were forced to defend their point of view if that position was not in the mainstream like it is today? Would they be as bold? Would they ever see the light of truth if the social structure no longer upheld the shroud that now shields them from it?

This is the guiding concept that moved me to conceive *Let There Be Light,* the Sorbo family's first film together.

Hannindipity

Kevin

"Kevin, I have an idea for a movie."

It wasn't the first time Sam had an idea to do something, but ideas are worth only the paper they are printed on in Hollywood, which is to say, ideas are a dime a dozen.

The year before, Sam had had an idea for a faith-based television program. Although my manager told her there was little hope of getting the thing on the air without a *bona fide* writer, Sam remained undeterred.

Part of her drive stemmed from her aspiration to see morally principled entertainment on TV and part from her desire to see me working full-time again on a show. She knows how much my type-A personality craves steady work. Funnily, part of her ambition was not to become a TV writer.

In any case, she set out to find a writer by turning to a producer friend. He was the only producer she was friendly with, of course. Sam never hung out in Hollywood circles, and as a mom to three, she never really cultivated those connections that are vital in this industry.

We met him for lunch at a restaurant close by, and he listened intently to Sam's pitch—the first one she'd ever given. He was duly impressed and offered the name of a writer he thought would be an excellent choice, Dan Gordon, who had been the showrunner on *Highway to Heaven* for Michael Landon. We set up another meeting.

Sam and I both really hit it off with Dan. He loved the idea—particularly the faith-based aspect of it—and decided to work on it with us.

Sadly, early on in the very involved and frustratingly slow process of show development, circumstances dictated that Dan recuse himself from the project. The friendship persevered despite that.

We pitched the show fervently with our new writer and sold it to NBC and Sony, but timing or politics or just plain nonsense moved it onto a shelf, instead of into prime time.

Sam's attitude at the time was that although she had conceived an excellent idea for the show, she would not be show running or even writing on it. True, we needed someone with a proven track record to run the show, but that she ceded her power in that realm so easily might have contributed to the eventual sputtering of the engine. At the time, she had her radio show and was stretched thin. She considered herself a liability rather than an asset.

She was wrong.

So, when Sam came to me with yet another idea, I did not respond with the typical, "That's nice, dear," and go back to my work on the computer.

Sam was sitting in the oversized carved-wood antique chair she bought us in New Zealand, in my small, green bedroom-office upstairs. The afternoon sun was streaming through the window, splashing on my desk, and reflecting in the photos that peppered my walls. I love to surround myself with pictures of my kids and family.

"Okay, tell me about it," I replied, turning my seat to face her.

She smiled. "The world's greatest atheist has a near-death experience that completely contradicts his disbelief, and he has to rethink his entire purpose in life."

Wow. It wasn't at all what I was expecting, but I learned long ago that Sam easily surprises me. "Interesting. What are you going to do with it?"

"I want to write it as a script, obviously. You like it?"

"Of course, I like it. It's got so much potential. I love it."

"I need a writer, though. My name won't sell it. Plus, I'm not that good, frankly."

"Sam, you're too modest. But if you want a writer, I have a few names you can call. What about the guy we got for *Miracle Man*?"

"Yeah, I'm going to reach out to him, and I have another idea, too. I'm excited." She got up from the chair and stood in the doorway, giddy.

"Good! But, Sam, can you take this on, with everything else?"

"Aw, Kevy, if only I had the choice." She leaned over my desk as she spoke. I smiled at the fire in her brown eyes. "I'd sit back and eat bonbons all day long and read. But the way this idea just came to me... it was a gift from God, obviously, and I am obliged to see it through." Sam puckered her lips for a peck.

I kissed her, and she smiled, looking in my eyes. Then she added, as she turned to walk away, "Plus, it's fun!"

"Okay," I said, laughing. "Keep me posted!" I resumed working on my computer.

About two weeks later, Sam came back from lunch positively ebullient. "I have awesome news!"

"I love awesome news! What is it?"

"I've got a writer to work with me on the script!" she said gleefully.

"That's fantastic! Who is it?"

"Okay, so I called Dan Gordon," she began. "You know how he worked on *Miracle Man* for like a moment, but I really liked him, so I called and said, 'Hey, Dan, I've got an idea for a movie. Would you consider writing it with me?' And he said," she paused here, for effect, then leaned into me, "No!"

I must admit, I was confused. She was still smiling. Typically, "No" is not the word we are hoping for when pitching a new idea. "No?"

Still animated, Sam shook her head slowly from side to side.

"Okay..."

"But he did say, 'Sam, we haven't seen each other for a while. Let's have lunch.' We just had lunch!"

I could tell she was enjoying my confusion, but my patience was wearing thin. "And?"

"He regaled me with the story in the screenplay he just sold for one point two five million dollars, which is why he doesn't need me to write with him, obviously."

"I know you're enjoying this, but I'm not. Can you just shortcut it for me? Why are you so happy when all I'm hearing is bad news?"

"At the end of lunch, Dan says, 'So, tell me your idea for a movie.' I'm thinking maybe he'll give me a tip or something because he's an awesome storyteller. I mean, wait till you hear about this movie he just did. I can't wait to read his new book, either."

She was doing it on purpose. There was good news in there somewhere, and she was purposely stringing me along to hear it. It was a good thing I loved her because she was sorely testing my forbearance.

"I pitched him the short version of my idea. He thought about it for a moment, nodded, and then said, 'I like it. We'll write it together. And I know how we can get it produced, too.' He thinks he can help get it produced!"

Okay, the payoff was worth it.

Neither Sam nor I believe in serendipity, or what some people call chance. Lady Luck, the roll of the dice, karma, none of those are real things. Things only appear to happen by chance because our perspective is too close. Sometimes this is more evident than at other times. Often, we can't hope to catch a glimpse of a plan determined to remain unseen, until, fully executed, we stand back in awe an exclaim on its magnificence. God is good, all of the time.

A couple of weeks after Sam's great news, she was nearly finished writing the first draft of her movie. That's when I got a phone call from Sean Hannity. Now, that's pretty cool. I like Sean, and I've known him for a while. I've appeared on his show and enjoyed his support of my faith-based movies, but honestly, it wasn't a regular occurrence that he would give me a call.

He spoke in a clipped, straight-to-the-point manner. "Hello, Kevin. How are you?"

"Doing good, thanks, Sean. How are you?"

"I'm great, thanks."

We chatted briefly about golf and tennis, his favorite sports, and then he cut to the chase.

"You know, I've been thinking of getting into movie production. It's a powerful medium, and you've got a great handle on it. I want to produce a movie with you. One of those faith-based ones, like *God's Not Dead* or *Soul Surfer*. What do you say?"

To say I was flattered does not do my emotions any justice. My soul smiled.

But I wasn't thinking of Sam's script, truth be told. I was so blown away by this phone call, firstly, and second, I have a plethora of good movie scripts that I wanted to make, and I had no idea what specifically Sean might be interested in. We left the conversation with the idea that I would be getting back to him with a proposal in the next few weeks.

Later that day, I was in the kitchen making dinner. Yes, I cook. No, I'm not too studied about it, but I enjoy making tacos or grilling chicken, and with Sam on the radio three hours each morning, and all the work she does with the kids for school, I pick up the slack sometimes in the kitchen.

Sam wandered in as the rice finished cooking, and I pulled it off the stove. She handed me the rice scoop.

"Sean Hannity called me today," I said casually and self-important.

"You're kidding?" Sam responded lightly. "What did he have to report? Are you going back on his show?"

"No, it wasn't about his show. He said to me that he wants to produce movies with me."

Sam was about to pop a taste of the grilled steak in her mouth, but my words stopped her in her tracks. She actually got a tear in her eye, put down the steak, and faced me.

"That's my movie," she smiled.

I thought about it for a moment. Of course, it was, but then, I didn't want to get her hopes up needlessly, either.

"Sam, I've got a whole mountain of good scripts upstairs. We don't really know what he wants to produce in the way of films…"

She got a very serious look in her watery eyes and frowned at me, insisting, "Kevin, that's my movie, and you know it. It was given to me so that we could do this and written for Sean to produce. There is no such thing as random chance, just opportunities."

I had no arguments. It just seemed so right. "Well, then, congratulations. Let's make it so."

We high-fived and called the kids to dinner.

Movie Culture

Sean Hannity

You know, I'm a simple guy. I enjoy watching movies when I get the chance, especially those that are inspirational. There is nothing better than a movie that leaves you uplifted, the type of film where everyone is talking about it afterwards discussing how it affected them.

But, hey, what do I know? I'm a radio and television personality. My focus is on politics, terrorism, and the future of America. The Hollywood film industry is a completely separate field from my news and political world, but every once in a while, the two actually intersect. Take the few occasions when I can interview a Hollywood celebrity on my show; those brave enough to talk to a conservative, of course. I deal in truth and reality, while most of the Hollywood crowd live on Fantasy Island.

Kevin Sorbo is one of those exceptions, and he has never been accused of fearing the truth. He's a no-nonsense, guys' guy, straightforward and honest. The first time he joined me on my show, we hit it off. Over his visits to my studios, Kevin and I developed a friendship and mutual respect for one another.

I saw *God's Not Dead*, and it was a truly powerful film. Kevin's role in the movie played a large part in that. It was an emotionally impactful story where the audience left the theater feeling challenged and uplifted.

I called Kevin to congratulate him on the great success of the movie, and I said to him, "If you ever get a project that is interesting, something contemporary, that will inspire people, give me a call." I wanted to be a part of something that was positive and gave people hope again. Little did I know then that his wife had just conceived an idea she was planning to write with Dan Gordon called *Let There Be Light.*

Kevin called me back a month later, and we arranged to meet at my office in New York City.

What was I getting myself into? It's one thing to say you might be interested in funding a movie project, but honestly, only crazy people get in the film industry! By most accounts, it's a corrupt, slimy business. We've all read the papers, seen the lawsuits.

Still, movies can have a powerful effect on culture, and I had an honest desire to contribute to that intangible force. There is something valuable that happens when a good film impacts hearts and minds, and when a message resonates. The idea of participating in this production became something I really wanted to do, even though my skepticism about this new venture made me cautious.

Kevin came into my office first. Dan and Sam followed, and Kevin introduced Dan, who was clearly their designated storyteller. Normally the talkative one, I just sat still, listening to Dan. Our meeting lasted a full half-hour, and by its conclusion, I was sold. From Dan, I had heard a movie that I wanted to see. The plot and story convinced me, so my gut said, "go," while my business brain said, "wait!"

Against all my better, rational judgment, we had a handshake deal when they left my office. To say I was conflicted doesn't put it in the right light. I'm a decisive person, and I committed to the idea behind the project as much as to the film itself. I knew it was a roll of the dice. I felt like I would be part of something big, all the while recognizing it could go south in a moment.

As they began their search for the location of the shoot, they kept me apprised, but I didn't want to meddle. What did I know about producing a dramatic movie? I gave them my trust and left them alone.

The team started shooting in August in Birmingham.

The script called for me to play a small role in the movie as myself. That's a stretch! We scheduled them to film in New York at the very end of the month. My two scenes could be shot in one day, and so we scheduled the office scene for the morning, and then the broadcasting scene for right after I finished my television show that night.

I showed up at the office set, which was on a high floor in the Fox building in New York, and everything was ready to go. The place was abuzz with their crew moving equipment, testing microphones.

I said to Kevin, "Look, I'm not the memory guru, here, so, bear with me."

He was his typical affable self. "Don't sweat it. We'll keep it loose. Remember, it's not live television! There's always another take."

That was an understatement. There were so many people around, and the space was a bit cramped in the office suite, which was a long ascetic hallway with some individual offices off it. One had been transformed into the hair and make-up room. The outer reception area, where the hallway ended, was crammed with equipment and technical experts. The sound cart was there, and the video guys had set up camp. The final door at the end of the suite gave into a white office that had been transformed into "my" space, one windowed wall with a high city view, some framed show posters, and a conference table.

I walked in with Kevin and Sam to rehearse. Kevin made some joke about shooting the rehearsal. Apparently, sometimes as an actor, you do your best work in the rehearsal!

We shot the same scene about twenty times because we had to do each take twice. I realized why I never became an actor (among many other reasons): I don't have the patience!

I will say this: the thing that blew me away that day was Sam's talent. At one point during the film, her character Katy is going through some intense stuff, and when I offer to provide publicity for the app that she and Sol are designing, she tears up—real tears! I was stunned. I'm not someone who cries, certainly not on cue. And what I found most poignant about her crying wasn't just the tears; it was that I believed her. It wasn't some trick, to just cry on cue. Each time we ran the scene, she became truly emotional. Even today, I don't know how she did that.

Shortly after the election of Donald Trump, I received an email from Kevin. "Hey, Sean, we have the movie completed in a rough form, and we'd love to come to New York and do a screening for you. How can we set that up to best fit into your schedule?"

My emails tend more toward "brief." I sent back, "Send a screener, please. Just prefer to watch alone, thanks."

They provided a link for me.

It was with intense trepidation that I sat down, alone, in my office, to watch the screener. Now, here's the weird part, I knew what was going to happen in the movie. I had read the script, of course, so none of it was surprising, and yet...

There are so many twists and turns in this movie. I couldn't turn away. It's an emotional roller coaster. And, this is, for me, the test of a great movie: it stayed with me. I kept thinking about it. The next day, I showed it to some friends and watched it again.

I wrote the gang this:

Ok, I watched the entire movie beginning to end. This is always something I need to do alone, just how I roll. To say that I am blown away is an understatement.

Like I wrote at the beginning of this story, I am a simple man. I set out with a goal to be part of a production that would affect people in a positive way. I am so proud to be involved in this movie and for the opportunity to work with these gifted individuals. If this movie brings *light* to just one person, it has been successful. But I believe it will provide a light for each person who sees it.

The Meeting

Kevin

Scheduling the meeting with Sean Hannity posed several challenges. First, he is a very busy man. At that time, the American presidential election was in full bloom, and he was in the thick of it. With three hours of live radio and an hour of on-air television each weekday, his schedule was packed. He was completely preoccupied with American politics, and rightly so. I don't think someone could do his job and not be intensely focused. It was left to us—Sam, Dan, and me—to identify a moment when we could be in New York to meet with Hannity and finagle a few seconds in his demanding life.

We finally did, and the big day arrived.

As anyone who has ever sought capital to start a business knows, it's one thing for someone to say they would like to fund a movie production and an entirely different thing for him or her to write the check.

I can easily say that for the number of film productions I've participated in, there has never been a finance meeting that went more smoothly. We sat in Hannity's small, windowed office and pitched the movie's story. Dan is undoubtedly the best pitch guy in the business. He took his time relating the main elements of the story in a humorous and emotional way. I had already read the script and can attest to crying as I moved through it. I was on a plane, and the guy sitting next to me kept looking at me to see if I needed help. Dan didn't exactly make Sean cry, but his pitch was perfect anyway. Before we left the meeting, Sean declared we were in business.

The three of us descended in the elevator, not speaking. Each of us internalizing the experience of a stressful but successful meeting, however, the deal was yet unwritten. We were excited, optimistic, and giddy. When we exited through the revolving brass and glass doors and stepped into the warm New York breeze and bustle, we could barely conceal our joy. Hugs and handshakes ensued!

Now it would be up to the lawyers to write up the details of the deal.

When I became a public figure, I was performing on the show *Hercules*, which we shot in New Zealand. Initially, the show didn't air in New Zealand, and that small aspect postponed my inevitable awareness that I was famous. Nobody in Auckland knew or cared who I was, and I liked it that way. But when the show really hit, word started to get around, and people's behavior toward me changed. I had always stood out, but now they identified me, and that came with some presuppositions.

Fame is a double-edged sword. It is both an asset and a liability. One evening in the early days of *Hercules*, I was sitting at a local bar with some cast-members, celebrating the end of a long week of work. A swarthy guy, wearing a five-day growth and a muscle shirt swaggered up to me at the bar. He was carrying his pool cue menacingly.

"So, you're Hercules, are you?" he taunted in a heavy Kiwi accent.

"No," I answered carefully. "That's a TV show. I am an actor playing a character named Hercules. I have no ambitions on being a Demigod."

"You think you're tough?"

I inspected him, his foul alcoholic breath, his beady, searching eyes. He stood about six-foot-one in his boots, firm on the ground, aching for a fight. I had at least three inches on him and likely a few pounds of muscle as well. I'd been a bouncer at the hottest Dallas nightclub back in the day, and although the fights on *Hercules* were choreographed, I knew perfectly well how to subdue a hostile opponent. I could take him and the horse he rode in on (speaking metaphorically, of course), but to what end? I had never been the guy who wanted a fight, something I shared with the character I played on TV.

"No way, man. I'm just a wuss. They practically paint my muscles on each morning."

"America's not that great. I'll fight you..."

"What? That's not..."

Wow, the guy wasn't listening, either. I decided to do the right thing. I put my hands up in the universal sign of surrender. "Wait a minute. Hold up there. Let me say something here."

I stood up on the footrest at the bar, so I was a bit taller and spoke my announcement boldly. "Listen, everyone. This guy here wants to fight me, but I'm not going to, because he can kick my a--. Seriously, I can't fight him. He's tougher and stronger than I am." I got down off the stool to a stunned crowd of onlookers and turned to my would-be opponent. "There, does that make you feel better because I know how insecure us mates can get about our manhood."

Mr. Tough-guy glared at me for a long moment, then looked around the pub. He threw his pool cue on the table in disgust and left the bar.

It was funny to me, but it affected me on a profound level as well. I had officially become a target, justified by my celebrity. In other words, my renown became an invitation to criticize and attack me. Fame offers opportunity—for both sides, in both ways.

For me, fame offered the obvious things: wealth, security, the prospect of doing more, and a soapbox if I wanted it. For the fans, my fame offered them someone to admire and emulate or at least inspire them. But it also offered the detractors a permissible foil. Being the strongest man in the world meant they ought to try to knock me down if only to disprove that assertion. The fact that it was merely make-believe was, to them, more provocative than insignificant. I found this so ridiculously stupid, to nurse that much insecurity, and a waste of time and energy, but it's all tied up in the ego.

Of course, the upside of having celebrity status cannot be overstated, so I don't lament the attackers. I welcome them. As long as they're paying attention, right?

Starring in the number one show in the world for a major studio, Universal, and appearing on television in 176 countries made it hard to comprehend the number of fans I had garnered worldwide. The Tribune Company, which was based in Chicago, owned many of the TV stations that aired my show, including their main flagship station WGN in Chicago. They also owned the city's Major League Baseball team, the Chicago Cubs, at that time. As a promotional event, Tribune graciously invited me to throw out the first pitch at a Cubs' home game at Wrigley Field.

I was by the Cubs' dugout talking to a few players before going out to throw the ceremonial "first" pitch, which they do at almost every game across America at every ballpark, often with some kind of celebrity or special guest, for whatever reason. This day, they'd given the first pitch to a little eleven-year-old girl. They announced her as the winner of the random pick for a fan to try to toss one across home plate. Called right out of the stands in the stadium, she came on the field. They moved her up about twenty feet in front of the pitcher's mound to give here at least a chance to get the ball to the catcher. With no warmup, she threw the ball in the general direction of home plate, but it landed way short!

What happened next shocked me. Those Chicago fans booed her! An innocent little child! I imagined she would be in therapy for the rest of her life.

I looked at the Cubs player I had been talking to. He shrugged and advised me, "Get it over the plate."

They announced my name and showed a quick clip of *Hercules* on the big screen in the outfield and then switched to me, live, walking out to the mound. I was nervous. As I walked out, amongst the cheers, I heard, "F- you, Hercules." "Pussy!" "I will kick your a**!" and other fun stuff. These fans were serious and uninhibited—

always brave in a mob. The menacing crowd in the stadium loomed over me like a thirteen-story-high wave about to crash down.

I stood on the mound, and I looked at the catcher. Vertigo took over, and home plate drifted about a mile away. Now, I used to be a pitcher back in my school days, and I had practiced a bit before coming to the park for this. When I finally focused on the catcher, I did my best major league wind up and threw the ball. I guess I'm a pretty good actor because although it was high for a ball, it sailed over the plate. That was a relief.

After throwing out that first pitch, Tribune had arranged for me to join Harry Caray in the announcer box. While walking through the stadium, some fans ran up for autographs.

"Tough crowd, in this town," I quipped.

"Yeah. We had to heckle you, give you some crap, you know?"

"Wait, you were some of the guys taunting me?"

"Sure! It's the Chicago way! We were just having fun with you," they laughed.

I'm still not sure why, but I posed for a few pictures and signed a few baseballs.

After that, the publicity team brought me up to the Bird's Nest to meet Harry Caray and do an inning of live radio with him.

Now, you have to understand, Harry is a treasure to Chicago and the Cubs. He had been the play-by-play announcer for them for decades. Known to be a bit of a character, and also known to tip a drink or more during his broadcasts, his unusual style of banter made him one of the best-known and most beloved sportscasters in the business. Part of his charm was his complete lack of guile, which was aided by his imbibing great doses of what some call truth serum. To the rest of us, it's alcohol. It was well known that he drank pretty much the entire game, despite his being the announcer.

Up in the booth, Harry Caray asked me seven times during that one inning if Sorbo was an Italian name. It is definitely not. I am one hundred percent Norwegian, and I pointed that out numerous times. It was pretty funny because Harry kept circling back around to ask me again as if it had just occurred to him to ask.

As I walked out of the booth, he turned to his assistant and said, "I could have sworn he was an Italian boy."

While I enjoyed my time in the booth, my experience on the field strongly impacted me with an odd recognition. I had become a target, simply because I was famous. It didn't seem fair, but there it was. The only question was, what to do with this new understanding?

Once I fully absorbed my changed status, I figured my notoriety was a tool that I could leave on the workbench of life or take up to carve some good in the cultural marble. My show was a morally principled show, and I was in the ideal position to assure that as its star. I did it because it was my name and face out there, and I believed in the wholesome and fun aspect of the show. Although sometimes it was a fight to keep this fully "G-rated" standard over time, I received countless letters from fans about how I positively influenced them. Even the editor of *TV Guide* wrote me a kind note explaining that mine was the only show his family watched together. Understanding that my fame could give more impact to a message I might want to relay was the launching point of a new career goal for me. While I didn't delve too deeply into the specifics, I figured out that there was a message I needed to communicate through my acting.

Suffering three strokes during season five of the show derailed me for a long time. My audacious designs for a fabulous Hollywood career lay dashed on the pavement. Having the paramedics whisk me off the film set in Atlanta was not a constructive career move, obviously, and it took me a good long time to accept my new paradigm. In some ways, I still reject it. I certainly regret the strokes, while at the same time, I appreciate that they were God's plan for me.

After I had healed, I still struggled with figuring out 'why.' What was the purpose behind my suffering? What was God's plan? I prayed for an answer.

My three strokes brought me very close to death. This experience afforded me a new perspective on life. But it didn't explain what I should use it for, and, let's face it, I thought I was doing great before all this happened. I begged for enlightenment, for reasons, explanations. I floundered in my spiritual life. It felt like God might be trying to tell me something, but I couldn't hear Him.

One day I was sitting at my desk when I got a call from my manager saying that I was being offered a small part in *Soul Surfer*. She was sending me the script.

Shortly after that, Sam came into my office. My office is a former bedroom, upstairs at the opposite end of a large bonus room, which separates me from much of the daily chaos. Sam often shows up just to touch base when she gets home from chauffeuring the kids around or running errands. If she didn't, we'd probably just be email pals at this point. I'm kidding, of course, but it's nice that we have separate offices in the same building.

This day, Sam hovered in the doorway. "How's it going?"

"Good. I just got offered a part in this movie, *Soul Surfer*. It's the true story of Bethany Hamilton, that girl who lost her arm to the shark."

"Wow. Is it a faith-based movie?"

"I don't know. Why do you ask?"

"She testifies."

"What do you mean, she testifies? You know her?" I was confused. I'd heard a bit of the story, but clearly, not as much as Sam knew.

"Sure, I remember when it happened. She was like twelve or thirteen, right? I remember vividly she went on the *Today Show*, or whatever, and they interviewed her. It was Matt Lauer, I think, and she sat there, pointing up to God. He asked her if she was angry or something, and she answered along the lines of, 'No, God has a plan for me, and I just have to walk in faith.' It was amazing because Lauer lost his words for a moment. Faced with such tremendous faith, he didn't know what to say." Sam laughed. "I have to say, she challenged me, too. That girl knows God. It was amazing."

"Well, I'll let you read the script, but I don't know if I should do the movie. I'm supposed to be the one who saves her from the water, right after the attack. I don't surf."

Sam gave me her most patient looks and smiled. "That's what stunt doubles are for. If this is a faith-based movie, you should do it, Kevin. Plus, it'll shoot in Hawaii, right?" Sam knew Bethany was from Hawaii, I guess.

"Yeah, I was getting to that."

"Uhm, yeah. You take the part because Hawaii!"

"Really," I pushed back.

"Really! The kids and I want to go to Hawaii!" She started to hula. She wasn't very good, but she was awfully cute.

I laughed.

"Read the script, and then decide."

We both read the script and discovered it was a very powerful, emotional drama. There was no way I wouldn't do the movie. Plus, several weeks in Hawaii for the kids was the icing on the cake. It would star Helen Hunt and Dennis Quaid, with AnnaSophia Robb playing Bethany.

I traveled to Hawaii ahead of the family, a week before shooting started so I could take some surfing lessons and look half-way decent in the water. What can I say? I'm a lake child, not a surfer, and as athletic as I am, surfing requires a whole other muscle performance set than what I grew up with. I fared well, but I won't be competing anytime soon.

As it turned out, we filmed in the very bay where the ailing shark attacked Bethany. They say that shark was unwell, which is why it behaved abnormally.

Floating in the water where a fourteen-foot-long shark snatched off a thirteen-year-old's arm was eerie, to say the least. We all sat on our surfboards four hundred meters from the shore. I examined the other actors who were to shoot the scene with me and noticed the quiet. No one spoke.

The camera crew was setting up the cameras. I finally broke the silence and said, "I know we aren't worried about a shark attack right now, but we are all thinking about it, right?"

Everyone laughed and nodded yes.

We filmed the scene of Bethany's rescue over a two-day period. I had an opportunity to meet and converse with the man I was playing. He recounted to me that on the day of the attack, the water was unusually calm. He was out there with his son, daughter, and Bethany, just waiting for a decent set of waves to come in. His daughter and Bethany were best friends. Bethany had been twenty meters away from him and his children, just in her own world, lying on her board, lazily swishing the seawater with her arm. Suddenly, they saw her paddling toward them with only one arm, as best as she could. They hadn't seen or even heard the shark attack, it happened so quickly, but as she tried to get to them, they all saw the gaping wound where her other arm ought to have been, and the gushing blood.

He immediately sent his children to paddle in to shore as fast as they could, instructing them to phone 911. His main concern was that with all that blood in the water, it would initiate a feeding frenzy. He paddled as fast as he could toward this little thirteen-year-old girl, who was already in shock, believing that they both would be dying on this day.

He maneuvered his board to the correct side of her so she could hold on to his shorts while he paddled as hard as he could to get them both in to shore. Bethany was praying aloud the entire way in, even while in shock. Thank God it was high tide, so the reef in front of them had a couple of feet of water over it. He ripped off his rash guard, the long-sleeved top for surfing, and tied it as tightly as he could around her stump to staunch the blood flow from her shoulder, and then ran across the reef, Bethany still on her surfboard, with the sharp corals ripping the bottoms of his feet open as he ran.

The movie scene that depicted that day captures well the intense trauma of that experience and is a powerful part of the movie, to say the least.

A water shoot in the actual bay, fake blood, trauma and terror, all of these things made for an exhausting time. Worst of all, water got into the cameras and destroyed much of the footage, so very little of the scene that we shot was left on screen. Somehow the editors managed to eke out enough from the surviving footage that the audience wouldn't notice what was missing. I did. I was there.

But the final version, even without much of what we shot, is penetrating and effective storytelling. I'm proud of this movie.

One part of the movie that confounded me was the ambulance scene. In the real story, Bethany had lost over sixty percent of her blood, and her blood pressure was deathly low. As the ambulance whisked her off to the hospital, the paramedic asked her, "Have you accepted Jesus into your heart?"

"Yes," she replied simply.

That scene was in the script version of the movie, but studio producers wanted it out. I was there the day we shot the scene, so I asked them, "So, if I want to say, 'Jesus' as a swear word, that's okay, but not if it's got a religious tone?" They basically nodded.

In Hollywood, even the true stories suffer at the whims of the storytellers. It's the corollary to, *the victor writes the history of the battle.* I suppose that was when I decided I had to rewrite that dynamic. When the producers admitted that they purposefully left out an important part of the story because it supported strong Christian faith, I took it a little bit personally.

I started actively looking for projects that were less abashed in proclamations of faith. These would not be studio pictures, because for whatever reason, perhaps it stems from the more secular worldview that is prevalent in our culture today, studios typically shy away from bold faith statements in films. More than that, they often produce films that openly mock or denigrate the Christian faith, or that push other ideologies, with negligible adverse repercussions.

I have found many films with strong supportive messages to be part of. These aren't the big Hollywood pay-day types of films, but they are gratifying to be able to contribute to. What's even more satisfying are the numerous fans who praise my work, gushing about how much they appreciate these kinds of films, and then ask me to keep doing them.

I wasn't shocked that Sean called to say he wanted to get involved in the film industry—I was only modestly surprised he wanted to work with me. Storytelling is the way to preserve or destroy a culture. There is a good reason much of Jesus's speaking

180

in the Bible is in allegory. Stories move us like nothing else will. Hannity knew that. And in me, my wife, and Dan, he found eager and ready partners.

"Faith Film"

Dan Gordon

"Faith Film" is an interesting phrase. In the motion picture business, it has a definite meaning. It is a film intended for a niche audience: people of faith. The faith for which it is specifically intended is Christianity, and the audience is its adherents.

There are times when it's a fairly crass term. It's intended to calculate a more-or-less guaranteed return if the target audience is reached.

But there's another kind of faith film and, sometimes, the two coincide. It is the kind of film not only intended for a faith audience, but a film literally made *by* faith.

Let There Be Light is exactly such a film.

To start with, there was not only never really a chance of seeing it get made. There wasn't even a unanimous intent on getting it made. I've been a screenwriter for longer than I care to admit. In May of this year, I will mark my fiftieth year in the biz, as they say. I have always been a studio writer, and have written such films as *The Hurricane*, with Denzel Washington; *Wyatt Earp*, with Kevin Costner; *Passenger 57*, with Wesley Snipes, and *Murder in the First*, with Kevin Bacon. *Let There Be Light* marks my seventeenth feature-length film. I have also done around two to three hundred hours of network, cable, and premium cable television along the way, starting out as the head writer of Michael Landon's *Highway to Heaven* on NBC over thirty years ago.

In each and every case, absolutely without exception, either I had an idea for a movie and pitched it or someone contacted my agent and said, "We've just optioned a book or the subject of a life story, and think Dan Gordon might be right for this." You are one on a short list of writers. You put together your "take" on the subject, then go to the studio and pitch your idea. You basically audition for every job you get.

Those are the only two ways it works.

Or at least, those are the only two ways its ever worked in my career.

That is, up until *Let There Be Light*.

From the beginning, *Let There Be Light* fit no mold and proceeded, not according to my plan, nor that of any studio or network, but, I firmly believe, according to God's plan. That's an awfully arrogant statement to make, I know. But since I've spent my life as a storyteller, let me tell you a story.

One day, I get a call from Sam Sorbo, wife of Kevin Sorbo. They're a lovely couple, and we were introduced by a mutual friend. We flirted with a television series idea or two. As I recall, we even pitched one of them. And, as is the case with more than ninety percent of all the projects I've ever been involved with, absolutely nothing came of it.

Actually, that's not true.

A deep friendship I have come to treasure came of it. But that doesn't pay the rent, keep the lights on, or get a film made. And those kinds of friendships, many times, crash on the rocks of the pressures of actually making a movie.

But from the get-go, this one was different.

I get a call from Sam Sorbo. She says, "Would you be interested in writing a screenplay with me?"

"No."

"How come?"

"Because I don't write with other people. And in kindergarten, I never shared my toys or played well with others."

"Well, would you consider meeting with me for coffee?"

"No."

"How come?"

"I don't drink coffee."

"Tea?"

"Don't drink tea. But I'll meet you, and I'll bring a bottle of water. You can drink what you like." So, I meet her at a shopping mall in Calabasas, and she tells me a story. And I said, "OK. Here's what I'll consider doing. There's something in this. You write the first draft and then give it to me, and I get to do what I want. And then, we'll both look at it and see if we think it's a movie."

Well, we didn't proceed to writing a screenplay because almost exactly at the same time we were meeting, Sean Hannity had a conversation with Kevin Sorbo, who had appeared on his show on FOX News, probably plugging *God's Not Dead*, and Sean says, "If you ever have a faith-based movie that you think I might be interested in, bring it to me because I think movies can do more than anything else to influence culture, and that's something I'd be interested in."

Now, may I say, that's just plain goofy. The money never chases you. You ALWAYS chase the money, and, usually, you run out of breath before it does. But here's one of the most well-known television personalities in the entire world saying, "If you've got something, I'd be interested in financing it."

Of course, we didn't have something. All we had was the story that Sam and I had agreed to write, which we had not yet written.

So the three of us fly to New York, and we pitch Sean in his office at FOX News. Now, outside of the President of the United States and a one-armed paper hanger, there is probably no person on earth busier than Sean Hannity. He doesn't have a lot of time, and he doesn't like to spend a lot of time just talking. He is a very dynamic doer. I basically have twenty minutes to a half-hour between his three-hour radio show and his one-hour nightly television show in which to pitch him the story of a screenplay that doesn't yet exist.

But it is a heck of a story.

Its genesis was in Sam's pure heart, and for me, it was probably one of the most personal stories I've ever done. It dealt with the death of a much-loved, first-born child. It contained the heartbreaking bitterness of two people who once loved each other and who had been torn apart by loss. It dealt with lacking faith and finding faith. It delved deep into the hours I have known of PTSD, of washing down pain pills with vodka and still feeling the pain. Of what F. Scott Fitzgerald called, the "real dark night of the soul" where "it is always three o'clock in the morning, day after day."

On those nights, after a rather nasty car accident which tore my rotator cuff, fractured a collar bone, and triggered some horrific memories both of my son's fatal car accident, and of wars in which I've participated, I would sit, zonked out in a chair, since I could not sleep lying down for three months, blitzed out of my mind, watching infomercials. And the next day, I would find, to my amazement, I had ordered six cases of whatever the previous night's huckster had been selling.

So the story contained a combination of the purity of Sam's soul and a few hard-won truths. It also contained the story of a pal of mine, who used to be a mobbed-up wise guy and found Christ in solitary confinement during the time he was euphemistically residing in government housing. It made a heck of a story, and I managed to tell it before Sean had to go on the air for his radio show or start prepping his nightly television program.

There are a lot of indecisive people on earth. A lot who do not follow the truth of their own convictions and even more who have no convictions to follow.

Sean Hannity fits into none of those categories. He said okay on the spot.

He asked what the budget was, and we told him.

He simply said, "OK." Just like that.

He then said, with the hard glint in his eye of an Irish construction worker, "Don't come back to me for a penny more because you're over budget."

And as easy as that, we were in business.

Without realizing it, the Big G was orchestrating everything all along. People came to be a part of our film, not just because it was another gig but because it was their heart-wrenching story, as well.

Our story touches upon cancer because my brother died in my arms of a brain tumor. And as he did, his last words were about what he was, apparently, catching a glimpse of. "It's so beautiful," he said. "It's so beautiful!" I had never seen a smile like that before on his face.

A young actress who was to play a pivotal role in the film auditioned for us. It wasn't just a gig for her, though. Despite her youth, she was a cancer survivor, and this was her story as much as ours.

Another young woman who turned in a magnificent performance had to be done by a certain hour because she needed eight hours of dialysis. It was her faith that kept her going, and she poured every ounce of hers into it.

Our producer-slash-line-producer was nothing less than a Jedi warrior. He made miracles happen on the set. Usually, you search for locations. Our locations searched for us and found us.

Every step of the way, through every crisis, the Big G made it better, and there was always a lesson for all of us to learn.

Sam had never produced a movie in her life, and she carried this one across the finish line... on faith.

Kevin had to carry the load of starring and directing, and he did them both... on faith.

And Sean Hannity was the best boss anyone could ask for. He left us completely alone. He never visited the set, never even called. He just said, "Bring me back a good movie." And he did it... on faith.

The end result is a film that makes audiences laugh, cry, stand up, and cheer. And, I do believe, it renews in them that most precious of all commodities... Faith.

Let There be Light is, you might say, a faith film.

Making Friends

Sam

Some people think that making movies is magic. They're right.

There's a special kind of magic that goes into the filmmaking process. First of all, a single film has several tremendously different iterations. Like an adult that only vaguely resembles the baby it originally was, the film begins as an idea first and then becomes the script.

After the script is written, the process of deciding on and procuring the locations for the shoot begins to define in physical terms the aspects only previously imagined by the screenwriters and producers. This changes the film significantly, typically for the better.

Shooting again alters the film from the written page as so many other elements combine to produce what ends up on the screen. Then through the editing process, the film again is completely transformed. They say films are truly made in the editing room, and I have personally seen films saved by the editor.

On one project, the editing team, comprised of the director and editor, was so frustrated by an actor's complete lack of expression during a scene, they searched the ends of the takes, for the movements and facial expressions he displayed after the director said, "Cut!" Those moments presented simple *truth*, the actor's reaction to what was really happening instead of his imagined perfection of *acting* within the scene when he was trying to convince the audience that he cared.

I watched dumbfounded as they grabbed the end clips from each take and sandwiched them into the scene as his reaction shots to the other actor. This sleight-of-hand made the entire scene, and the character, much more compelling. At the premiere of the movie, I recall hearing someone ask the other actor how great it must have been to act opposite such a caring and compassionate individual and an "obviously gifted" actor. I saw the twinkle of confusion in his eyes because his experience on set was of an entirely different, untalented individual. Editing can remake a movie in profound ways.

Once we got the green light to start the process of making our film *Let There Be Light,* the race was on. It's an odd part of the business, which is probably true of most entrepreneurial ventures, that there's a lot of chatter, waiting, twiddling your thumbs, and discussions until the point of "go," (or the money hits the account), and then it's kind of a race to the finish line after that.

Kevin, Dan, and I started making calls. One conversation led to another. We didn't even have our location nailed down. Atlanta seemed like a good lead. They had a great tax credit going, but we discovered that Atlanta had so much production happening there that the credit might be used up, and the crews were all working on other projects. In other words, the amount of talent available there had dwindled, and we were better served looking elsewhere. But where?

South Carolina? Louisiana? As it worked out, Kevin gave me the name of a friend of a friend who lived in Alabama, saying, "Bob said to call this guy and ask him about Alabama. They've got a rebate going. Maybe that'll work for us."

I called.

"Patrick? Bob gave me your number to call about shooting a film in Alabama."

"Yeah, sure. I can help you with that. This is the greatest state to shoot in, bar none, and we'll get you set up here in no time."

Patrick had a charming southern drawl and a kind voice. He spent several minutes on the phone explaining the tax rebate system and all the great qualities of his beloved state.

"Okay, I get all that, but I need Connecticut and New York City. Can I find that down there?"

"Absolutely, darlin'. I'll send you some photos tomorrow."

True to his word, Patrick emailed several photos. They showed buildings like a city and countryside like Connecticut, but nothing like what we were hoping for. The buildings were not "New York" enough. They lacked the glitzy side of New York that we were looking for, and I told that to Patrick. He remained undaunted.

"No? Not exactly? That's okay because that's just Mobile. I'll tell you what, you want Birmingham. They got exactly what you want over there. Let me put you in touch with someone up there in their film commission, and he'll get you just what you need. Plus, you want to meet my good buddy, James. He lives out your way in Los Angeles. I've been trying to get him to move out here to this beautiful state, but he's still out there."

"Well, why don't we do a phone introduction when you get the chance, please."

"I surely will. I will try him right now and call you back."

Patrick hung up. and five minutes later, my phone rang. "Sam, my good friend James Quattrochi is on with us. James, say hi to Sam Sorbo."

"James, you have an Italian last name. I love it!"

"Believe me, it was no picnic, growing up. It means 'four eyes,' and for all that, my vision isn't all that great!"

And that's how James came to be our producer. Of course, we met and interviewed, but ultimately, it was through this series of phone calls that we found ourselves with James, shooting our New York and Connecticut movie in beautiful and friendly Birmingham, Alabama.

Meet the Sorbos

James Quattrochi

It was a sunny April spring afternoon in southern California. I had agreed to take a meeting at a local Starbucks with an ingratiating producer who was trying to convince me to write a movie for him "on spec." In my business, "speculation" means free: No pay!

I noticed the Starbucks was predictably quiet for a weekday mid-morning. My hot coffee warmed my hands, but my heart stayed cool. We were seated at a corner table near the door. As I listened to his plea, my mind drifted. The idea was unremarkable and unengaging, and I realized that although I wanted a job—I'm the kind of guy who genuinely needs to work—I truly did not want this job.

As he droned on about the story and how fantastic it was (it wasn't), my cell phone rang. I glanced at the number but didn't recognize it. Still, it made a great excuse.

"I'm so sorry," I said as politely as I could. "I really need to take this."

My companion smiled indulgently.

I stood and walked a few paces from the table, immediately feeling freedom wash over me. "Hello," I said, and instantly recognized the voice on the other end, an old acquaintance.

"Hey, pal, long time no speak!" He was an industry guy I've known for a long time, and he runs hot and cold, so I never know which individual I'll be dealing with. He sometimes likes playing little head games. I find it annoying. I'm a straight shooter, with no time for dumb stuff, but over the years I've done a few projects with him, so I heard him out.

He began cryptically (no surprise, there), "Hey, Jaimie, do you know who Kevin Sorbo is?"

I replied, "Sure I do. The Hercules guy with the long hair!"

"Good! Today's your lucky day. I just found out he's looking for a producer on his new movie. They reached me, and I thought of you. I'm having them call you, so be expecting."

"Okay, thanks." I hung up my phone and thought about the odds. Who knew if this was a greenlit film or just a fishing expedition? No use asking my friend, because in this business you don't really know until the money's in your account, but I got a warm feeling for it, like the heat from my coffee had finally reached my heart.

I returned to the quiet Starbucks table, sat down, and the producer began to speak again.

"So, the thing about this screenplay that makes it so different is the protagonist and the antagonist are related!"

I felt a chilly breeze on the back of my neck, prickly and discomforting, despite the heated rays of sun through the windows.

I politely declined the offer to write a free screenplay. "I just can't see it fitting into my schedule within your timeframe, so I think you'd be better off finding someone else." I walked out of the Starbucks with a discreet joy in my step.

A few days later, I parked my big red truck in the Sorbo driveway. When I rang the bell, it was Sam Sorbo who answered the door and invited me in. She led me to a dining room with a large inlaid-wood table that reminded me of the noble knights in the medieval days of chivalry and shining armor. I took a seat, noting a life-sized painting of Kevin as Hercules. It was an impressive piece, reminiscent of the days when noblemen posed for painted portraits. I started imagining a Connecticut lock-jawed Kevin entering in his white tennis togs with a scotch and soda in hand, saying things like "Daddy's got the Rolls today, so I'm taking the Jag-u-ar," rolling Jaguar into three syllables on his spirit-loosened tongue.

Sam noticed me gawking. "It was a farewell gift from the crew of Hercules. Where else can I put it?" she explained, laughing. "Kevin doesn't like it, but he rarely contributes to any decorating decisions, so I guess he figured, 'Why start now?' For years, it sat in storage. When I finally painted this room, I realized I needed a very large, reddish piece of art for this large wall, and, well, remembered I still had him in the closet!"

"So, Kevin came out of the closet? I always wondered about him..." I joked feebly.

Sam fixed me with an intense, uncomfortable stare. Then she cracked a wry grin and laughed. "Oh, you have a sense of humor. We'll get along just fine."

Just then, Kevin entered all smiles and char—and sweat, having just come from the gym. He was disarmingly unlike the somber image in the painting. I can't lie, it was a little intimidating. We shook hands, and he thanked me for coming on such short notice.

I remembered aloud a weird little morsel. "Hey, Kevin, you and I actually studied acting with the same teacher way back when."

Small talk, but Kevin immediately engaged me on our mutual experiences in that class. I began breathing a little easier.

Then Sam started the interview process. It seemed like a classic "good cop, bad cop" routine. Kevin lulled me into a sense of security, and then Sam pounced with the tough questions! I soon realized that it was her I would have to impress to get the job.

Our meeting lasted about 30 minutes, and Sam was sure to let me know I would have to supply her with several references. It was clear she maintains high expectations—nothing but near-perfection—from those who she works with. Yipes!

Sam then asked me how much I would want to be paid to travel with them for several days to scout locations. We needed to determine what city would work best for the film's budget to unlock the full funding of the movie.

At that point, I'll be honest, writing a free screenplay was looking a lot easier! I pondered for a moment, and then I said to myself, "I will rise to this challenge and win her over!"

Of course, I had impeccable references, and Sam checked every one. First hurdle vaulted.

I traveled to Alabama with The Sorbos at no charge. That was my way of showing them I was a team player and committed to our project. The trip to Birmingham was full of hidden blessings and strikingly favorable discoveries, plus the food was incredibly delicious. After a fantastic scouting trip—probably the best one I've ever experienced, from the locations to the environment to the companions—we decided to film our movie there.

Once we returned from Alabama, I was hired to produce this amazing film titled *Let There Be Light* that I am so very proud of.

I spent April, May, and June on the phone several hours each day soft prepping the movie, interviewing and hiring locals, and hammering down the budget and screenplay. I handed in my final budget on July 4th at 11 am and then went to the Sorbo's home for their annual 4th of July party, where Sam and I determined I needed to fly out the next day to start pre-production in Birmingham.

I must say, I was very proud of the team I had assembled before I got there. By the time the Sorbos finally arrived, we had everything in place. Our offices were fully established and functional; phones were ringing, equipment was humming, production assistants were running between the set designer's office, accounting, and photography department. A furnished apartment stood ready for the Sorbo family, locations were lined up on the schedule, catering contracts were locked and loaded—the list seemed endless. Producing is like eating an elephant: one bite at a time.

The "aha!" moment for me came when we three pulled up on set the very first day. We drove down the beautiful tree-lined street we had originally located purely by accident, and turned the corner, revealing the beehive of activity and film paraphernalia. Several different trucks were parked along the road, the crane was moving slowly into position, and the crew was busy shuttling gaffing gear and adjusting camera equipment. A crowd of onlookers had gathered in the street as well. It was an impressive sight, and everything was working as planned.

Sam turned to me and said, "James, this is amazing! You are amazing! I could kiss you, but my husband is sitting right here next to me."

Kevin laughed. "Don't answer that, Jamie."

"I wasn't going to!" I confessed.

He clapped me on the shoulder when we got out of the car, enjoying the full impact of a working set. "Wow, James. You really pulled it off. Now it's my turn to make some magic happen."

"That's what it's all about, why we do what we do," I answered with a good degree of self-satisfaction.

It had taken a few months for our faith in each other to build, but from that moment on, I felt like the Sorbos and their wonderful children would be in my heart and life forever.

August in Birmingham

Sam

The climate in this nation is such that although there are people of faith everywhere, they tend to be shy about admitting it. This inhibition stems predominantly from our current society's and media's implicit contention that the Bible is a fairytale book, and that evolution is the "scientific" explanation for our existence. Never-you-mind that evolution, as a theory, leaves far too many questions unexplored and unanswered to begin to replace the creation story and the Bible. Years ago, we removed the Bible from our schools. What should we expect as all school children became disciples in secular humanism—the worldview that Man is his own answer, despite the obvious contradictions of history? After all, each modern society that eschewed the Word of God to turn inward to the Rule of Man. Mao Zedong and the "Great Leap Forward" communists of China, Lenin/Stalin and the communists of the United Soviet Socialist Republic, Hitler and the National Socialists (NAZI party) of Germany, and Pol Pot of the communist Khmer Rouge in Cambodia, all became enormous death camps, with over a hundred million dead in their movements' collective wakes. Why? Because in order for Man to rule man, Man (the one in charge, that is) must become all-powerful, and power corrupts. Absolute power corrupts absolutely, to put it bluntly.

Evil itself is a spiritual force not to be trifled with. In the United States, we have our own movement, in the very same direction as Pol Pot and Mao, and we are currently teaching it in our schools. The proof for this is Candidate Bernie Sanders, an octogenarian "democratic socialist," and, let's not mince words, because Bernie Sanders only inserts "democratic" as a modifier to make socialism *sound* more appealing. There is nothing truly democratic about what he advocates, yet he received more votes in 2016 from American youth than Hillary Clinton and Donald Trump combined. To sum up, the young people are voting for the oldest candidate because they've been instructed in our educational institutions that socialism is "grandpa with candy," and who epitomizes that image better than Mr. Sanders?

They've also learned to rely on appearances over substance, color vs. character. The election and popularity of Alexandria Ocasio Cortez is also ample evidence of this travesty. A young woman working in a bar, instead of her chosen line of study, ascending into public office and then presuming to lecture the rest of the country and her fellow public servants on how best to run the country is astonishing, but it's to be expected. A good portion of the public believes in the merits of socialism, despite ample evidence the world over to the contrary. The power of the schools to persuade an ignorant youth of untruths cannot be underestimated.

Those opposed to truth disparage the Bible, insisting it is simply a fairytale because the Bible maintains that there are rules to live by—rules which are reasonable and necessary for a populous that has a contract to self-govern. Self-government implies a society that lives by a moral creed, and therefore understands that laws are a contract between one citizen and another. Without this fundamental understanding and the morality that underpins it, we will lose the very freedoms we fought to covet and protect. Voluntary adherence to our laws is the only thing standing between us and chaos.

But in public school, our youth no longer learn civics, the proper responsibilities of the public, and the prescribed role of government. Instead, they learn that government is the solution to all ills. This is the long-term recipe for power to shift more and more to our federal government, which seems already to have assumed a great deal more than was ever envisioned by this nation's incredibly gifted and brilliantly strategic founders, most of whom, if not all, were professing and devotedly practicing Christians.

Thus, we find ourselves at a bit of a crossroads in our country today. As the children are taught that socialism will cure their woes and that God is not the answer but man is, they're less and less tolerant of Bible-believing Christians. This is due to a lack of comprehension, to be sure, and to an education that teaches that words have as much, or more, power than either blunt or sharp instruments. This renders a new culture in which children demand "safe spaces" and "free speech zones" to segregate themselves from any verbal expressions or even thoughts that contradict their current ideologies or challenge their worldviews. To forces of evil, Biblical truth and morality is a weapon, so the enemy seeks to banish that message and abolish even the mention of its name. Enemies of truth accomplish this by shutting down any debate and by ridicule. The purveyors of evil actively persecute Christians who profess the truth and stand in the breach in the public marketplace. It has degenerated to the point that California is considering a bill which would outlaw Christian counseling for sexual behavior, despite even the patient's desire for such! In other words, "You may *be* Christian, but you may not *express* Christian beliefs or *perform* Christian works, or even *hold* Christian views." It turns our First Amendment on its head.

While this is not the focus of our book, its exemplifies the underlying intention in our movie. Religion, or *worldview*, informs everything a person does. I've often said, "Show me a politician who makes policy decisions *not* based on his religion (his worldview), and I'll show you a hypocrite." Although the culture tries to persuade us to relinquish our religion before entering the marketplace of ideas, what it actually demands is hypocrisy, a bridge Kevin and I refuse to cross. Instead, we seek to encourage others to stand firm in their Christian convictions, especially as a means to a more peaceful and loving environment. After all, there are many religions, but only one that preaches and practices peace and love as its main tenets.

It was a hot day in June as our small crew drove around Birmingham to do our location scouting. The crew consisted of Kevin and me, James, our set designer Anthony, and Buddy, a local good ol' boy who ran the film office for Birmingham. Patrick had introduced me to Buddy once we established that Mobile, his hometown, was not going to answer our requirements. Buddy worked tirelessly, researching and identifying the various locations that we needed:

- New York style loft: Expensively decorated, high rise, city-view
- Connecticut house: Pretty and quaint, traditional
- Party venue
- Wedding venue
- Pretty church
- Coffee shop
- Theater 1
- Theater 2
- Hospital room (three of them!), plus an exterior and hallways

That was our starting list, and Buddy was busy being our tour guide and showing us the venues he had found while I served as designated driver in our red minivan rental.

The Birmingham Museum of Art was one of our first stops. It was a modern granite edifice that presided over a wide street, across from a verdant park. I crossed the street to take it in, picturing the red carpet and throngs of paparazzi and flashing cameras outside the building as we watch our erstwhile hero enter for his book launch party with the glitterati of New York City to celebrate him. It was perfect!

We stepped inside and met an older woman whom Buddy had previously contacted. Petite and casually dressed, she showed us their main gallery, which was white and spacious with lofty ceilings and fabulous pieces of art hung on the walls. It was just inside from the street and had a large staircase that gave onto a surrounding second-floor mezzanine. Sol's book-launch party would be beautiful in here, and we immediately fell in love. The possible camera angles from the balcony down, the book announcement from the stair landing, which offered a great vantage point from which to survey the entire space, and the brightness and ease the room offered for lighting, all convinced us we needed to make this deal happen. The clincher was when we learned that they would be only too happy to host us for a very modest fee, or our hostess genially whispered, "Perhaps no fee at all." After all, everyone wanted Birmingham to become the next big center for filmmaking, so if the local art museum could help entice us to film there and bring some attention to their city, they were thrilled to contribute.

Then Buddy said, "Let's show them the theater."

Our hostess enthusiastically walked us toward the back of the building and through a set of pale-wood double doors into a beautiful, modern, honey-stained, wood-paneled theater. We gasped with delight.

Jackpot!

"This is perfect for the debate!" Kevin remarked to Dan, who readily agreed.

"Where do I sign?" I quipped.

Some of our locations were going to be challenging, we knew. This was not one of them. Check!

With that settled, Buddy directed me to drive through some of Birmingham's residential communities, to better discern the kind of house we needed. Birmingham has some lovely architecture, and much of it would pass for Connecticut, even for the more specific statement we were trying to make for Katy's house. I'll admit that I was personally invested in finding my character her ideal home, but I wasn't being overly particular. We just couldn't find the right one.

There are many issues to consider when location scouting for a movie, not least of all being traffic. A film crew, even a small one like ours, requires several trucks, a place for the wardrobe, makeup and hair, a set office for the production staff, ample room for props, sound, and what we call the "video village," where the directing team can view playback and the script supervisor, continuity, hair and makeup, and others can watch in real-time, out of the way, but close enough to run onto set when necessary.

The next day, I was on the air doing my live broadcast for the first three hours in the morning, but the gang insisted on texting me pictures of houses they were finding. One house was particularly charming, and the boys set their sights on it. Painted a pale powder blue, this house was unusual in that the front door stood off to the left side, under a cozy little archway, while most of the house lay to the right. Once I got off the air, the gang picked me up and excitedly assured me they had found the perfect house. They gave me the wheel.

We pulled up to the house, which looked less interesting to me than the photos showed. That typical, frankly. But it wasn't the house itself, that discouraged me, it was the street.

"Well, the house is pretty enough," I began, looking around as cars whizzed past us. "But Guys, we can't shoot on this street. Look at it! It's on a curve, right off a busy thoroughfare, and it's busy, too. We'd just as soon shoot ourselves in the head than get tangled up in this mess."

They immediately saw my point. In their zeal to find the property, they hadn't yet considered all the parameters that are involved in choosing a filming location. It's important not to lose sight of accessibility, noise, traffic, and many other things. Where can we park the cast trailers? If it's too far away, getting cast to and from location becomes a logistical nightmare. Those practicalities meant that house wouldn't work as a prospect and sent us venturing outside of Birmingham into her quieter suburbs.

We stopped for lunch and visited a church afterward. Buddy navigated us to one he had previously investigated, saying, "You let me know if this one is in the right direction, or if you are looking for something different."

All we had said was "Connecticut" and "maybe white clapboard." When we pulled up, we all cast our eyes upon a more beautiful white clapboard church than any of us had ventured to imagine finding for our little project. We toured inside but quickly settled on shooting all exteriors because the white picket fence and fieldstone foundations beckoned. We had found our church, and we were no longer in Birmingham city.

"Buddy, I think the problem with the houses inside the city of Birmingham is, although they are very pretty, we're going to have all kinds of traffic and logistical issues, and noise as well. Maybe we should find a sleepy suburban housing development, or something more relaxed?"

"There are a few places near here that we can tool around in if y'all want to look."

The group assented easily. "Let's go."

As we drove where Buddy indicated, I noticed the houses were very much 1970's tract homes, or older. The neighborhoods lacked the distinct charm we sought for Katy's house. Others in our van agreed with me. No one saw anything that made them shout, "Stop the car!"

We were tired, hungry, and disappointed. Finding Katy's house seemed to be our biggest challenge, but as a locus for the movie and the setting for so many scenes—the initial argument and our introduction to Katy and the kids, the setting of the dissolution of their marriage, and then the family's reunion and the healing and forgiveness it housed—Katy's house demanded distinction and became a lynchpin in our location needs. For my own part, I was determined that it be an enchanting expression of Katy herself.

"Buddy, I'm just not seeing it," I offered, dejected.

"I'll make some more calls tonight, and we'll find something tomorrow."

"So, we'll head back to the hotel now? Agreed?"

The boys mumbled their okays.

Instinctively, I turned onto a smaller road back to the main drag I knew lay off to my left. "Tomorrow is another day. I know there's a house for us here. We just haven't found it yet."

I pulled up to a stoplight at a firehouse. Across from the fire station, to my left, a small street wound down and out of sight. The houses on it were a little different from what we had previously examined, and I was immediately intrigued.

"Does anyone mind if I turn down here for a moment? I just want to explore a little more…"

They encouraged me. It seemed none of us were eager to give up the chase. I think we just all felt like we needed some sign of encouragement. The light changed, and I turned left.

The houses sat above the street on the right and below the street on the left. They were nicer than what we had seen, but still not anything special. That street ended at a T, and the houses that then faced us had charm. I turned left again, to discover we were on a cul-de-sac. The homes were small and spaced at a generous distance. The home at the end of the street had an overhanging roof and a deep, inviting front porch. It was, in a word, charming.

The dead-end quality of the road was a tremendous boon, as traffic would already be quite limited. I parked the car, and we got out, breathing the cooling late afternoon air deeply.

"I gotta say, this is more like it." I was smiling, heartened that I had found a house with curb-appeal but hesitant in my knowledge that "pretty" wasn't enough to close the deal.

"Send Kevin to the door. They won't know what hit' em," Dan offered.

"I'll go. Anthony, why don't you come with me?" Kevin offered.

Kevin, Anthony, and I approached the cute little house, and we knocked on the door. No one was home. I peeked in the window and saw construction, then noticed some construction wood piled down on the driveway. If they were mid-construction, using this house would likely present some hurdles. We turned around, facing up the entire street, taking in the wonderful, neighborhood-y vibe. It was lush and green, with flowers and some children's toys lying in a yard. A dog barked in the distance. There was definitely a Connecticut feel to it, too, and I felt more certain we were closing in on something special.

The neighbors to the house I had first spied drove up and waved at us as they parked their car next door. I walked over to them to inquire about the pretty house we were interested in. The tall woman who got out of the car was dressed in an embroidered top and jeans and smiled through her gracious southern greeting.

"We're making a film and scouting locations, and this house interests us. Do you know your neighbors?"

She explained they had recently bought the house and were renovating it, and that the wife would likely be back soon, but in the meantime, she could relay a message and perhaps my phone number? I agreed and wrote a note for her.

I strolled back to the car feeling more positive than I had for a while and recounted the pertinent elements of my conversation to the group.

Dan said, "Well, great. But there are other houses on this street, too."

Three houses down on the left stood a gorgeous cream house with a beautiful hedge and glass front door.

"What about that house?" Anthony offered.

"Yes. That one would do. It's really pretty with that tree in the front." I started walking. Kevin joined me while Anthony hung back. No need to completely overwhelm whoever might answer the door.

I stepped onto the small front porch and rang the bell. I watched a small, older, well-dressed woman walk toward me and open the door. She did not smile, but stood there, expectantly.

"Yes?" she demanded in a southern drawl.

I put on my most friendly smile. "Hi, my name is Sam Sorbo, and this is my husband, Kevin."

"Hello," Kevin interjected.

"We're in Birmingham to shoot a film, and we think your house is gorgeous. We were wondering if you might be interested in allowing us to film here."

Full disclosure: anyone who lets a film crew into their house is crazy, and I know it. But we needed a house, and some people like the idea of having their domicile featured in a movie. Furthermore, who am I to judge?

She looked up at me with skeptical, searching eyes. She folded her arms and spoke pointedly, with a terse Southern accent and drawn out words for exaggeration.

"Oh, so y'all are from *Hollywood*? Do yew know *Courtney Cox*?"

"You mean, from *Friends,* the TV show?"

"Mmm *hmm*," she nodded. "Do y'all do *drugs*? I heard she does. I know those *Hollywood* types…"

Kevin said, "No, we're not that kind of Hollywood. This is a faith-based film that we're shooting."

"Oh, *really*?" She cut him off. "*Faith*-based, huh? Are yew all *Bible*-thumpers?"

That gave us both pause. "Well…"

She didn't let up, though. "So, you're not going to have *orgies* in the movie? Is there at least a *murder*?"

"Uh, nope," Kevin answered simply.

"Wait a minute. Are you *famous*?" She seemed to have just recognized Kevin.

"To some people I am," Kevin answered, always modest. "Maybe you know me from *Hercules* or *God's Not Dead*?"

"No, I don't recognize you, I was just checking if you were *really* from Hollywood. I guess you are. So, I suppose you want to see the *inside* of my house?"

I was surprised and thrilled. "Well, yes, if you don't mind."

"Well, I'll show you. Come on in." She held the door open but leaned out in front of us. Two gardeners worked in her front yard, just behind us. "You boys stay *close by*, ya' hear? These people are from *Hollywood*, and they may intend to *rape* me or what *have* you. So I may need you to *save* me, okay?"

The gardeners, seemingly equally perplexed as us, nodded decisively. I laughed then. I just got the joke she was having on us.

Her house was exquisite. Irma, of course her name could only be Irma with her near-bouffant hair and studied makeup, was an interior decorator with impeccable taste. She was remodeling her kitchen, so there were dishes piled high in the dining room. This did not detract from the rest of the house, which thrummed with a mild buttery color scheme with some mild fawn and fern colors tossed in. It whispered serene and sophisticated. In short, it was exactly what I'd dreamed of.

The fact that it was situated on a quiet cul-de-sac was an added bonus. No traffic to speak of, and the surrounding neighborhood was tranquil and charming.

The punchline came when, while we were shooting at the house, I had the opportunity to chat with Irma's neighbors.

"So you're the producer who talked Irma into lending her house for a movie shoot? How did you do that?" they quizzed me.

I shared the story of our first meeting Irma, and we laughed together.

"Seriously," one nicely-dressed woman with delicate gold earrings responded, in a smooth southern intonation. "Of all people, Irma is the *last* person anyone would expect to have you folks into her house— no disrespect. We heard about it, and after recovering from our initial shock, we had to come out to see. How *ever* did you convince her?"

This question stumped me, too, especially in light of our initial introduction. The next day, Irma herself came to the set. Production had lodged her at a nice place nearby so the crew could have full access to the house for the few days of shooting.

I liked Irma as much for her intense humor as her frosty worldliness, but her house was so beautiful, I did wonder at her willingness to let a burly, indifferent film crew in there.

"Why did you agree to let us use your house?" I asked her after mentioning the neighborhood's response.

"Oh, those busybodies! They're just jealous because they've never been invited over!" She was joking, in her inimitable style.

I laughed.

Then she became a bit more serious. "It's true, I would never do this, normally." She looked me intently in the eye. "I just figured, if the good Lord had led you to my door, it wasn't my place to refuse. I mean, I'd have to be really dense to miss His voice in all this, and I ain't that stupid. I read your script, too, and it profoundly affected me. I have sat at the bedside of people who have passed away. I've met death face-to-face, and God is there in the details of that. People have to know that God exists. Oh, who are we kidding? They *know* it, they just don't want to *admit* it! Maybe this film will get them dense ones the message, right?"

God is Good

Donielle Artese

It's always exciting to get that call from your agent: "You have an audition!"

Your mind immediately starts to race. What's it for? What should I wear? How much time will it take me to learn my lines?

Typically, the audition is the following day, so the clock starts ticking from the moment you pick up the phone. *Don't forget your picture and resume. Don't forget your lines. Don't let them see you're nervous!*

When you arrive at the casting agent's office, the waiting room is full of other actresses, some of whom you may even recognize. Insincere smiles all around. This is a cutthroat business, even among friends.

After signing in, you sit, nervously. *Just breathe,* you counsel yourself. The casting assistant calls your name after what seems to be an eon. You enter the room, putting your best smile forward, answer some supercilious questions, perform hopefully as best you can, and then it's over—just a typical audition. And even more typical, you never hear another word about the project until it comes out on television or in the theater and you lament, *that's that role I auditioned for!*

The only thing is, I am anything but typical.

206

I got that call that every actor dreams of: "You booked the job!"

To be perfectly honest, it had been so long since my audition, I didn't even know what job it was that I had booked! My manager called to give me the details of the job. She discussed the various parameters of the job, the pay, and the shoot dates. Then, very casually, she mentioned I would be shooting 3 weeks in Birmingham, Alabama.

WHAT???

You see, this is where that atypical-ness I have comes in. More precisely, my kidneys are unordinary in that they do not function. I do 8 hours of home dialysis every night. Yes, you read that right, EVERY night!

What could I do? They had cast me for the role, so it was up to me to make the necessary arrangements to be able to travel and perform my part. After doing the calculations for equipment and supplies, I asked my manager to discreetly obtain my hotel info. I explained the reason for my inquiry; I needed to ship over 300 pounds of dialysis formula to the hotel, but of course, I needed her to keep my health problems confidential. Kidney failure, like any life-threatening illness, is not something its victims shout from the rooftops. Although I had my condition under control, most people struggle to comprehend how an illness like mine manifests in real-life, and more importantly, how it affects my work. (It doesn't.)

My manager did exactly the thing I dreaded. She called casting and blabbed my entire situation. Apparently, discreet isn't part of her working vocabulary.

"Hi, I'm Donielle's manager, calling to get her hotel information for the shoot in Alabama for *Let There Be Light.* She needs to send a bunch of dialysis equipment out there, so it gets in before her."

The reaction from the other end of the phone line astonished and alarmed her. They took my condition much more seriously than she had, and that brought my manager up short.

She called me back directly to breathlessly report that casting was rethinking the whole choice. In her saddest, most contrite voice, she explained that she had to side with them in their trepidation of appointing a significant medical case for a key part in a movie.

I knew it had been an innocent mistake, however, it sent me into a panic. I was certain they would fire me before I even got started. For me, the role was like a mercury-glass medal. My manager's *faux pas* had seemingly shattered it into a million fragments.

I needed to at least try to piece it together again. After all, *I can do all things through Christ who strengthens me.*

I prayed for God to give me the strength to be able to do this film, to allow me to keep the job. I thought of Jesus in the Garden of Gethsemane, praying for the cup to be taken from Him, if it was God's will. I revised my prayer. "God, if it is your will to allow me to keep the role, then I am certain I can perform it well. But if the role is taken from me, I can rest in your perfect will." Strangely, despite my intense apprehension about the future, I experienced a quiet peace.

In His infinite knowledge and flawless grace, God responded. My doctor cleared me to work. Casting was on my side and kept my secret from production. After that, everything else fell perfectly in place. My mother, who lives in Atlanta, happened to have the exact amount of dialysis supplies I needed. Like a marvelous angel, she packed them in her car and drove them to me in Birmingham.

Just as all my panic truly subsided, I received the script. When I auditioned *for Let There Be Light*, I had absolutely no idea that this was a faith-based film. Nothing in my audition dialogue gave me any clues, and titles can be deceptive. I read the script in one sitting and couldn't believe it. My first lead role in a film would be a faith-based film, and a fantastic one, at that! God was unquestionably directing my steps.

I am steadfast in my faith; Jesus Christ is the center of my life. That is surely not an emblematic characteristic of Hollywood actors. No matter. I am who I am because He is Who He is.

Doing this movie, I felt the presence of God carrying me through. I suffered absolutely no health issues during the filming, and working was a breeze. Everything was so seamless; I was grateful and full of praise.

At the wrap party, Sam and I started chatting about the production and final days of shooting remaining. God put it in my heart to share my situation with her though I had no idea how she might react.

With some trepidation, I offered, "You know, there's an entire back story to this shoot that I could share with you."

"Really? Tell me!" Sam fixed me with an open, curious gaze.

I took a deep breath. "Well, you don't know this about me, but I have renal failure."

Her eyelids flew open wide, and she immediately responded. "You're kidding me! When do you do dialysis?"

"Every night, for eight hours."

"Oh, for heavenly days! Every night? You're a walking miracle!"

I knew then that the casting agent had been true to her word, not telling anyone about my condition, because it was mine alone to manage. I don't know what I had expected from Sam, but she received my information with compassion and empathy. For that I am grateful.

Auditioning for roles, my days are fraught with insecurity and apprehension. As someone dependent on today's miraculous medical advances, my life is filled with marvels and amazements. God is good. Working on *Let There Be Light* changed me. I left the film with a newfound confidence. Not in myself, but in God. That film was a gift from God to let me know that His word is the truth. I felt His presence, and I felt His grace and mercy in a way I had never felt it before.

Let There Be Light will forever be the gift that keeps on giving. Every time I see the film, I am reminded of God's great love.

Faith-Based Films

Daniel Roebuck

Hollywood is all about trends; there is no doubt about it. Have you ever wondered why, suddenly, our movie screens are filled with countless movies, all of which are indistinguishable from one another? Now it's Superhero movies, a few years back it was teenage girls with cancer movies. Back in the '80s, we were all subjected to films in which the dad and son switched places—like eight of them!

Recently a new theme has hit tinsel town: faith-based films. Now, for a faith-based human, you'd think this would be a welcome relief from the multiple caped crusaders demolishing New York City time and time again. Wait, while we're on that subject, please allow me a slight digression from my point.

Why must we see New York City reduced to rubble in every third movie that comes to the big screen? Where is the entertainment in that? Don't tell me it's Gotham or Metropolis, it's NYC and, guess what, we already saw part of this glorious city crumble at the hands of a callous but effective small group of murderers. It was thousands of lives lost in minutes, and when the building fell, NO ONE was miraculously saved by movie-star-du-jour stepping out in black underwear and a mask! So, please, can we

210

stop destroying the Big Apple or pretending that when skyscrapers fall, there aren't countless horrible deaths?

Thanks, I feel better. Now back to my point.

There's this new trend, and as a Christian man and actor, it excites me beyond measure to know that—finally—some great faith-based films are being generated. Better than the fact that they are being made is the reality that they are being watched in full theaters by audiences excited to receive the message. But since it's a trend, my fear is that, just like the superhero movies, one film will simply fade into the other, and soon the message will be lost to an audience whose eagerness for communion with the uplifting message will soon be replaced with the same apathy by which I greet the news of Thor 7.

Now, I'm not just an actor, I, too, am a filmmaker whose heart is in bringing the message of God's eternal love and forgiveness to the masses, but my aim isn't the converted. I don't want to only "preach to the choir."

My personal hope is to entertain moviegoers and let the glorious message seep into the story when they least expect it. Then, a couple of days later, when in a moment of clarity while ruminating on the movie, they connect their good fortune with God's promise to them, and voilà, they are one step closer to salvation. That's my ideal but, believe me, being part of any religious-themed film excites me like a zealot on a Sunday.

Last year, I had the distinct good fortune to move from one faith-based movie to another. Let's be clear, moving from one secular film to another is a "lottery win" for an actor, so jumping from one faith-based film to another is nothing short of a miracle! The first film was *Getting Grace*, a movie I made using my own tactic of subterfuge filmmaking to get the message out. We are nanoseconds away from the completion of that film, but for those who have seen the workprint so far, my tactic seems to be working. I look forward to the day that I can share it with the readers of this piece.

The second film was the one we celebrate here, *Let There Be Light*—yes, celebrate because this film was obviously meant to be made. And dare I suggest it—willed to be made by the very God we choose to honor in the story.

The mechanics of making a movie are myriad and never easy. Never. Not ever. My film took nine years to make. Granted, once that ball was rolling downhill, it also seemed like God's hand was at work all the time.

However, *Let There Be Light* was clearly meant to be from the get-go. It was the perfect storm of events that led to the creation of a wonderful film by a group of wonderful people, all of whom believe whole-heartedly in the message.

I can tell you that most filmmakers go their entire lives hoping to meet a guy who says something like, "You know, I think we need more faith-based movies, I'd be interested in funding something like that!"

The truth is that this never happens. It's a fantasy. Yet, in a chance conversation between a respected journalist and an equally respected filmmaker, that very thing did happen, and out of it, *Let There Be Light* was born.

Not being Columbo, I don't have "all the facts," but to the best of my understanding, Sean Hannity made the offer, Kevin Sorbo (the filmmaker) jumped at the chance and Sam Sorbo, Kevin's whirling dervish of a wife, reminded him that if such a thing were to happen, the obvious story to tell would be *Let There Be Light*. Thank God, she did. What a wonderful story it is. Nothing hits home like a conversion story (let's face it, we're all sinners), and what better story about the subject than one about the world's most famous atheist realizing his own fallibility and God's love and forgiveness, simultaneously?

Sam Sorbo was blessed to have the master storyteller Dan Gordon to guide her on her writer's journey. He has shaped many a wonderful story over the last four decades in Hollywood. Together, they have fashioned quite a powerful tale in *Let There Be Light*, an unforgettable story that most certainly lives up to the faith-based trend.

Yet, as I keep writing those words, "faith-based," something else occurs to me, which is that every film might really be considered an effort predicated on faith. No matter what the subject matter of the film, to convince others of its value and to create a work of art with as many moving parts as a feature film requires necessitates a herculean amount of faith. Granted, there are any number of filmmakers who believe that it's faith in themselves that propels a movie along. But I can tell you from my experience of three-plus decades in this business, no *one* person ever makes a movie, and no *one* person could ever marshal the talent necessary to achieve such a thing. Everyone who signs on to the project has faith that it will work and entertain, otherwise what would be the point?

When I was asked to take part in *Let There Be Light,* it was very near the end of my own movie, and carving out two hours to read the script was a virtual impossibility as I was serving as writer, producer, director, and lead actor on *Getting Grace.* So it was that dynamic duo of Kevin and Sam Sorbo in whom I initially put my faith. These two can do anything they put their minds to, as is evidenced by their wonderful careers and, more importantly, their beautiful family. Also, Dan Gordon is a name I knew and a talent I appreciated from a series I took part in nearly 30 years earlier, *The Dirty Dozen.* Lastly, Kevin and I share a very well-respected agent named Harry Gold, and Harry thought it would be a good match as well. Thus, I accepted the job knowing all would be right as these talented people couldn't let me down.

It wasn't until I was on the airplane traveling to Birmingham, Alabama, that I finally had the time to read the movie. What a powerful tale Sam and Dan had concocted, this story about salvation, forgiveness, and acceptance, and I was so happy that I would be part of it. My faith, it seems paid off.

I play Kevin's character's agent in the film, and right there on the plane, I had this wild idea that it might be more interesting if he was English. There's no real explanation for why actors come up with such things, we just do. I would argue that it's God's hand directing me on a righteous path that would lead me to fulfill the character as best I could. Another actor might say he thought of it after eating an English Muffin for breakfast. Whatever the case, I saw Norm as English in manner and attitude.

From an actor's standpoint, thinking of these kinds of character things is the easiest part of the equation. Harder is getting all the other creatives on board. How does one convince the "powers that be" that your radical idea is the best idea? Norm wasn't written as an Englishman. In fact, it turns out that the role was based on a real guy who was certainly an American.

As we landed and I collected my luggage, I pondered my actor's conundrum. Like in the *Wizard of Oz*, these things have to be handled "delicately." You don't just storm on to another person's set and make demands. Especially if that "other person" once played Hercules and could twist you into a pretzel faster than you could say, "Stanislavsky."

Well, it turned out fate and faith both played a hand in the matter. I got to my costume fitting, and the designer, Gwendolyn Stukely (a proper English woman, herself) had, unbeknownst to me or anyone else, pulled a decidedly European style of clothing for the character. Yes, you are correct, England is in Europe, and the clothing she chose was fabulous and exactly what I was thinking on the plane. Imagine that—I had a random but extremely specific character idea, and she had a random and extremely specific character idea, and thanks to a force known to me as God, we ended up in the same "place!"

I was ecstatic at our good fortune, mine and hers, but how could we convince the big guy (not that Big Guy, He was obviously on our side because He helped Gwendolyn and me draw the same conclusion about the character even though we were separated by time and space)?

An ingenious plan presented itself out of necessity. The very next day, I had to go to the set to say hello, and Kevin had to approve the costume I would wear. Usually, directors look at pictures. Instead, we decided to present the character in full detail. I put on one of Gwen's great costumes, grabbed my glasses out of my bag, and had the hair department style my hair to look like Peter Sellers circa 1965. Together we went to the set with high hopes. With nothing to lose but the job, I greeted Kevin and Sam in my best

English accent. I was a nervous wreck as I had an actual English person standing 12 inches away.

Kevin's first question was, "Are you going to do it that way?"

"Only if you'll let me," I answered, and that was that.

How wonderful when a plan comes together. Better still when you realize that the plan wasn't ever your plan to begin with. It's through faith that so much in life is presented to us. We have to believe in a greater power and accept that God's plan is always the righteous one. Don't fool yourself into thinking that God wouldn't care what accent I used to play Norm. Yes, of course, He's got His eye on the Middle East, but I sleep better knowing he has His eye on me, too.

When I am acting, fully alive in a role, I feel His love. Because of that, I am always open to His input. There is an old saying attributed to the French novelist Andre Gide that I love and refer to often. "Art is a collaboration between God and the artist. The less the artist does, the better."

Truer words have never been spoken!

God's Response

Gwendolyn (Jac) Stukely

I know the plans I have for you, plans for you to prosper, plans to give you hope and a future.
- Jeremiah 29:11

For about a year before *Let There Be Light,* I was praying and talking to God about wanting to design costumes for a faith-based film. "God, please bring me a project with meaning that honors You."

I had been costume designing films, TV shows, commercial shoots, and other projects, but I was in a season of discontent. My projects were fun, and I enjoyed the creativity required to conceive the fashion expression for a movie, but for some reason, I had a nagging need to work on a project that delivered a message of hope or promoted an underlying sense of the eternal. I wanted to contribute to a project that sought to inspire, something with more meaning than your run-of-the-mill entertainment, as fun as that is.

Cut to a year from this initial place of dissatisfaction. I received a call out of the blue from a friend who asked me if I was available to design a feature film that she was going to be working on.

Now, whenever I get a job offer, my first question is always, "What's it about?" and so I asked that right off the bat.

My friend answered in her typical casual style, "Well, it's one of those faith-based films."

At that moment, I knew—I just knew—God had not only heard my prayers, but He answered them as well.

The script arrived, and I fell into my concept for these characters immediately. I prayed that God would be with me, guide me, and give me the wisdom throughout this visual process. I asked God to show me these characters and how to dress them before the costume fittings. (Trust is something I diligently work on.)

I desired for the film to be an extension of my faith, meaning fabrics, cut, color, the way I see clothing, etc. and I also wanted it to resonate differently than most other faith-based films. As a costume designer, I experience most faith-based films with some disappointment. They often depict characters with a sense of dressing old-fashioned or too goody-two-shoes. I did that for some characters, but I wanted the edginess that God gave me to come across for the other characters. That's real life, and that's who I am.

One morning during the shoot, I prayed to God and asked him to bless me that day for my fitting with Daniel Roebuck. The schedule was tight, and I wouldn't have time to re-shop his clothes, so I just had to get it right immediately—no small task! I got on my knees, and I prayed hard that everything that I had brought to this fitting would be well-received. The actor typically has the final say on what he wears, so my ideas needed to resonate with him, and the clothes had to fit well for me to pull this off. I almost held my breath as we started the fitting. I had no more time, and I was stressed. This is where that trust issue is so difficult for me, so my anxiety ruled.

Well, we started the fitting, and all the suits fit him *perfectly*! What are the chances of that happening? I'll tell you: slim to none. As he regarded himself in the mirror, Daniel paused and declared, "I didn't have a firm grasp on this character until today, seeing what you put together. I could have gone a myriad of different ways with him, but it is now clear to me who I am going to become." When we had finished, he said, "In all my years, I have never had a costume fitting that was this successful." It wasn't me, though. I knew God's hand was all over the costume department.

I had prayed, "God, I want you to be proud of this film and with the work that I'm doing." He answered my prayers.

The story of my life is wrought with turmoil and pain. There is no reason for me to share in detail here, but suffice it to say that God has done so much for me, I could fill another book!

That He brought me this film and allowed me to serve Him in this small way, doing what I love where I find fulfillment, is an incredible blessing. I'm tremendously grateful and proud to have been a part of this film.

The verse at the beginning of this chapter is one of three I keep with me at all times. I have them on a small, yellowed laminated card that I carry in my bag on set and in my purse. Once, my card became too mutilated from wear that I needed to replace it. I toyed with changing the verses—the Bible is full of so many good ones— but the comfort these provide cannot be overstated, and so, I remade the card exactly as it had been. These three strong phrases give me hope, strength, and peace, and in my business, those are three commodities in short supply. My other two favorite guiding verses are:

I can do all things through Christ who strengthens me.
– Philippians 4:13

If God is for us, who can be against us?
– Romans 8:31

Entertaining, family-friendly, faith-based films are essential because they search each of us down to our core. They plant seeds— seeds of forgiveness, seeds of renewal, seeds of peace within us. And sometimes, like with *Let There Be Light,* they can even cause us to dig deep into what we believe and why.

Life will challenge you. It's better to be prepared with a solid, unwavering answer. I'm so grateful that I know what mine is.

Infinite Hope

By Olivia Fox

Never give up infinite hope.
– Rev. Dr. Martin Luther King

It was early July of 2016. I was enjoying a mug of hot chamomile tea in the warm shade of an old oak tree with my dear friend Bailey, trying to swallow my feelings of discouragement and despondency. My career seemed derailed, and my prospects were dwindling.

"Everything changes all the time. What you are experiencing right now will shift, as sure as the leaves fall in the autumn, Liv," Bailey said, encouragingly.

My phone rang. My new manager briefly described a movie audition. Vanessa, a Russian supermodel in her early twenties, was the love interest of the star, Kevin Sorbo, who was also directing. I was stunned—and thrilled! I'd spent much of my formative years watching Kevin Sorbo on television in one of my favorite shows, *Hercules: The Legendary Journeys*. Now I had an opportunity to work with him.

It seemed more like a fantasy than a real answer to a prayer.

In 2008, my career had been off to a great start. I had just appeared on a network television show and had done a few impressive campaigns as a model. I reveled in my newfound success while I planned a ski vacation to celebrate my twenty-first birthday.

Then I noticed a little pain in my leg and saw the doctor about it, thinking it was nothing but a nuisance. Overnight and with no warning, I went from dreaming of magazine covers and thespian awards to the nightmare of being a young cancer patient facing a grim future.

A nine-inch-long malignant tumor encircled my right femur. They diagnosed a rare, aggressive, osteosarcoma—bone cancer—and immediately prescribed the first of sixty rounds of chemotherapy.

My career and my promising future dissolved in a cytotoxic solution.

After thirty rounds of fierce, debilitating chemo, I underwent my first operation. A titanium implant replaced most of my femur, part of my knee, and extended deep into my shin. I literally became a three-million-dollar woman (without the TV show.)

Post-surgery, I endured weeks of painful physical therapy and another thirty rounds of incapacitating chemo. Nausea, vomiting, dizziness, weakness—I had every side effect known to mankind, and though my body showed no further signs of cancer, I was hairless, depressed, and in constant, biting pain. I remember an acquaintance commenting that shaving my head was a bold fashion choice. Little did she know.

Within the year, I underwent another invasive and complicated surgery on my knee to alleviate some of the pain, to no avail. Nothing helped—not pain medication, physical therapy, acupuncture, chiropractic treatment, or any of the myriad other protocols I tried.

Though my hair grew back, years later, I was still limping badly and spending much of my time in a wheelchair. The x-rays didn't show it, but the implant had failed to fuse with my bone, and, consequently, every step I took caused excruciating pain.

I hit rock bottom. My perceived options narrowed. I even prayed for death—anything to escape the intense, incessant pain.

Finally, after seeing a dozen other impotent specialists, I met with the world's leading orthopedic surgeon for my type of cancer in New York. We decided to replace my deficient prosthesis with a new technology that he had recently developed.

To my complete amazement, immediately after surgery, I felt relief! Pain was still present, but it wasn't like the previous piercing agony. And though the surgeries left me with a long, shriveled scar that slithered up my leg, after some difficult physical therapy, I could walk.

But could I still work? I signed with new management after losing almost a decade of my life. I fretted. Was it too late to begin again?

As I read the details of the audition for *Let There Be Light*, trepidation and insecurity kicked in. I'd never done a foreign accent on film, and the meeting with the casting directors was the next morning. I didn't think I could pull this off on such short notice and started talking myself out of going to the audition.

Luckily, my best friend was with me. She always inspires me to be my best. The first time we met, I was speaking about myself in a very self-deprecating way, with a "victim" attitude.

She admonished me, "Stop it, Olivia." Instead of allowing me to wallow in negativity, or worse, joining me there, she encouraged me to focus on the positive, live in appreciation for my blessings, and look for the synchronicities in life. She helped me understand that the role of Vanessa was actually meant for me: one of my grandfathers was Russian, I can do a Russian accent with ease, and I had been modeling since the age of fourteen. The fact that I had long adored watching *Hercules* was the clincher.

I conquered my fears and started studying. I went over my lines a hundred times. My good friend accompanied me to the audition for support, but it almost wasn't necessary.

The casting directors greeted me warmly. That was a change of pace! They were so kind and patient, making me feel as if they wanted this to work out for me. I left the audition with a feeling of acceptance, excited about my prospects for the first time in a long time.

Days later, I got a call that I was on hold for this incredible role. This was the affirmation I had been seeking. After a few more days, they booked me! I felt hugged and uplifted.

From the beginning, Gwendolyn Jac, the costumer, was in my corner. I confessed to her that some of the clothes made me feel self-conscious. I was worried that my scar would show and anxious to play my villainess as multi-dimensional. We finally found an eye-catching, elegant dress that Jac assured me would fit the bill.

When I arrived on set in Alabama, I still had some apprehension about working long hours with the pain in my leg and the long scar that began at my knee and snaked its way up my thigh, but the positivity I felt on the set buoyed me. Every person on the crew was friendlier than the previous one. One of the other actresses confessed to me the challenging illness she had faced, and we became very close. I was relieved that I could be my authentic self with these people, and though I was still nervous about meeting my girlhood hero, Kevin Sorbo treated me like family.

Sam came into the trailer to meet me and talk about the script and the wardrobe, and I knew I had to be honest with her about my leg. I had auditioned in a long gown, but my wardrobe was a short dress, and I dreaded a big reaction about the visible damage on my thigh. As co-writer, producer, and co-star, in many ways, this was Sam's baby. My lingering insecurity made my voice tremble as I told her my story and gingerly showed her the scar.

Sam looked at my leg, then looked in my eyes and smiled. She said that she saw nothing there; all that she saw was perfection. At that moment, I wanted to cry and hug her in gratitude. Sam's warmth and inclusiveness astonished me and gave me confidence.

Though I've never been a particularly religious person, in that moment, I felt God reaching out to me. The divine energy that drew the talented and loving people to this project is beyond words.

I've learned that adversity is part of life. But the more positive people we surround ourselves with, like the people in this film, the more positivity we experience. When I was depressed and despondent, I wasn't taking risks or making the most of life. I needed my inspiring friend to guide me back to a state of optimism, and that led to opportunity.

I am so proud to have been involved in this production. The hope that I've gleaned from this experience continues to carry me forward. My advice to anyone experiencing difficulties or obstacles is to refuse to give up hope. Though I spend much of my time in and out of doctor's offices seeking a solution for my constant pain, and perhaps always will, I recognize, respect, and offer thanks to the people in my life who inspire me to get up and make the best of every day and situation.

Community and compassion are the best medicines.

Shine the Light

Damon Elliot

When my manager called me about the movie *Let There Be Light,* I thought to myself, *Hmm, I wonder direction what God is moving me towards.* I had not yet seen *God's Not Dead,* and faith-based movies were a bit out of my norm workwise. However, being a Christian, the proposal to work on one seemed more like a message than just a routine job offer.

Patrick, likely misreading my hesitation, sent me the script, saying, "Just read it, and let me know what you think. But don't take too long. These guys are anxious to figure this thing out musically, and I'm convinced you'd be great for this."

Well, let me tell you, from page one, I was hooked! I could relate so much to this story. It wasn't because I'm an atheist—I'm anything but—it was the idea about giving up hope. I've been there, at a complete loss of hope, lacking any ability to see through the ominous clouds that block God's comforting rays of sunlight.

When the script progressed into that message of reaching for the unconditional love only God can give, my head began to nod. *Been there, done that,* as they say.

I forwarded it to my mom, Dionne Warwick, who also read it with an appreciation that went beyond the words on the page. We drafted her to sing the theme song and be in the movie because she was the perfect person! Mom is why my faith is as strong as it is today.

Once the project moved into post, the time after principal photography is finished and the editor and director are piecing together all the moving parts of the film, and it was time to choose the musical cues and lay down song tracks, I scheduled a meeting with the team for our initial work-through for music cues.

That's when catastrophe hit. I was working out—I'm in pretty good shape, and my wife is a fitness instructor, so my whole household keeps pretty healthy—but all of a sudden, I started feeling these pains down my arm. I slowed up on the machine, thinking *what the heck?* Maybe there was a little voice inside me that knew what was happening, but my denial kicked in pretty strongly, shouting that little voice into submission. I tried a few more paces on the equipment, and I started to have trouble breathing. *Uh, oh.*

I called my wife and said, simply, "I think I need you to take me to the hospital."

I have a little girl who is my joy. I was so worried that I might not *make it. What would happen to her without me?* I sent a prayer up to God to help me through whatever storm was coming my way.

I was, in fact, having a major heart attack, and it's kind of a miracle that I survived. Even my doctors were in awe of my recovery, which was faster than they predicted.

I believe that my involvement in this film truly helped save my life because I have found new hope and used that as a tool while lying in the recovery room after receiving two stents.

The day after my release from the hospital, I recorded the demo for the title song for this beautiful film entitled *Let There Be Light*. I was full of happy tears: tears of life, tears of light. I cannot wait for the world to feel the hope I feel from being a part of this movement. This film, more than any other project I've worked on in the past, expresses my light, my hope, and my faith.

Worth It

Kevin

I was on a plane, heading back from Brisbane, Australia, to Los Angeles—home. This was a long haul: thirteen hours trapped on the plane. And while I normally have plenty to do on any plane ride, somehow, the daunting prospect of that entire half-day stymied me. I felt exhausted, even before we reached our cruising altitude.

Maybe it was because this trip had been a working vacation. Maybe it was because I missed home. I travel too much, though I do love to travel. I guess it's a love/hate relationship. My wanderlust invigorates and enervates me simultaneously. Some people drink coffee, and some people are workaholics. I crave new horizons. They beckon to me like the sirens' call to Odysseus, but I hear them and answer back. And Sam, ever the faithful Penelope, awaits my triumphant return.

I started bringing my children with me on some of my trips when my oldest was about seven. Sam and I, as part of our home education strategy, realized not only the importance to the father-child bond and the potential for fun, but that travel was educational, and the ability to travel well was something to be cultivated.

As international models in our previous careers, Sam and I had constantly been on the move, so we both learned the art of voyaging. We also recognized that the ability to journey well—

packing appropriately, finding the way without losing confidence, and appreciating strangers by sometimes relying on them for information—is an acquired skill. Managing personal belongings through crowded airports, handling tickets and hotels, organizing a changing schedule on the go, enjoying new foods and different cultures, all are learned behaviors that we aspired for our children to grasp. Not least of all our reasons for desiring to raise good travelers is that we both believe, because we've made the comparisons ourselves and experienced foreign lands, that our nation is amazing. We want our children to have an intrinsic gratitude for their homeland, something that seems more and more eroded with each generation.

I had been asked to travel to Australia for a public appearance and instantly recognized the opportunity this presented for my boys. Braeden and Shane had been very enthusiastic about joining me when I approached them with the idea. Though Shane is more reluctant to travel because he suffers homesickness more than any other family member, the chance to see Australia with me presented too much of a temptation to resist. (This might be because I've always had a soft spot for the land down under, and the kids know this.)

My appearance was only a part of our trip, and I had ample time to go exploring with the boys. We hiked. We surfed at the beach. We saw wallabies and kangaroos close-up. We held all kinds of critters like snakes, lizards, and even koalas. We had a stupendous time that the boys and I will not soon forget.

Now, on the plane ride home, after an exciting, eventful excursion, I tried to sleep. Unfortunately, even in my own bed I'm not a good sleeper, and the plane didn't relax me either. Since my days on *Hercules*, and even before, I would struggle to get more than five hours a night. Maybe it was the paper route growing up, or just my dad's farm-life work ethic, trained into me from a young age, but when the sun rises, my feet hit the floor. Having three strokes also didn't help my brain learn to relax better, and so there seems to be a fight in my head where my brain maybe *wants* to sleep, but concurrently *craves* a sense of accomplishment, of doing something meaningful—it craves work. I work hard and I play hard, and that's just who I am.

So, it was a battle in my brain on the plane ride back home, where I was dead tired, but my mind restlessly raced with thoughts about getting back and working on the various projects I had going, all at different stages. Into this miasma of thought, the captain's voice broke over the tinny, squawky speakers. Why are the speakers on airplanes so bad? He announced something about Los Angeles, flight time, some other standard (I hoped) muffled mumbo-jumbo that is typically so hard to understand, and, yes, I heard the words, "breakfast will be served."

That tidbit of information made me pop up from my premiere economy seat to freshen up before the big rush. It felt good to stretch and move a little. I checked on my boys who were knocked out and sleeping like rocks. *Wait a minute*, I mused, *do rocks sleep?* Wow, I reflected, I really am tired! For perhaps the thirtieth time this flight alone, I envied their ability to just crash out like that. They had been sleeping for 9-10 hours by this time, little bastards! I also envied their youth, come to think of it. What's that phrase? *Youth is wasted on the young.*

I walked forward in the plane to the closest washrooms, approaching those intimidating curtains that separate the lower-grade seats from the premium ones. The small sign on the door said "Occupied" in glowing red.

The purser, Richard according to his name badge, was in the galley preparing his station with our breakfast items. In his mid-fifties, he boasted a slight but athletic build, and his movements were a study in fluidity and precision. Maybe because I didn't really sleep, I felt hungrier than I would otherwise be. The smell was more tantalizing than appearances, but boredom and sleep deprivation made it all seem fantastic. *Bacon is named so because it was a cross between "beckon" and "beacon."* In my half-dozing insomniac brain, I'm sure that's really meaningful.

Richard looked up at me and then back down at his bacon work. Then he looked up again. And again. And yet again. Oh, yes, even though I was looking only at the bacon, I could feel his gaze.

I am used to the double-takes people perform when they see me in a mall, grocery store, airports, or on sidewalks. *Hercules* was a very popular show, and *Andromeda* was no slouch, either. Of course, my successful movies only added to the recognition factor. It's funny to see some people's reactions, especially in those places when they are shocked at such an appearance. Airports and hotels are one thing. People travel. But at the bank, a Home Depot, or Chick-fil-A, the shocked faces can be quite entertaining. I've been told more than once that I look like "that guy who plays Hercules on TV."

"You mean Kevin Sorbo? Yeah. I get that *a lot!*" I just mess with them a bit, sometimes. Can you blame me? Typically, people are very complimentary, respectful, and kind. If they're fans, it's not just because they enjoy watching me perform, but because of the values my shows promote. Most of my projects embrace my values, and that comes across to the viewers. They appreciate what I stand for. Sure, they want a photo, but, more importantly, many just want to shake my hand. I was in a Walmart in Shreveport, Louisiana, once, and a big ol' boy walked up to me, scrutinized me, and then said, "You're that Hercules fella, aren't 'cha?"

I said I was.

"Whatcha doin' in Walmart?" He looked totally astounded.

I laughed. "Well, I needed some provisions..."

"But in Shreveport? This here's the armpit of America!"

Let me just say, I don't agree with his assessment of Shreveport. I spent several weeks there with the family, and despite having to suspend shooting at one point due to a tornado that took out the town's clock tower, we all really enjoyed it.

On the plane, the flight attendant Richard finally commits. He smiles at me, friendly, and says, "You're Kevin Sorbo."

"Guilty," I reply.

"Well, sir. I really enjoy your movies." The lavatory occupant exits and squeezes by me. I thank Richard while indicating my desperate need for the facilities! He smiles and nods, as I pass him to get to the toilet before the wakeup rush from the other passengers that will surely follow soon. I brush my teeth and do my dripping-hands-through-my-hair habit that has been with me since my Jackson Browne haircut days when I was a teen. Now I am truly refreshed and awake.

When I come back out past the galley, Richard stops me again ,and I notice a pain in his eyes that makes me step back.

"When I was in the States a little while ago, I went to see *Let There Be Light*," he confides. "I have to thank you for that. That movie, it gave me hope."

"Well, thank you for saying so. In what way do you mean, hope?" I had to ask. His eyes begged me to. In fact, the look on his face spoke volumes, and although our typical response to someone else's emotion is to run away, sensing the profundity of his pain, I knew I had a duty to allow him to express himself.

His eyes welled with tears as he related the story of his young daughter who had committed suicide six months prior at the tender age of seventeen. She had hung herself in her bedroom. Richard walked into her room to announce dinner, and discovered her body, lifeless. He took her body down, laid her on her bed and sat with her, reminiscing through the years of her short life in his mind

Some philosopher said that murder is killing an individual, but suicide is killing the whole world. For a seventeen-year-old to want to do that indicates an intense amount of either anger or agony or both. I've been to the edge where I have glimpsed the isolation of that kind of struggle. I pray, often, for those who battle with it. I pray they find the strength they need to win. I know that strength comes not from within, but from God.

I asked Richard if he was a Christian. He replied that he was spiritual and believed there was something out there. Then he told me how one night he prayed. He wanted her to leave him a sign. Any kind of sign that would let him know she was alright, that she wasn't hurting anymore. Soon after that, one evening in his living room, he sat down in his favorite chair and smelled his daughter's fragrance. He ran to tell his wife and brought her into the room to sit in the chair, but she couldn't smell anything. He was tremendously moved by the fragrance. With it, he understood that he had been given his "message," and he knew it was from his daughter. Wherever she was, she was okay, and he knew it.

I asked him in what way our movie gave him hope.

He replied it was the scene where my character nearly dies for a few minutes and sees the vision of his eight year old son, who tells him that it is not his time, saying, "Daddy, let there be light." That moment in the movie gave him the hope that one day he would hug his daughter again.

I replied that the entire book of the Bible is built on that one word. Christ came to give us all *hope.*

He nodded and smiled, as he recomposed himself. He had work to do, after all.

For him to share his very private and personal, tragic story touched me deeply. I thanked him for honoring me and the *Light* team, and we parted with a handshake.

When the boys and I returned home, I told Sam the story. Honestly, I had a hard time getting it out before choking up myself. It was a wonderful reminder as to why I love doing the movies I have been filming. Being able to tell stories that bring comfort and hope makes it all worthwhile.

Searching

Sam

What else does this craving, and this helplessness, proclaim but that there was once in man a true happiness, of which all that now remains is the empty print and trace? This he tries in vain to fill with everything around him, seeking in things that are not there the help he cannot find in those that are, though none can help, since this infinite abyss can be filled only with an infinite and immutable object; in other words by God himself.

- Blaise Pascal, *Pensées* VII(425)[12]

We all search for something. In his 1670 book in defense of the Christian faith, writer, mathematician, philosopher, inventor, and Catholic theologian, Blaise Pascal wrote about this search as a quest to fill a void within. Since then, this idea has morphed into the concept of a God-shaped hole within each individual. In other words, only God can fill that particular emptiness that exists inside everyone, although many people experiment with the material

---

12 http://christianity.stackexchange.com/questions/2746/where-does-the-concept-of-a-god-shaped-hole-originate

things of this world, be it food, alcohol, pornography, or money. While the concept itself isn't Biblical, it can certainly be supported Biblically.

Eventually we realize, through perhaps no intentional efforts of our own, that life comes down to only one thing: relationship. We are gregarious, social animals.

"Teacher, which is the greatest commandment in the Law?" Jesus replied: "'Love the Lord your God with all your heart and with all your soul and with all your mind.' This is the first and greatest commandment. And the second is like it: 'Love your neighbor as yourself.' All the Law and the Prophets hang on these two commandments."

Matthew 22:36-40 New International Version (NIV)

Is there any doubt that God created man to love, more than anything else? If a life is built on things of man—money, power, homes, jobs and vacations—what is left at the end but memories? Memories of material possessions or past accomplishments are impermanent. Memories necessarily denote the past. They are imperfect placeholders reinforcing in bas-relief how lifeless and void they really are. In essence, they are cold, melancholy, and rife with loss, while personal fellowship is warm, love-filled, and overflowing with hope. Relationships are not temporal but spiritual.

Some people might challenge my assertion that hugs are full of hope, but think about it. An embrace is an acknowledgement that the human is present and accepted. Acceptance is the hole in ourselves we seek to fill—from the time we are small children and we go off to school and face the judgment of other little ones, when we go to college and face the peer pressure to conform, and as we seek approval from our bosses, our spouses, and even our children.

It's true, some people succumb to their great desire for approval and appreciation more easily or readily than others, indicating that the void inside them is more profound or challenging than for other people. Perhaps it isn't the size of the emptiness, but the intensity with which it is felt that differentiates the behavior of those who readily conform for the approval of others from those who stand back, waiting for some proof of return on investment. It is the profundity of that gaping blankness, drawn down within an individual, which originally derives from the experiences he has outside it but associated with it: his relation to other human beings. His encounters with loving and being loved by others inevitably determine his passion to identify and address this "God-shaped hole."

For this reason, many people may never experience a particular desire for completion, though I would argue it still exists, as Pascal did. Those are the unfortunate ones who go blissfully ignorant into their old age, never understanding nor experiencing the greatest love story of their lives.

For the majority who struggle to find some solace, who declare a hunger for attention and love despite any self-generated confidence, composure, and conviction, there is a prescription: God's love.

The hole is filled in community with God, at local churches and within the pages of the greatest best seller, the most excellent self-help book out there. Because the void is not simply shaped like God but defined by Him. No imposter, either self-generated or society-approved, will ever fit well enough to seal the fissures generated in the absence of God's life-sustaining, infinite love.

I once spoke with a young woman who was a reformed and remade madame. She had been groomed into sex-trafficking by a man who alternately built her up and tore her down. "You are gorgeous, strong, and mine," he would tell her on a good day. The next day he might grab her by the hair and crack her head against the wall, screaming profanities and declaring, "You're a piece of sh*t! You're *nothing* without me!"

After the storm passed, he would come back to her, gently, protesting that it was her beauty or his intense love for her that made him so jealous. He became her pimp by nurturing in her a need for his approval, his love, and then creatively satisfying or denying her.

One day, authorities put the pimp in prison on drug charges. At that point, the now-reformed madam knew the business quite well. She started a brothel in his absence, running as many as five hundred women who sold themselves in the sex trade. For years, she insisted she was an independent, self-sufficient businesswoman and convinced many of the girls working for her that they, too, were strong females in charge of their lives (drug use and depression notwithstanding).

This woman eventually found her way out of the swamp of the sex trade when she suffered a breakdown and heard what she describes as "Jesus's voice." That profound transformation happened within her, overnight. The following day she shut down her business, encouraged by a newfound faith and a dedication to the one true God. I'm not making this stuff up. She told me she had no idea how she would survive financially, but she was so convicted by that *voice*, that she just put her trust in God and closed shop.

And God provided.

After being out of the business for a while, she realized through prayer that she was the perfect person to go back in and help save other young women from utterly destroying their lives.

The statistics don't lie. A whopping eighty-five percent of prostitutes and their clients say they were victims of sexual abuse in their childhood, and seventy percent experienced incest.[13] These are examples of betrayal on the physical level as well as the emotional one. The devaluation of these victims seemingly leads them to search out an antidote to their spiritual pain. Being 'in control' of their bodies may be the most convenient answer, although it is, in a sense, "the hair of the dog that bit them." It is the ruse that keeps them engaged without addressing the deep spiritual need for succor.

13

http://www.rapeis.org/activism/prostitution/prostitutionfacts.html

The reformed madam started an organization dedicated to shepherding and sheltering young women out of the sex trade. She said to me, "Sam, I've never seen a young woman escape successfully without Jesus Christ. If they don't discover the love of our Savior, which profoundly transforms, the rate of recidivism is *one hundred percent*."

Angola Prison earned the reputation of being the most dangerous prison in America. Then Burl Cain instituted inmate Bible studies and Angola experienced a drop in institutional violence. He established seminaries within the walls of the prison and the murder rate went down to zero.

Reportedly, Dennis Prager toured the facility in 2008. After seeing the work that the study of God's Word had accomplished, he was asked for his thoughts. He answered that he was angry.

In disbelief, the interviewer asked him to elaborate, so he did, remarking that he had seen the cure for cancer, but because there was a moral element to it, society at large rejected it. Burl Cain believed that education was the way to offer even life-long convicts the opportunity to live a meaningful life and that we should be instructing in morality before young men become convicts, instead of treating the disease of sin *post facto*.

Human desire for love is nearly insatiable. It's an intense spiritual itch that requires something equally ethereal for relief. It cannot be satisfied with a material response, however temporarily satisfying the worldly answer might be. A new car is only new for a few days. A new adventure may be stimulating, but merely for a limited time. The most powerful job can never satisfy our innately human desire for love—for companionship. But the material trappings of worldly success temp and taunt us, for we are very much physical creatures.

Humans are also gregarious creatures. That ought to tell you something. We crave relationship. Lacking the palliating cream to salve and soften this significant longing for love, a human being will turn to a terrestrial, temporary response instead. It is all too easy to pretend that our yearnings are purely material and can be satisfied by human things, but the evidence proves otherwise.

I had chosen to study biomedical engineering at Duke University for my higher education. I struggled mightily with test-taking and anxiety, having grown up terrified I wouldn't be able to provide for myself. I had everything riding on my grades and found myself working on an ulcer my sophomore year. So, I took some time off, and started a modeling career, at which I excelled. Modeling internationally earned a lot of money—more than "enough," I figured. I had "arrived," in the sense that I had my career and had proven my ability to self-sustain. I began wondering, "Is this *it*? Is *this* all there is to life? You work, you make money, you have some fun, you die?" I embarked on a journey to find a reason for my life—a reason for anyone to keep living, in a sense.

To do so, I exercised my determined, mathematical mind. I lauded truth and logic above all, so I started with an examination of books about life. I began by buying books on near-death experiences. Shirley MacLaine led me to everything from astrology to Zoroastrianism. I'll be honest, I never dipped too deeply into that special Kool-Aid, but I read voraciously, and because I was traveling nearly constantly, often working with strangers, spending only a few days in any one place, I appreciated airplanes and airports, hotels, and car rides as opportunities to read. I wasn't a recluse, but traveling alone, I had a lot of time on my hands. The culmination of all my research was quite simple: I confirmed that there is order in the universe that can only result from an order-creator, because the natural state of things in this world is decay into chaos.

That order-bringer is, of course, God. I mean, you can call Him anything you want, and some people do: spirit, force, being… but I tend not to beat around the bush, and God was as good a name as any.

So, if God created me, to what end? To live and then die, is that all? It simply makes no sense. In the Old Testament, God's first four commandments involve humanity's relationship with Him. God created us to love Him, because He loved us first, and still does. And because we are created for this purpose, we can only satisfy our craving for love by loving God as He prescribed for us.

That's how we fill that God-shaped hole inside: with our own faith and relationship with God.

Love

Kevin

Have you ever noticed that love can be satisfied, but hatred cannot?

We quench our love in the presence of the one we love, by doing loving things, even just by thinking about love. We wallow in love's glow and find peace in having our adoring feelings reciprocated or simply reflected upon us.

Hatred, however, is another story. Hatred tends to grow like a cancer if we allow it free reign. It festers like an open sore, while throbbing and aching inside. Attempts to assuage it by exacting revenge or otherwise punishing the offending party only feeds it like gasoline on a fire. It grows more spiteful and irritated, like a boil on the brain. There are no moments of peace for the hateful who indulge such consuming emotions. Hatred can become a full-time occupation, and often, the hater feels powerless to limit it. He becomes so entrenched in his personal war he fails to recognize the greater battle.

They say the opposite of love is not hatred, but indifference. That is because love is an intense emotion, and its reverse would be a complete lack of feeling, i.e. not caring a whit. Hatred is full of passion, like love, but it's misplaced rage. It's on the emotional scale, and, like any emotion, it affects the person feeling it more intimately than it ultimately affects its object.

It's no secret that when I was in high school, I was jock. I played football, basketball, baseball, and golf. I would get home after football practice and shoot hoops for a couple of hours. Frankly, it's a wonder I got any schoolwork done, but I managed to eke out some decent grades between games.

People know that football is a contact sport, and that it takes an assertive attitude to be successful. Less recognized, perhaps, is basketball's evolution into more of a contact sport, with increasing aggression happening on the courts, bumping and shoving, than how the game was originally designed. Sure, they can always call a foul, but with so much of this behavior happening, well, they simply can't, or won't, call every foul, and with players dedicated to the 'win,' there's going to be some contact.

When I was playing football and basketball, I developed a healthy competitive approach, and I must admit I cultivated a tough aggressive attitude. It was important, going into a game, to develop a strong will to win. I nurtured those intense emotions of desire and hostility, under control, to acquire a superior position for the win. Football, for me, was a series of battles every time I took the field. I played much of the entire game, for both offense and defense. It pitted me in a match of strength, wits, and sheer determination, against the player opposite me. There are head games between the players, trash talk that you can hear now that they mic players. You try to psych out your opponents on the field, get inside their heads, anticipate their next moves. Basketball was similarly a test of will and cunning. You attack your adversary in ways that the regulations allow, but aggression rules the day.

My athleticism, always informed by the fighting spirit I developed during my time on the field or on the court, remained a part of me, even after college. When I started my acting career in Los Angeles, I joined three different basketball leagues to keep up my game. Then, shooting *Hercules,* of course my days were filled with stunts, fight scenes, and a lot of time in the gym. When my strokes broadsided me during season five of the show, my intensity as an athlete served to propel my hard-fought, prolonged recovery.

While aggression is an integral part of my personal definition of being a man, I've learned also the importance of keeping it at bay. I use it as a tool, but I don't allow it to control me. It's a constant companion, like the callouses on the palms of my hands. It's in the road dust I've accumulated on my travels through life, but I find myself more likely to be brushing it off rather than rolling in it. I've studied the deleterious effects of the anger and aggression that had served me so well for so long, and they are many. Now, I afford them less opportunity to settle on me.

There's a reason the two commandments Jesus intoned both begin with loving. Love is the emotion that offers the soul harmony and fulfillment. There is a reason the Lord's Prayer insists on forgiveness of others, not to *earn* our own forgiveness, but to emulate God, who will "forgive us our trespasses *as* we forgive those who trespass against us." Forgiveness is often equated with letting go. Releasing anger allows the soul to be calmed and to offer love. Harboring bitterness blocks the soul and infects any love offering.

My journey into a deeper faith was distracted by rage and resentment. I was battling a beleaguered and broken brain that itself was unsuccessfully struggling to maintain a balance of emotion. I had heard that voice, solemn and deliberate, whispering, "Don't let him crack your neck," but I had failed to pay attention. I was angry at God, at the unfairness of the world, at the doctors who had failed to complete their tasks. But most of all, I was angry at myself.

But God had faith in me, and He had a plan to bring me close, with my faith in Him. He led me to the brink. He permitted me to peer over the precipice and ponder His purpose for me. Teetering on the edge of that void, I discovered my strength and rediscovered my faith.

Pragmatism

Sam

"I just think, I'm totally fine with them removing either the Pledge of Allegiance or just the words 'under God' from the pledge, if they choose. I think it's dangerous to try to force children to believe in God, especially if it goes against their parents' wishes..."

I was standing in my kitchen with Annette discussing, among other things, the role of religion in the schools. The sun shone outside, and I was just cleaning up after our hummus and carrots. The kids were in the backyard playing, so I had been keeping one eye on them, but at this proclamation, I turned to my dear friend. The diminutive blond was obviously of the opinion that religion had no place in schools. She didn't believe in God at all, in fact. That she should think this way should not have surprised me, but I struggled for a moment. How to address her with a reasonable but persuasive response? And at what cost?

Friendships are hard to come by, after all. It's seldom that we really 'hit it off' with someone, enough to forge a long-standing, deeply committed relationship, and Annette and I were on our way to having that, despite our differences in beliefs. I've always enjoyed knowing people with differing opinions because I've found that when everyone agrees, you soon run out of things to talk about. I recognize that, sometimes, I can seem too harsh in my strong opinions, even strident, and so I checked myself. I had only broached the subject based on an article I had read, so it wasn't even going to affect us locally. I thought for another moment before speaking.

"I guess that makes sense. I just wonder about it because how will the children learn right from wrong?"

Annette smiled. This is why I was drawn to her. She didn't take things personally. Aristotle said the mark of an educated mind was the ability to entertain a thought without accepting it. Robert Frost agreed, saying "Education is the ability to listen to almost anything without losing your temper or your self-confidence."

Annette answered, "I did, didn't I? You weren't raised in the church, either, right? We don't need the church to teach us what's right. No one likes to be force-fed religion."

"True enough. But I have one little problem, then."

"Oh, do tell!" She pursed her lips as if savoring the debate. "But let's have another cup of tea. I've got no place else to go for another half-hour, if that's okay with you."

"Of course, stay! Okay, so, before I go into that, where did you learn your morals? You don't lie, cheat, steal, etcetera, right? So, how did you turn out that way?"

"My mother raised me right." Another charming smile.

"So, it was just your mom who taught you those things? What about your dad?" The kettle boiled in the background, and I snatched up two tea bags from their flimsy box to put in our mugs.

"Yeah, him, too. He was a strong disciplinarian, as well. So, if my sister or I messed up, he came down hard on us. Although, to his credit, the punishment almost always fit the crime. The one time he lost his temper and swatted my behind with a brush, well, that was just that one time."

"Why do you suppose it was important to them for you to have good morals?" I poured the water and brought the tea over from the counter so we could both sit at the kitchen table. Igwet, my seven-pound black Brussels Griffon, followed us over, unwilling to be left out of the conversation it seemed.

"Well, they believed in doing the right thing. You know, the church taught them that. But they seldom took us to church. I guess it's just the way they were raised." Annette seemed almost to ask.

I'd gone back to fetch the honey and now I took my seat opposite her. "Annette, we have a social contract in our culture that requires morals and honesty—observing that what is not yours you may not take by force, that kind of thing. Your parents were doing what they saw as right, because of that. I like to call it 'moral capital.' And they likely inherited it from their parents, and so on back, but it all started with the Church and the Bible."

She stared at me. "I just know what's right, is all. I know right from wrong. It's that simple."

"Hmmm," I interjected, skeptically. "That's a pretty shaky definition of right and wrong. I'm just sayin'. Don't get me wrong. I know you well enough to have experienced your desire to do good in the world. I was even the recipient of it when you brought me that big tub of chicken soup a few months back when I was sick. I'm sure you're set, morally, right? I just wonder about all the kids who don't have your parents to teach them right from wrong, you know? Good from evil."

"But you don't need God for that. You certainly don't need the Bible," she lobbed, laughing a little. "I know I don't."

"Yes, you don't. And neither do a lot of people, because of that moral capital thing, thank goodness. But think of this. You're walking down a dark alley, late at night. There's no one around. That is, until a group of large men come out of a door about twenty yards away. You realize quickly you have nowhere to flee. You study them. Are they malicious? Would they harm you? They are a complete unknown, kind of rowdy. You keep walking, slowly, calculating your risks and your options, right? Then you see, above the doorway they exited, a sign that says, *Midnight Bible Study*. Do you relax?"

Annette laughed for real this time. "C'mon... Yeah, I guess I would be a bit more relaxed, but—"

"Annette, there are no buts about it. You know that the Bible teaches peace, the golden rule, love thy neighbor kind of stuff. You know that Christians tend to be, how should I put this, more helpful

244

than hurtful. It's because of the rules for society set up in the Bible that we even have a successful society at all. But never mind that for now, just put it aside. The reason I want the *idea* of God to remain in our classrooms, in our schools, is because although *you* are intrinsically moral and just because of how you were raised, I want other people's children to feel like someone, or something, is watching them—seeing if they are doing good, or doing bad. Someone or at least the idea of a potential someone, keeping them in line or holding them to a higher standard. Wouldn't that be preferable to what we'd have if they removed the very last vestiges of God from our culture, which, I believe, is exactly what they're trying to do?"

Annette shrugged and sipped. "I guess it couldn't hurt," she said. "It is historical, anyway, so, why change it now?"

"Agreed," I countered. "Now, if they had only thought of that when they removed the Bible from schools."

"But that was openly religious! That's what they should have done, because it was like the State dictating a *religion* for the citizens."

"Nope, sorry. That's incorrect. It was the State prescribing proper behavior for the citizens. That's kind of the *job* of the State, in actuality. What do you think laws are, anyway? Every law we have is a moral assertion. Every stop sign testifies to the values of life and personal property." I paused and watched her struggle with what I was saying. "But they didn't simply remove the Bible from our schools. They replaced *Judeo-Christianity* with *irreligion* which is the absence of belief in a higher power. I see that as intrinsically dangerous because it easily devolves into a *whatever's-good-for-me* type of deal. Or worse, it leads to totalitarianism. With nothing to rule that some things are wrong, it's survival of the strongest, and typically, the strong like to reign with absolute power. Let me say that just because you're a good person doesn't mean that anyone else is going to be, naturally. I think that's the great experiment, frankly, whether these United States can survive the loss of our heritage, our founders' religion, the, uhm, threads of the woven fabric of our civilization. Can we endure as a free society even after forfeiting the basis for our very culture?"

She looked at me, shook her head as if that were too profound a question, but she pondered it.

"Or," I continued, "will the strongest take the reins, change the laws to suit themselves, leaving the rest of us to fend for ourselves amidst corruption and the degradation of our value system until the only thing to value becomes proximity to the king? It's weird, because I feel kind of like that's already happening. Some laws apply to some of us, but others get a free pass depending on their affluence or influence, right?"

"Agreed. That's true. But so many of those folks who take advantage call themselves Christians! They are such hypocrites! That's what really irks me with those people."

"Yes, true." I paused. We were diving into rough waters—sensitive subjects. My friend was antagonistic toward the church for reasons dating back to her childhood. She didn't want to hear that religion was a solution. But the facts didn't lie, either. I knew the truth. Wasn't it my responsibility to level with her, even at certain cost? I wrestled with myself. What cost? Our friendship? I had been in this kind of position recently, and I nearly lost a good friend.

"So, what good is religion when people don't observe it for real, you know? There are so many fake and phony Christians out there with their 'holier-than-thou' attitudes looking down their noses at others when they themselves are thieves, adulterers and," she paused, searching, "Fornicators!" At that last word, she cracked up. I laughed, too. It was such an old word and so outdated to be coming out of her mouth.

"Yes," I answered, sipping my tea. I stuck out my pinky for emphasis. "The fornicators are a plenty! And the blasphemers, and liars, and, well, we are all sinners—"

She cut me off. "See? That's what I'm talking about! I don't get the whole, 'everyone's a sinner' blah, blah... when if that's the case, then what good is your religion?"

"An excellent question! My religion holds me to a higher standard and offers me the chance for redemption, telling me that I cannot merit heaven on my own. But through the sacrifice of Christ and my acknowledgement and acceptance of Him, I can receive forgiveness. This is the difference between Christianity and virtually every other religion. Because in other religions, people are trying to earn salvation, but you can't earn it because you're already so flawed. In Christianity, you can receive it, while attempting to be worthy, because the gift of grace makes you want to be worthy, want to at least try. It is through love, not threats or coercion, that people behave."

"Okay." Annette sat for a moment contemplating. Then she got up to clear her tea mug. "So, what am I missing, then? Why are so many in the Church—even church leaders—so dis*grace*ful?"

I laughed. "That was a very nice turn of phrase! Okay, you probably won't like this, but I think it's because the Church has retreated from the culture to the point that you've got young women sitting in abortion facilities while insisting they themselves are Evangelical. You've got self-proclaimed Catholics supporting Planned Parenthood, and the Catholic Church seems to have nothing to say about them, at least publicly. Divorce is rampant, because no Church would dare tell tithing parishioners they shouldn't do something. The irony is that people crave being told what to do! Children certainly need discipline, but even as adults, we seek guidance, and yet the one place that is designed to give the best guidance seems to fall down on the job. It is a failing of the Church, in part of its own free choice and induced in part by society's relegating it to the sidelines." I took the teacups, rinsed them and put them in the dishwasher as Annette checked her phone.

"So, then, what good is it?"

"Annette, I don't do religion because it's good for me. It's good for me because it's true. I do it because it's true, and I do it the best that I can, and I assure you that most of the people out there doing Christianity are doing the best they can at it. It's not easy, frankly, and until you've tried it, you can't possibly know, but once you know, you can't go back."

"Well, what about those guys who were like leaders in the church and just walked away, recently? The one who wrote that book, and the singer or musician or something, right?"

"Yes! Yes! Yes!" I got excited and Annette looked at me, shocked. "I'm sorry, but that's exactly what I was talking about when we began! The problem the Church—big C—has today is this wishy-washiness that has invaded, like a cancer. It's like socialism for the Church, and in fact it has its roots in Marxism—Liberation Theology. So the Marxists actually targeted the South American Church after World War II, and now you have so much of those politics that have seeped in from all sides into the American churches that churches are losing their direction. Then you also have the Johnson Amendment that promised to punish pastors for addressing politics from the pulpit! That scared and subdued pastors into remaining quiet when that was the last thing they should have done! And the fact is, the Johnson amendment has never been enforced or ever prosecuted, but the effect was castration of the Church in the US. Then we took the Bible out of our schools. Who teaches our children morals these days? No one in particular. We just hope they absorb some from the culture and maybe an hour a week of Sunday School. It's a recipe for disaster!"

"Okay, Sam, calm down now!" Annette showed a mischievous glint in her eyes. "You get so passionate about this stuff, but it's why I like you."

"That and my politics."

"Yes, your politics, too."

"But you recognize that politics cannot be separate from religion, because your worldview, which is your religion, informs your politics. If a politician says he won't let his religion influence his policy decisions, he's either a hypocrite or a liar."

"But if he has no religion?"

"No such thing. Irreligion is itself a worldview, a religion. It's actually in the top three."

"What do you mean? Oh, shoot, that's my phone." Her phone had just started buzzing. The ringer was off. She showed it to me. "Lover" showed up—with her husband's photo.

I smiled. She answered and indicated she needed to go, so I grabbed her bag from the table and walked her out while she spoke lovingly to her husband.

By the time we made our way to the doorway, he had hung up. Annette looked at me a smiled her impish smile. "I love that man!"

"I know you do!" I responded, part of our little game. "Think about this, why are you faithful to him?"

"That's easy! Because I love him." She was laughing at me, probably because the question seemed so banal.

"But marriage is a biblical institution, created by God. It's first and foremost a religious conjoining of two people in a covenant before God. But you're not religious, so why do it?"

That stopped her short. She tilted her head, much the way a dog does when he hears an odd noise. "Ah!" She had hit on the solution, she supposed. "Because it's really a *societal* institution, not only biblical! So I'm conforming culturally."

"You are, but first, it's a religious one. And you are conforming to a religious standard because the culture did first. And the culture did because it recognized that the biblical standard is for the good of the people. I'll just leave you with that. The Bible gets it right, a lot. Including on all our moral imperatives. That's all I'm saying."

"Okay, darling. Thanks for the chat. I love our chats!" She hugged me goodbye.

"Yeah," I smiled and sighed. "Me, too."

After she left, I pondered our conversation and realized the dilemma we face in today's culture. We've been sold a lie, that religion is a disposable crutch, a choice, like whether to use sugar or sweetener in your coffee. Choosing sweetener is simply a different choice, and some people choose not to sweeten their coffee at all. All this is a chimera. Religion is not the sweetener or sugar. Religion is the water of life. In fact, Jesus said he was the antidote to thirst itself. And the idea that we've had generations imbued with the assumption that they can do life, that we can have a functional society without a set of accepted morals and standards, or worse—that morals and standards can be set internally, by

Man—well, that is the equivalent of allowing the patients to run the asylum.

I guess we've known that all along, Kevin and me. We just failed to articulate it in so many words. It wasn't until I started really discussing this kind of thing on air and I delved into home education that I understood the profundity of these ideas and the impact they wreak on society in general. The conversation I had just had with Annette was a dialogue America needed to have with herself.

This is predominantly a discussion about faith. When I started the radio show, I was determined to talk about "politics and religion, the only things worth talking about. Religion is who we are and where we're going, and politics is how we get there." We have forgotten that our faith is the whole cloth from which our culture is tailored. Now that we are wearing the suit, we think we can discard the fabric, but then we are just enacting *The Emperor's New Clothes.*

When we uncouple our morals from our Judeo-Christian faith, we are saying, "Here's a good set of rules by which to live," but we're removing the ultimate impetus of enforcement—the reverence for the higher power that devised the entire system. Eliminating God makes the rules themselves seem more or less arbitrary. This gives citizens the impression that the rubric is arbitrary. A majority agreed upon it a long time ago, but ultimately, each individual is his own god, and therefore has the right to ordain his own policies as necessary. *Sure, those are good guidelines, but sometimes I just need to do what's good for me.* It's a dangerous path we are walking, and we can see the results of this approach as societal mores and standards break down.

Take, for instance, the erosion of respect for authority in schools. We see more and more disturbing videos of students beating up teachers. We also are witnessing a growing disdain for law enforcement. According to the National Police Support Fund and an FBI study, violent deaths of police officers in the US rose 36% from 2015 to 2016. Ambush attacks rose 61% and recently we've started seeing video footage of hoodlums throwing water on police and rescue services out trying to do their jobs. The fabric is fraying, but we remain convinced that we can resolve this with kumbaya moments and the usual pablum of understanding that criminals are victims, too.

It's high time we admit that people don't instinctively adopt notions of right and wrong on a societal level, but on a personal and selfish one. And once the culture breaks down to *each man for himself,* there's no coming back from that. We should sooner return to the religions moorings that allowed this nation to prosper. After all, the Golden Rule that everyone is so fond of began when Jesus admonished us all to love our neighbors as ourselves.

Israel

Kevin

"Is it running?" I asked Sam as she tweaked the iPhone on its stand.

She checked the shot, and, satisfied, pushed the 'record' button. "It is, now!" Sam ducked over and into frame, sandwiched between me and my oldest son, Braeden. "Okay." Sam looked expectantly at me. And I, back at her. I smiled at her, and turned back toward the camera, chuckling.

"We're the Sorbos. I'm Kevin."

"And I'm Sam, and we're so excited to be going to Israel!"

Our trip to Israel had been over a year in the making, but truth be told, it was a trip I always had on my list but seldom got around to even contemplating. I'm a traveler, and I always have been, it seems. In fact, when you look in that big astrological birthday book, the one that describes each person born on a certain day, well, my day is titled "The Traveler." Not that I put much stock in those things, of course, but it was pretty eerie when I read that.

The year before, I had met some guys who said to me I should lead a trip to Israel. Me? Lead a tour? In a country I'd never been before? I hardly thought that sounded appropriate. But I'll admit, I was intrigued. I talked to Sam. She decided to check the guys out, and it turned out she already knew one of them. After a few phone calls to plan things, we were committed. That's when we got funded for the movie, of course!

Don't you know that as an actor, or any kind of worker-for-hire, the moment you book a vacation is when a great job comes in? It always seems to happen that way, and this time was no different. Just when we needed to make our decision, the funding for our new movie came through and we had to postpone our trip, so we rescheduled it for a year later.

Now, the family was shooting some video for a documentary Sam had decided to produce about our tour. She seems to never have enough to do, my wife. She's always taking on new challenges and novel projects, and this trip to Israel was no different for her. So, she found some new friends who wanted to come and also do the documentary with her. That was fine by me as long as it wouldn't distract from the expedition or slow us down in places.

I'm including Israel as the last chapter in this book because it was the birthplace of our Judeo-Christian faith, and it seems a fitting place to leave off a discussion of the role of faith in our lives. Sam's idea for the documentary was, in part, to explore how people view faith these days, what has changed in the way we approach faith, and whether faith is really under attack, as so many believe.

The answers are, in order: very important, losing sight of it, and very much so!

On our trip to the Holy Land, which was engineered to be a journey in the footsteps of Jesus, we crossed the Sea of Galilee and saw a two-thousand-year-old boat. This was a recovered and preserved wooden boat from the time of Christ, that had been found in the sands of the shore of that sea, and so very likely was a boat that Christ could have used.

We stopped at the town of Magdalena, where evidence indicates Mary Magdalene was raised, and also the town of Caesarea. It was a profound historical experience, capped by a visit to the private side of the Garden of Gethsemane, where our group sat for forty-five minutes and virtual strangers shared stories of miracles in their lives. We read from scripture and shared communion at the site of the tomb. We sang songs on the bus, and connected at night after dinner, sometimes recapping the events of the trip, other times listening to arranged speakers.

Having just shot a documentary in Israel with the great John Lennox, Professor of Mathematics at Cambridge and a leading apologist, I was by no means an expert, although I had visited some of the sites for the first time only a few months before. This time, though, it was very hot!

We were sitting on the steps. You know the ones, the steps into the temple where Jesus confronted the money changers and overturned their tables. Tom, Carla and Roni, our guides, had just given us their run-down of the history that had taken place at that very spot. I was sitting next to Sam. Our kids, who had made some good friends among the other youth on our tour, were seated nearby. I watched them for a moment to see if they were really taking in the profound moment of touching history—great, earth-shattering history. Satisfied that they were, I turned my attention to Sam, who was quietly gazing upward into the waning daylight. A tear spilled slowly down her cheek.

I put my arm around her shoulders. Everything okay?

She nodded, overcome with emotion. Yes, the steps, their robust size, and age, and the fact that they are still there, is profoundly moving. These are the steps where Jesus rebuked the money changers for defiling the house of His Father. They were warm from the sun and baked in more than two thousand years of history.

The visit to the Temple Mount the previous day had been fraught with controversy. From the start—with a security screening before going out onto the enormous platform built by Herod to show his magnanimity and grandeur—to the moment we left through the far gate, the outing had been contentious, to say the least. The Temple Mount is controlled by Muslims. Although they have no real power there, they exert the maximum that they can. So, while the dress that Sam had chosen to wear was calculated to be modest enough, and our guide said its length, well below her knees, would be long enough, the moment we stepped onto the nearly thirty-six acre platform, the Muslim "modesty police" were at hand.

They immediately gave Sam a long brown sackcloth "skirt" to wear, but, then again, they also handed the same thing to a group of four nuns wearing full, grey habits.

Carla then stood before us, lamenting that only a few months before Sam wouldn't have required the skirt, but that the modesty police were getting stricter and exercising more power. Carla, a feisty South African gal who had become an Israeli citizen, easily transitioned to explaining the history of the Mount, specifically when Israelis had taken it back after the 1967 Six Day War, but then, in a momentary lapse of judgement, the Knesset determined to give it back to Jordan. Now it was out of their hands, and the Islamists had been given the right to excavate under the main flooring, in the cavernous archways supporting the grand structure. Soon after, Israelis had found antiquities of the old synagogue in the dump not far from the site. Carla showed us an Islamic tour booklet that denied there had ever been a synagogue on the Temple Mount. We then toured the entire platform, approaching the *Dome of the Rock,* where we saw with our own eyes the piece of marble that so closely resembles the face of Satan on its one exterior wall. The attendants had placed an outdoor kiosk-type structure in front of the marble, but it failed to conceal the sinister image from our view or our cameras. I remarked to myself the oddity that one piece of marble would have so clear an image on it, while it's symmetric, corresponding piece on the left side would be clear of any imagery of any kind.

The whole visit to the Temple Mount was rife with conflict, which well mimics the entire nation of Israel. This small plot of land, sandwiched as it is between antagonistic nations, is a region of all kinds of struggle. But it is an area of resplendent beauty, prosperity and freedom, and for that we are so grateful. We were tremendously blessed by our trip to Israel, so much so that we are planning another journey back there already.

Faith gives us conviction—the ability to stay the course when struggles frustrate our progress and the strength to stand again after challenges knock us down. Faith brings us comfort—the knowledge that there is a divine plan regardless of our own misgivings and vexations. Faith offers us liberation—the proposition of forgiveness for misdeeds and the inspiration to forgive others, freeing ourselves and our enemies from the bonds of shame and guilt. Faith provides the backdrop for the scenery of our lives, the flavor in life's stew, the bass notes for our personal soundtracks. If faith is important, and Sam and I think it is of utmost importance, then traveling to the birthplace of our faith is foundational.

But Sam put it best, I think, on the steps of the Temple Mount. As she looked up to the sky, with a tear making a lazy rivulet down her cheek, I kissed her face and she turned to me.

I smiled and said, "Did you learn something today?"

She looked in my eyes, wiped her face, and said, "I learned the most amazing thing in this astounding country, darling, and you know what that is?"

"What?"

"I learned to really love people. I feel *called* to love people. I love people so much more today than I did before coming to this land. I can't explain it, although I can guess why. I think the Holy Spirit just filled me with God's love for humanity, and now I feel it overflowing."

"You've always loved people. That's why I can never get you to say goodbye when we are leaving somewhere."

She giggled, her eyes still glistening from the emotions coursing through her. "True enough. Could it be that I love people *more,* now? I think so."

"Well, that's a good thing, then, right?"

"You betcha," she answered, just like my dad used to say.

About Kevin and Sam

Kevin is best known as Hercules in *Hercules: The Legendary Journeys,* Captain Dylan Hunt from *Gene Roddenberry's Andromeda,* and as Professor Radisson in *God's Not Dead.* In his fifth year of playing the strongest man in the world, Kevin suffered three strokes that initiated his three-year trial to complete healing and which inspired his first book, *True Strength: My Journey from Half-God to Mere Mortal – and How nearly Dying Saved my Life.* His fiancée, Sam (née Jenkins), saw recovery in him even when he couldn't. They were married just four months into his healing. He says she got the "worse" part first, from their vows, "for better or for worse." Since his full recovery, Kevin has acted in over sixty films and various television shows.

Sam performed in many films like *Bonfire of the Vanities* and *Twenty Bucks*, and television, including *Jag* and *Chicago Hope* before guest-starring on *Hercules.* Kevin swept her off her feet and they married in 1998. Sam is an impassioned advocate for home education. She wrote *They're YOUR Kids: My Journey from Self-Doubter to Home School Advocate* to empower parents to reimagine their children's education standards and accept the responsibility, challenge, and joy of teaching them. While she continues acting and hosting a daily radio show, she is an education activist who inspires us to rethink how we approach education as a culture and a nation.

Together, the Sorbos produced and starred in the surprise hit *Let There Be Light,* a film highlighting family, faith, and forgiveness. Kevin directed it and their new film, *Miracle in East Texas: A Tall Tale Inspired by an Absolutely True Story,* which launches in spring of 2020. With their Sorbo Family Film Studios, they seek to elevate Christian values, inspire hope, and restore the culture. Kevin and Sam have three children who are home educated.

www.SamSorbo.com

www.KevinSorbo.net

Facebook.com/SamSorbo
Facebook.com/KevinSorbo

@TheSamSorboShow
@KSorbs

@Sam_Sorbo
@KSorbo

CPSIA information can be obtained
at www.ICGtesting.com
Printed in the USA
LVHW091105170320
650296LV00001B/70

9 780982 800119